the *new* europe series

General Editor: Helen Wallace

Drawing upon the latest research, this major new series of concise thematically organized texts is designed to provide state-of-the-art overviews of the key aspects of contemporary Europe from the Atlantic to the Urals for a broad student and serious general readership. Written by leading authorities in a lively and accessible style without assuming prior knowledge, each title is designed to synthesize and contribute to current knowledge and debate in its particular field.

Published

Andrew Cottey: *Security in the New Europe*
Christopher Lord and Erika Harris: *Democracy in the New Europe*

Forthcoming

Klaus Goetz: *Governing the New Europe*
Colin Hay and Daniel Wincott: *Welfare in the New Europe*
Ben Rosamond: *Globalization and the European Union*
Vivien Schmidt: *Political Economy of the New Europe*
Anna Triandafyllidou: *What is Europe?*

In preparation

Citizenship and Identity in the New Europe
Nationalism and the State in the New Europe
Europe and the World
Society and Social Change in the New Europe
Making Sense of the New Europe

The New Europe Series
Series Standing Order
ISBN 0–333–96042-4 hardback
ISBN 0–333–96043–2 paperback
(*outside North America only*)

You can receive future titles in this series as they are published. To place a standing order please contact your bookseller or, in the case of difficulty, write to us at the address below with your name and address, the title of the series and an ISBN quoted above.

Customer Services Department, Macmillan Distribution Ltd
Houndmills, Basingstoke, Hampshire RG21 6XS, England

Security in the New Europe

Andrew Cottey

First published 2007 by
PALGRAVE MACMILLAN
Houndmills, Basingstoke, Hampshire RG21 6XS and
175 Fifth Avenue, New York, N.Y. 10010
Companies and representatives throughout the world

PALGRAVE MACMILLAN is the global academic imprint of the Palgrave
Macmillan division of St. Martin's Press, LLC and of Palgrave Macmillan Ltd.
Macmillan® is a registered trademark in the United States, United Kingdom
and other countries. Palgrave is a registered trademark in the European
Union and other countries.

ISBN-13: 978-1-4039-8648-1   hardback
ISBN-10: 1-4039-8648-7   hardback
ISBN-13: 978-1-4039-8649-8   paperback
ISBN-10: 1-4039-8649-5   paperback

This book is printed on paper suitable for recycling and made from
fully managed and sustained forest sources. Logging, pulping and
manufacturing processes are expected to conform to the
environmental regulations of the country of origin.

A catalogue record for this book is available from the British Library.

A catalog record for this book is available from the Library of Congress.

10   9   8   7   6   5   4   3   2   1
16   15   14   13   12   11   10   09   08   07

Printed and bound in China

This book is dedicated to my wife, Maeve, and my sons, Eoin, Oisin and Ultan, in the hope that the region of the world in which we live may continue to be stable and secure, and that we can help to bring at least some of that stability and security to less fortunate parts of the world.

Contents

List of Tables and Boxes   x
Foreword by Helen Wallace   xi
Preface   xiii

Introduction   1

1   Security in the New Europe   5

Security: a problematical concept   6
The European security community   11
Institutionalized security co-operation   16
Enlargement and its consequences   18
Conclusion   28

2   The New Global Security Agenda   32

The new international (dis)order   33
The new wars   36
Proliferation: the second nuclear age   39
The 'new terrorism' and the 'war on terror'   42
Soft security   45
American hegemony   49
Conclusion   54

3   Europe and America: The End of an Era?   58

The post-Cold War era   59
The Bush Administration, 9/11 and the Iraq War   62
NATO: transformation and uncertainty   67
Interpreting transatlantic relations   71
Conclusion   77

4   The EU and the Europeanization of European Security   79

Towards a common foreign and security policy?   80
Euro-atlanticism versus Euro-Gaullism   86
Neighbourhood politics   88

A global role?   92
The military dimension: peacekeeping and beyond   95
Internal security: the EU's Area of Freedom, Security
    and Justice   97
Conclusion   99

5   Russia: Partner or Problem in European Security?   102

Russia: post-communism and foreign policy   103
Russia and the West: a troubled partnership   107
    Russia and NATO   109
    Russia and the EU   110
Russia and the former Soviet Union: the 'near abroad'?   112
The security problems of Russian weakness   116
Conclusion   120

6   The New Interventionism   123

The new interventionism   123
Intervention within Europe   130
    The Balkans   130
    The former Soviet Union   133
Europe and global interventions   136
NATO and the EU: global peacekeepers?   138
    NATO   138
    The European Union   142
Conclusion   146

7   Proliferation   149

Assessing the proliferation threat: European perspectives   150
Arms control   155
'Loose nukes' and co-operative threat reduction   158
Dealing with tough cases: diplomacy, sanctions and
    the use of force   160
Living with proliferation?   163
Conclusion   167

8   The 'New Terrorism' and the 'War on Terror'   169

Europe and terrorism – 'old' and 'new'   170
Europe and the US 'war on terror'   174
Counter-terrorism I: the homeland security agenda   177

Europe's Islamic population: an internal terrorist threat?   182
Counter-terrorism II: foreign policy and the root causes
    of terrorism   187
Conclusion   190

9 **Soft Security**   **192**

Economic development policy   193
Global warming   198
Population movements   206
Conclusion   215

10 **Conclusion**   **217**

The new European security order   217
New threats?   219
Europe and America, NATO and the EU   221
Europe and global security   223

Bibliography   225
Index   250

List of Tables and Boxes

Tables

1.1	Regions of Europe and membership of European security organizations, 2007	20
2.1	The global balance of power in the early twenty-first century	51
6.1	Intervention in conflicts in the former Soviet space	134
6.2	NATO peacekeeping and crisis management operations	140
6.3	EU peacekeeping and crisis management operations	143
7.1	WMD proliferation: the state of play, 2007	151
8.1	Europe's Muslim population	183
9.1	European, Japanese and US contributions to development aid	195
9.2	Past, present and future greenhouse gas (GHG) emissions	202
9.3	EU greenhouse gas (GHG) emissions and the Kyoto target	205
9.4	Migration: inflows of foreign population into EU and selected OECD countries	208
9.5	Inflows of asylum seekers into EU and selected OECD countries	209

Boxes

4.1	Co-operation under the EU's Area of Freedom, Security and Justice	98
7.1	The EU, Iran and nuclear proliferation	163
8.1	EU counter-terrorism measures post-9/11	178
8.2	US–EU counter-terrorism co-operation post-9/11	181
9.1	The consequences of global warming	200

Foreword

We live in troubling times. In the period of euphoria following the collapse of the Soviet imperium in Europe there was a wave of optimism that the ending of the Cold War would lead to a period of peace, calm and reconstruction. It would, we thought, now be possible to scale back military expenditure and to reap a defence dividend that would enable resources and human energies to be transferred to other fields. Our societies would be able to relax as our governments were enabled to direct their attention to other concerns and policy areas.

How wrong we were. Since communism unravelled in Europe in the 1980s, we have instead experienced war in Europe again, albeit confined to the former Yugoslavia. Across the world we have witnessed a proliferation of armed conflict both between states and, even more worryingly, deep inside societies. For those directly involved in military activities the price is high – active duties in dangerous places have displaced the previous period of training operations designed to deter conflict but not to join combat. Sharp tensions have spread at the societal level with the transnational projection of the consequences of armed conflicts, which have included the rising number of displaced persons seeking to evade conflicts in their own countries or to escape the consequences of failed states and stateless countries. Moreover the vocabulary of 'security' and 'insecurity' has spread to many other dimensions of society, as the so-called 'soft security' agenda has expanded.

All of these developments present huge challenges to the national, European and international policy-makers and politicians in search of remedies. These are challenges of analysis and understanding as much as they are challenges of when, where and how to develop policies to increase security and to decrease insecurity.

Andrew Cottey's book explains the troubled evolution of recent years, the ways in which the issues of security have been reshaped, and the kinds of responses that have been produced by public policies. It not only provides a carefully crafted analysis of a complex subject but one which succeeds in illuminating on several levels. On the one hand, his account, though nuanced and thoughtful, provides a straightforward explanation both accessible to the general reader and provocative for the specialist. On the other hand, he writes with an empathy for the dilemmas facing policy-makers and citizens alike as they struggle to make sense of this confusing and unsettling new world.

The volume is focused deliberately on how these security challenges impact on Europe and Europeans. They are framed by reference to the wider global context and then analysed in depth across the range from harder to softer security issues. Cottey writes with a careful tone on the difficulties for Europeans of reframing the transatlantic relationship or of formulating collective European policies and capabilities. His account is thus an invaluable and measured appraisal of just how much has to be done to enable Europe and Europeans to become more secure.

HELEN WALLACE

Preface

This book is the product of many years' interest in and research on European and global security. As such, I owe a debt of gratitude to the wider community of academics and policy-makers who have contributed to my thinking during that time. I would like to extend particular thanks to my colleagues in the Department of Government, University College Cork, and before that in the Department of Peace Studies, University of Bradford, for providing both intellectual stimulation and supportive working environments. I also wish to thank series editor Helen Wallace and my publisher Steven Kennedy for providing me with the opportunity to write this book, and for many helpful suggestions on its development. A number of colleagues have read and provided detailed comments on all or part of drafts of the book: Derek Averre, Alyson Bailes, Pal Dunay, Anthony Forster, Sean Kay and an anonymous reviewer – I am especially grateful to them, both for their willingness to give their time and for their insights. The final contents of the book are, of course, my responsibility.

ANDREW COTTEY

Introduction

Security poses some of the most prominent and controversial challenges facing European societies. The 11 September 2001 terrorist attacks in the USA dramatically illustrated the vulnerability of advanced industrialized societies to so-called asymmetrical threats. The March 2004 terrorist attacks in Madrid showed that Europe, as well as America, was a target for globalized Islamic terrorism. In response to 9/11, the USA has launched a global 'war on terror' and major military interventions in Afghanistan and Iraq, creating global controversy and bitter disputes with some of its long-standing European allies. European governments are struggling with the dilemmas of how to tackle terrorism internationally, strike the appropriate balance between security and liberty domestically, and relate to an assertive and unilateralist America. A range of other security problems, some new, some longer-standing, also pose major challenges for European governments. The wars in the former Yugoslavia in the 1990s prompted deep divisions over international military intervention. Similar complex internal conflicts elsewhere in the world suggest that the dilemmas of intervention in these 'new wars' will not go away. The prospect that a widening group of states may obtain nuclear, biological or chemical weapons has generated much debate about the extent of the threat posed by weapons of mass destruction (WMD), and what can and should be done to prevent their proliferation. A range of non-military challenges – the global economic divide between rich and poor, environmental problems such as global warming, the spread of HIV/AIDs and other infectious diseases, mass migration and organized crime – are also viewed increasingly as security threats. Taken together, these developments herald the emergence of a new security agenda that is a central part of global politics in the early twenty-first century. However, the nature, extent and relative priority of the threats posed by these various security challenges (and the appropriate policy responses to them) remain deeply contested.

This book explores the nature of security in the new Europe of the early twenty-first century, and European responses to the new global security agenda. It examines the changing character of security in contemporary Europe, the nature and extent of the threats posed by

1

different security problems, and the policy challenges and dilemmas involved in responding to these problems. Its central argument is that European security is being reshaped fundamentally by the intersection between two developments: the end of the Cold War, symbolized by the tearing down of the Berlin Wall in 1989; and the emergence of the new global security agenda, symbolized by the 9/11 attacks on the USA. For forty years, from the late 1940s to the late 1980s, debates on European security were defined by the Cold War division of the continent and revolved around the conduct and management of the East–West conflict. The sudden end of the Cold War in 1989 was therefore a revolution for European security. Overnight, the old security challenge – the management of the East–West conflict – disappeared and Europe entered uncharted waters.

Chapter 1 of this book examines the impact of this revolution within Europe, arguing that the emergence of a security community– a zone of peace where war is inconceivable– in Western Europe since 1945 has fundamentally transformed the nature of European security. The term 'security community' is used here in the sense developed by Karl Deutsch, meaning a group of states between whom war and the use of force has become extremely unlikely, if not impossible (Deutsch, 1969; Adler and Barnett, 1998). The membership of the European security community is essentially the largely overlapping memberships of the EU and NATO, but while the EU and NATO may be central pillars of the European security community, that security community is not formally defined by or linked to either institution. With the end of the Cold War, that security community is now the defining feature of the new European security landscape. Whereas the historic problem for European security was the risk of war – above all, great power war – within Europe, at the beginning of the twenty-first century the likelihood of such conflict is low, and the traditional pattern of balance of power politics and competing alliances has been replaced by the European security community.

The period after 1989 triggered much debate on the nature of the post-Cold War world, but there was little consensus on what – if any – were the defining characteristics of this period in international politics, leading some observers to describe it as an interregnum – a transitional period of uncertainty, awaiting the emergence of a new era (Cox *et al.*, 1999). That interregnum came to an end on 11 September 2001. Following the end of the Cold War a decade earlier, 9/11 triggered a second revolution in global security, and illustrated in a dramatic way the vulnerability of the Western industrialized world, including

Europe, to threats from elsewhere in the globe. At the same time, the USA's pre-eminent position in terms of global power and its assertively unilateralist response to 9/11 mean that American power and choices increasingly frame the security agenda for all other states, including those of Europe.

Chapter 2 explores the nature of the new global security agenda and America's central role in shaping and responding to that agenda. In combination, these developments – the emergence of a security community or zone of peace across much of Europe, and the new post-9/11 global security agenda – mean that European security is likely to revolve increasingly around the issue of how Europe responds to global security challenges rather than the historic problem of war and peace within Europe.

These developments have also had a fundamental impact on the main security relationships and institutions in Europe, which are at the time of writing undergoing major transitions, the outcomes of which are uncertain. Divisions between the USA and Europe, especially over the 2003 Iraq War, have called into question the future of the transatlantic alliance that has been the bedrock of Western European security since the Second World War. Chapter 3 examines this relationship, arguing that transatlantic relations are likely to be characterized by a continuing uneasy mix of co-operation, divergence and conflict, and that the era when America and Europe were each other's default allies is coming to an end.

Parallel to this, the European Union (EU) has since the end of the Cold War assumed a growing security role. Chapter 4 examines the EU's emerging security role, arguing that while the Union faces significant constraints in this area, it is nevertheless likely to assume growing importance as the main security actor within Europe and an important security player globally.

Chapter 5 addresses Russia's position as the largest European power outside the European security community. It argues that Russia is not likely to become a full member of the European security community for the foreseeable future, and that Russia's relationship with that community is likely to continue to be characterized by an uneasy mix of co-operation and conflict. It also argues that both the security problems Russia faces and those it poses for others are likely to result from the unusual mix of great power strength and internal weakness that characterizes contemporary Russia.

The second half of the book – Chapters 6 to 9 – examines European perspectives on and responses to core aspects of the new global security

agenda: the dilemmas of intervention in 'new wars'; WMD proliferation; the 'new terrorism'; and non-military soft security problems.
These chapters show that European states and organizations, in particular the EU, are playing a growing role in addressing global security
challenges beyond Europe, but also that they are placing a strong
emphasis on multilateralism and soft power, in contrast to a US
approach that emphasizes unilateralism and hard power. Europe's role
in addressing the new global security agenda is, however, constrained
by its limited hard power capacity, and by the politically fragmented
nature of the EU as an international actor.

The book concludes by assessing the overall state of security in the
new Europe, and Europe's role as a global security actor. It argues that
while problems such as terrorism and WMD proliferation pose serious
threats to European states and their citizens, these are not comparable
in terms of consequences to the Cold War threat of nuclear annihilation
or to the historic danger of great power war in Europe. Although there
are important regional variations in security within Europe – the countries of the Balkans and the former Soviet Union, in particular, face
much more serious security threats than the rest of Europe – the low
likelihood of continent-wide great power war means that Europe and
European citizens are more secure than they have been at any time in
the continent's history. The existence of the European security community and the ongoing process of integration within the EU, further, have
created an increasing tendency towards the development of common
security policies relating to the world beyond that community, but the
very nature of that security community – a politically fragmented and
decentralized entity – also constrains it as a security actor. In global
terms, Europe, in particular the EU, is only one of a number of centres
of power in the twenty-first-century world, alongside the USA, China,
India, Japan and Russia, as well as other emerging powers such as
Brazil, Iran and South Africa. While Europe may thus be developing a
distinctive approach to global security, emphasizing multilateralism
and soft power, the extent to which this emerging European vision of
global security can be given substance will depend on Europe's ability
to persuade other powers to support that vision.

Chapter 1

Security in the New Europe

This chapter explores the nature of security in the new Europe of the early twenty-first century. The first section examines what we mean by security, highlighting the contested nature of the concept, the difficulty of assessing threats to security, and the inherent security policy dilemmas commonly faced by governments. The rest of the chapter addresses the changing character of security in contemporary Europe. The central argument presented here, and one of the core theses of this book, is that the emergence of a security community, a zone of peace where war is inconceivable, has fundamentally transformed Europe. This security community emerged in Western Europe after the Second World War and has expanded to include significant parts of Central and Eastern Europe since the end of the Cold War. Since the emergence of the modern nation-state system, the central problem of European security has been the risk of war, in particular of continent-wide great power war. The ever-present risk of war and the associated insecurity of states have also driven much of Europe's international politics, resulting in a system of balance of power politics and competing alliances. Although Cold War Europe differed from previous eras in important ways, the East–West conflict conformed to the historical pattern of a continent defined by balance of power politics, competing alliances and the risk of great power war. The end of the Cold War raised major questions about the prospects for war and peace in Europe, and the future direction of European security. Some argued that Europe was likely to return to its pre-Cold War pattern of a multi-polar balance of power and that this would increase the danger of war on the continent (Mearsheimer, 1990). Instead, the Western European security community that emerged during the Cold War has outlasted the historical circumstances that gave rise to it, and is now the defining feature of the new European security landscape. The emergence and consolidation of this security community has dramatically reduced the likelihood of war in Europe and in so doing fundamentally transformed the nature of security in Europe. This chapter explores the nature and implications of this transformation.

Security: a problematical concept

Analysis of security issues is inherently problematical, for a number of reasons. Although the term 'security' is widely used, it is broad and open-ended. The meaning of security is thus open to a variety of different interpretations and is often contested. In a general sense, security – being secure – implies the absence of threats or a lack of vulnerability. The *Oxford English Dictionary*, for example, defines security as being untroubled by danger or fear, safe against attack, or the safety of a state, company, etc., against espionage, theft, or other danger (Allen, 1990, p. 1093). Security is therefore a general term applicable to individuals or any social group and relating to a wide range of issues – from an individual's personal or psychological security, to a state's security against external attack, to humanity's security from global threats such as climate change. In international politics, however, security has come to have a narrower and more specific meaning centred on war and peace, and the protection of the territorial integrity and political independence of the nation-state from the threat or use of violent force. Writing during the Second World War, the American commentator Walter Lippman described security as the extent to which a nation is not in danger of having to sacrifice core values, if it wishes to avoid war, and is able, if challenged, to maintain them by victory in war (quoted in Wolfers, 1962, p. 150). This understanding of the term security became widespread in international politics in the wake of the Second World War and in the context of the Cold War. What has come to be described as the traditional or narrow definition of security (Buzan *et al.*, 1998, p. 21) thus focuses on the military security of states, but has an important political dimension in that it also relates to the ability of states to maintain their freedom, independence and values (such as democracy).

Critics of the traditional definition of security argue that invasion, war and violent coercion are not the only potential threats to states' security or necessarily the most serious or pressing security problems. A wide range of non-military problems – dependence on foreign economic resources (such as oil or finance), environmental degradation, mass migration, transnational organized crime and pandemic diseases such as HIV/AIDS – may threaten the security of states and their citizens. Such critics argue for the broadening of the concept to include 'soft' security challenges or a range of non-military 'sectors' (Tuchman Mathews, 1989; Buzan *et al.*, 1998). The danger with this logic is that security may come to include virtually all international problems and in so doing arguably becomes so broad as to be meaningless (Walt, 1991). In the end, what constitutes security or a threat to security is subjective – it depends on *perceptions* of which communities, values and institutions matter, and the threats to those communities, values and institutions. Security therefore is not something that can be objectively defined or of which there is likely to be an agreed definition.

The subjective nature of security points to another important issue: how and why do individuals or communities define some issues or problems (but not others) as security problems or threats? This process has been described as securitization and involves the definition of an issue as an existential threat requiring extraordinary or emergency measures above and beyond the bounds of normal day-to-day politics (Buzan *et al.*, 1998, pp. 23–6). Since the early 1990s, we have seen the securitization of a wide range of non-military issues including international economic relations, global environmental problems, mass migration, transnational organized crime and pandemic diseases(in particular HIV/AIDS), with governments and international organizations defining these problems as threats to security and seeking to mobilize action and resources on this basis. The nature and extent of the security threat posed by these problems and how states should respond to them, however, remain contentious. This issue is explored in more depth in the next chapter. European responses to this broader security agenda are returned to in Chapter 9.

A second problem with the concept of security revolves around the question of 'Whose security?' The traditional or narrow definition of security focuses on the nation-state as the 'referent object' (the entity facing threats and requiring protection) and is associated with the idea of national security. This state-centric focus, however, is problematical in two important ways. First, the focus on national security may in fact risk undermining security. Measures taken by one state to enhance its security risk provoking similar responses from other states, thus undermining the security of the first state and increasing the likelihood of war. This action–reaction dynamic is common in international politics and is referred to as the security dilemma, since states remain vulnerable if they do not take action to provide for their security but risk provoking damaging counter-actions if they act (Buzan, 1991a, pp. 294–327; Herz, 1950; Jervis, 1978). Critics have argued that the state-centric focus of national security needs to be replaced with a focus on co-operative approaches to the security of all states – variously termed collective security, international security, common security, co-operative security or a security regime (Jervis, 1982; Palme Commission, 1982; Jervis, 1985; Buzan, 1991a, pp. 328–62; Carter *et al.*, 1992; Zartman and Kremenyuk, 1995). Second, drawing on classical liberal thinking, the state-centric concept of national security assumes that the state provides security for its citizens by maintaining order within its borders and protection against external threats. In many cases, however, states fail to provide for the security of their citizens and may even be the primary threat to their security. Through authoritarian rule, human rights abuses and in extreme cases genocide, states often threaten the physical security, well-being and survival of their citizens. In multi-ethnic states, the state is often perceived as threatening by minority populations. Internally weak or failed states may be unable to provide the basic order necessary for security. Critics therefore argue that the state-centric concept of national security should be supplemented, or perhaps even replaced, by a focus on other referent objects such as the individual, or society or humanity as a whole (Buzan, 1991a, pp. 35–56; Waever *et al.*, 1993; Buzan *et al.*, 1998, pp. 36–42 and 145–50; Commission on Human Security, 2003). From a European perspective, this debate on referent objects raises questions as to how far the traditional nation-state focus of European security is being, or should be, replaced by a focus on the security of the European Union, or alternatively the broader European continent.

Assessing threats to security is also inherently problematical (Buzan, 1991a, pp. 112–45). Threat assessment depends on information about the external world, yet such information is inevitably uncertain. Information about other states' military capabilities is rarely fully reliable, since all states are secretive about their armed forces and governments must rely on various forms of intelligence. Even if we have reasonably accurate knowledge of other states' military capabilities, however, assessing the significance and implications of these is often difficult. Assessing other actors' intentions is even more problematical, depending on inferences drawn from material capabilities, intelligence information on those intentions, past experiences and our own prejudices (Jervis, 1976). Furthermore, intentions, are not static but may change over time and in response to changing external circumstances. In addition, others may try to deceive regarding their capabilities or intentions. Equally, our own assumptions and biases may give us a distorted view of the world. Given these problems, it is not surprising that history is replete with examples of threats that have been underestimated, exaggerated or misunderstood. While technological advances, in particular the development of reconnaissance satellites, may have significantly improved the information available to some states, the intelligence failures relating to Iraq's WMD capabilities prior to the 2003 Iraq War show that the underlying problems of threat assessment remain (Butler Committee, 2004; Gormley, 2004; Commission on the Intelligence Capabilities of the United States Regarding Weapons of Mass Destruction, 2005; Hart and Simon, 2006). More broadly, assessment of the relative importance and urgency of different threats depends on a diverse range of factors including geographical location, political values and socio-economic circumstances. In a global context, therefore, states' threat assessments are bound to differ.

Security policy choices are equally problematical. Since policy decisions depend on threat assessments, they are deeply vulnerable to all the problems of threat assessment noted above. And policy decisions involve not only analysing others' capabilities and intentions, but also their likely reaction to our own actions: 'If we do X, how will they react? Are they more likely to do Y or Z?' The problem of assessing the likely reactions of others to our actions multiplies the uncertainty inherent in security policy decision-making, and makes the security dilemma referred to above one of the defining problems of international politics. Security policy-making is further complicated by the broader problem of unintended consequences. Blowback, where a state's foreign or security policy choices have major unintended negative consequences for that state, is a common phenomenon (Johnson, 2000). Few if any observers, for example, predicted that the arming by the US of Islamic guerrillas fighting the Soviet Union in Afghanistan in the 1980s would help to fuel a global anti-American Islamic terrorist movement a decade later. The complexity and interconnectedness of the global political and economic system also means that it is vulnerable to 'system complexity effects', where a small action in one place can have indirect but major consequences elsewhere, or even on the system as a whole (Jervis, 1997).

Since actors also have other goals such as prosperity and freedom, security policy decision-making involves important trade-offs between competing goals. Analysts have argued that without survival the achievement of other goals is impossible, and that security – maintaining the survival of the state, society or community – is (or should be) the paramount goal. While states and other actors do sometimes face truly existential security crises, the choice between security and other goals is often not so definitive. Absolute security – complete invulnerability to a particular potential threat – is rarely, if ever, possible, so states and other actors normally have to live with a degree of insecurity. Security policy-making therefore often involves choices about the priority and resources to be allocated to security alongside other goals: what proportion of political, economic and other resources should be directed towards addressing a given security problem? What are the costs, both direct and indirect in terms of opportunity costs, of responding to this security problem? Two forms of trade-off are particularly commonplace, between security and welfare, and between security and freedom. The security–welfare (or 'guns versus butter') trade-off involves decisions about the allocation of limited economic resources: expenditure on armed forces, police, border controls or other material security measures reduces funding available for health, education and other collective goods, and vice versa (Russett, 1982; Buzan, 1991a, pp. 272–4). Since armed forces are usually one of the largest components of state expenditure, debates on the security–welfare trade-off are commonplace. Such debates were ever-present in Europe during the Cold War. With falling defence budgets since then, however, the salience of these debates has declined somewhat, but some critics now argue that European states are unwilling to spend the money necessary for adequate defences or Europe's wider military ambitions in areas such as peacekeeping (Gompert and Kugler, 1995). The security–freedom trade-off relates to the danger that measures taken to enhance security may undermine the freedom and values on which democratic societies are based. Surveillance of potential domestic threats, arrest and detention without trial, limits on free speech, and other intrusions into people's privacy and constraints on their liberty are quite often justified by political leaders as responses to security threats. Such measures, however, threaten fundamental democratic principles that limit the arbitrary power of the state. They can also easily descend into witch-hunts, as occurred in the USA during the McCarthy era of the 1950s. European democracies have long experienced such dilemmas in relation to terrorist threats. In the wake of the 9/11 terrorist attacks, however, balancing freedom and security has become a more acute problem.

Security is also open to abuse. Authoritarian regimes often justify repressive measures as being vital to the security of the state. Scapegoating, where leaders create or exaggerate external or internal threats in order to mobilize support, is commonplace in international politics and viewed by some analysts as an important cause of wars (Levy, 1989, pp. 92–8). Leaders may use the language of security to justify aggressive policies. State bureaucracies – defence and interior ministries, police and intelligence services – may develop institutional interest in particular security policies and the threats that underpin them. What governments and leaders do in the name of security should therefore not be taken at face value.

In summary, security is a deeply problematical concept. The problems identified here – the open-ended and disputed meaning of the term security, the question of whose security is being dealt with, the difficulty of assessing threats to security, the inherent security policy dilemmas faced by states, the trade-offs between security and other objectives, and the potential abuse of the concept – suggest that, for all its ubiquity, security is likely to remain a contested concept; that security poses some inherent dilemmas; and that security policies are likely to remain highly contentious.

The European security community

Historically, the defining problem of European security has been the danger of war, especially continent-wide war embracing Europe's major powers. As Kenneth Minogue (2000, p. 52) has put it, 'The history of Europe has largely been a story of war . . . preparing for war, waging war, or recovering from war.' Modern European history has been characterized by a series of continent-wide major wars: the Thirty Years' War in the early seventeenth century, the Seven Years' War in the mid-eighteenth century, the Napoleonic wars at the beginning of the nineteenth century, and the First and Second World Wars and the Cold War in the twentieth century. Even during periods of relative peace, lesser wars have been commonplace, while the risk of escalation to great-power war has loomed in the background. Wars and the resort to violent force have generally resulted from two types of threat. Major powers have periodically posed what may be termed hegemonic threats, seeking to dominate the entire European continent – as in the cases of Napoleonic France, Nazi Germany and arguably Soviet Russia. Aspiring hegemons have triggered wars either through their own efforts at aggrandizement or by provoking responses from other major powers trying to maintain the status quo. A second cause of war and resort to violent force may be termed revolutionary threats – that is, domestic political challenges to the status quo such as nationalist challenges to empires, democratic challenges to monarchies, and communism's challenge to capitalism. Such challenges have resulted in the violent overthrow of regimes (as with the revolutions of 1848 and

1917) or the use of force by rulers to suppress revolutionary movements. Often the two types of threat have been intertwined, with revolutionary domestic political change triggering both hegemonic
ambitions and threats to the wider political status quo. Within this
context, the dominant pattern of international relations in Europe has
been balance of power politics: states have sought to advance their own
interests and power, and balanced against potential hegemons, resulting in a shifting pattern of alliances reflecting changes in the distribution of power and/or domestic political regimes.

In security terms, Europe at the beginning of the twenty-first century
is radically different from its past, as the likelihood of war between
Europe's major powers is lower than at any time in modern history. In
contrast to the competing alliances of the past, Europe is dominated by
a process of political, economic and security integration centred on the
European Union (EU) and the North Atlantic Treaty Organization
(NATO). The key development underpinning this has been the emergence of a security community, or what Singer and Wildavsky (1993)
call a zone of peace. This security community emerged in Western
Europe during the Cold War, but has outlasted the end of this and
subsequently expanded into Central and Eastern Europe. A security
community is a group of states among whom conflicts are resolved by
peaceful means, there is a high expectation that this norm will be maintained and war is therefore extremely unlikely, if not inconceivable
(Deutsch, 1969; Adler and Barnett, 1998). In contrast to the historical
pattern of conflict and war between Britain, France, Germany and the
other states of Western Europe, an unprecedented period of peace has
now developed between these countries.

The emergence of this security community has fundamentally
altered the nature of European security. In the past, European security
was based on the possibility of war between Europe's major powers
and the resulting balance of power politics, alliance building and military preparations. Today, European security is based increasingly on
the assumption that primary security threats arise from outside the
security community. And the development of this security community
has gone hand-in-hand with the consolidation of democracy, unprecedented prosperity, and institutionalized co-operation and integration
in both the EU and NATO. As a consequence, the existence of a security community in the western half of the continent is the defining
feature of the new European security order, not only precluding war
between its members but also acting as a dominant pole of attraction
for most of the continent. This, furthermore, is a global rather than

purely European phenomenon: the USA and other Western states (such as Canada, Australia, New Zealand and Japan) are part of a larger security community among the major industrialized democracies (Mueller, 1990; Buzan, 1991b; Jervis, 1991–2, 2002; Goldgeier and McFaul, 1992). The existence of this security community has funda-mental implications for world politics.

Assessments of the origins of the Western European security community and of the prospects for peace in contemporary Europe depend in significant part on underlying assumptions about the nature of international politics. Realist theorists of international relations argue that the anarchic nature of the international system drives secu-rity competition among states, and issues of war and peace are deter-mined by the balance of power (Morgenthau, 1985; Waltz, 1979). From this perspective, the Cold War confrontation and nuclear deter-rence helped to keep the peace between East and West after 1945, while the existence of a unifying external threat (the Soviet Union), the support of a benign hegemonic power (the USA) and the division of Germany underpinned the development of peaceful co-operation in Western Europe (Gaddis, 1986; Kegley, 1991). Realists argued that, with the end of the Cold War, multiple centres of power would re-emerge, and an unstable multipolar balance of power and pattern of shifting alliances would be the result. Germany might be driven to develop nuclear weapons in order to provide for its own security, and the likelihood of war within Europe would increase significantly. In short, Europe might well return to the war-prone system that existed before 1945 (Mearsheimer, 1990).

In contrast, liberal theorists argue that security competition and war result not simply from the effects of international anarchy, but more from the aggressive ambitions of states and leaders and from the absence of mechanisms for managing relations between states. Liberals see common democratic values, close economic ties, free trade and international institutions as means of promoting peace between states (Keohane and Nye, 2001). From this perspective, while the Soviet threat, American hegemony and the division of Germany may have played an important role in facilitating the development of the Western European security community, that community is underpinned by other equally important factors. First, a high degree of interdependence – intensive international and transnational economic, political and societal ties – developed between the countries of Western Europe, increasing the costs of using force within the community and creating groups with an interest in the maintenance of peaceful co-operation.

Second, Western Europe has developed an unprecedented network of international institutions based around the EU and NATO that provide mechanisms for the resolution of disputes and reinforce perceptions of common interest (Keohane *et al.*, 1993). Third, the democratic peace hypothesis suggests that common democratic values and the constraints imposed by democratic governance make war between democracies unlikely (Brown *et al.*, 1999; Russett, 1993). Bruce Russett and John Oneal (2001) argue that interdependence, international institutions and democracy form a reinforcing tripod underpinning the European and wider Western security community. Liberals have therefore argued that the Western European security community will outlast the Cold War that helped to establish it (Van Evera, 1990–1; Jervis, 2002).

At the time of writing, nearly two decades after the end of the Cold War in 1989, the record vindicates the liberal perspective. Realist predictions of a return to old patterns of balance-of-power politics, competing alliances and an increased risk of major war in Europe have not proved to be well founded. The security community is deeply entrenched among the major Western powers, and war appears to be very unlikely among its members for the foreseeable future. Only very radical political or economic change indeed – economic collapse akin to the inter-war great depression or the collapse of democracy in one or more of the major Western powers – would seem likely to create circumstances that might trigger a return to the old patterns of international politics.

Indeed, far from breaking up, the Western security community is in fact expanding eastwards (Gambles, 1995). The collapse of communism and the end of the Cold War generated fears of a significantly increased likelihood of war and violent conflict in Central and Eastern Europe and the former Soviet Union (Nelson, 1991; Smith, 1991). The region was a potential tinderbox of unresolved disputes over borders and ethnic minorities. Difficult post-communist political and economic transitions might result in the emergence of demagogic nationalist and authoritarian regimes, exacerbating tensions with ethnic minorities and neighbouring states. Post-communist political and economic change might also generate new non-military security problems, such as mass migration and transnational organized crime. The problems of post-communist transition have led some to describe the region as a 'wild east' (Fishman, 2003; Swift, 2004), characterized by instability and violent conflict. Fears of an upsurge of conflict in post-communist Europe appeared to be confirmed by the onset of war in Yugoslavia

1991 and the subsequent conflicts in Bosnia in the mid-1990s and Kosovo in 1999.

Viewing the security situation in Central and Eastern Europe through the lens of the Yugoslav conflict, however, provides a misleading perspective. The worst-case scenario of endemic instability across the region, with multiple Yugoslav-style conflicts, a widespread collapse of democracy and massive population movements, has been avoided. Despite the Yugoslav conflict, setbacks to democracy in some states (such as Belarus) and conflicts in parts of the former Soviet Union, there has been progress towards democratic consolidation in Central and Eastern Europe, border and ethnic minority disputes have largely been managed without resort to violence and, while countries face serious economic and social challenges, these have not in most cases fundamentally destabilized states. The Western security community has also been a significant stabilizing influence in Central and Eastern Europe, providing a powerful impetus for reform and moderation within the region.

In the context of democratization and integration with Western institutions, Central and Eastern European states have made significant efforts to overcome historic disputes and develop new co-operative relationships (both bilaterally and multilaterally). Given the region's history, perhaps most significant has been the historic – but not always widely recognized – rapprochement between Germany and Poland. Since the early 1990s, Germany and Poland have developed a significant political, economic and military partnership (Cottey, 1995, pp. 40–2; Gardner Feldman, 1999). Although some tensions between the two countries have resurfaced in the 2000s (for example, over relations with Russia, and over compensation for Germans expelled from Poland after the Second World War – see Associated Press, 2006), Poland is now a member of NATO and the EU alongside Germany, and such tensions appear unlikely to lead to serious political (let alone military) conflict. War appears as unlikely today between Germany and Poland as it is between Germany and France – a remarkable development given the history of relations between the two countries. Elsewhere in the region, there have been significant improvements in historically conflictual relations between Hungary and its neighbours; Poland and its eastern neighbours; the Baltic States and Russia; and Romania, Bulgaria and their neighbours (Wohlfeld, 1997; Cottey, 1999b). New multilateral subregional co-operation frameworks such as the Visegrad group (which brings together Poland, the Czech Republic, Slovakia and Hungary), the

Council of Baltic Sea States and the Black Sea Economic Co-operation group have also been established (Cottey, 1999a). The Central and Eastern European states are also being institutionally and functionally integrated into the EU and NATO, a process that began with various co-operation arrangements established in the early and mid-1990s and culminating in full membership for a significant number of states since the late 1990s. Overall, these developments suggest that the process of security community building based around democratic consolidation, interdependence and institutional integration that occurred in Western Europe after the Second World War is now being repeated in post-communist Central and Eastern Europe. This process is extending Western Europe's zone of peace into Central and Eastern Europe.

Institutionalized security co-operation

A second defining feature of the new Europe is institutionalized security co-operation (Keohane *et al.*, 1993). Attempts at building co-operative security institutions are not new in European history, as the nineteenth-century Concert of Europe and the inter-war League of Nations illustrate. The extent and nature of institution building that has taken place since 1945, however, is radically different from that of previous eras. An unprecedented set of overlapping security institutions has been established, providing multiple frameworks in which states co-operate and co-ordinate their policies. Since 1949 NATO has provided a framework for military integration among its members and the co-ordination of policies towards external security challenges – the Soviet bloc during the Cold War, the new security problems of Central and Eastern Europe since the end of the Cold War, and more recently beyond Europe. The EU is a unique exercise in political and economic integration, driven – especially in its early years – by the implicit security goal of making war among its members impossible. Since the end of the Cold War, the EU has intensified efforts at building a common external foreign, security and defence policy, as well as enhancing internal security co-operation.

Beyond NATO and the EU, there are other less well-known European security institutions. The continent-wide Conference on Security and Co-operation in Europe (CSCE, renamed the Organization for Security and Co-operation in Europe – OSCE – in 1994) emerged as a framework for East–West détente during the

1970s, but has subsequently developed roles in promoting democracy and human rights, and in conflict prevention and post-conflict peace-building. The Council of Europe, which was initially a Western European organization but has now expanded to include most post-communist states, also plays a role in promoting democracy and human rights. The various subregional institutions noted above also address a variety of non-military security challenges, such as environmental problems and transnational crime. In short, European security at the beginning of the twenty-first century is deeply institutionalized: states co-operate with each other in a range of different institutions and across the spectrum of different security issues. In particular, the national security and defence policies of the members of the EU and NATO are increasingly co-ordinated and integrated into common policies towards external security challenges.

Some critics view these security institutions as a masque hiding more traditional calculations of state power and interest, and thus being of little substance (Zelikow, 1996). Realists may well be correct that the Soviet threat, US hegemony and the division of Germany made the establishment of NATO and the EU possible, but this does not necessarily mean that these institutions have no substance independent of these developments, or that they will not outlive the historical circumstances that gave rise to them. The existence and development of these institutions is in part a reflection of the emergence of the European security community: freed from the past risk of war with one another, the members of the security community (as noted earlier) now view external problems, rather than each other, as the primary threats to their security. Combined with the consolidation of common democratic values, this has facilitated the emergence of broad common security interests among the members of the European security community. In this context, it is hardly surprising that the countries of Western Europe, joined since the end of the Cold War by the new democracies of Central and Eastern Europe, have sought to conduct their national security policies through institutions such as the EU and NATO: these institutions provide a mechanism for countries to address common security challenges and to increase their leverage *vis-à-vis* those security challenges by acting collectively. The development of security institutions may also be a self-reinforcing process: membership of these institutions and the functional dynamics of co-operation reinforce perceptions of common interests and help to create the sense of common identity on which these institutions are in part based.

Enlargement and its consequences

The third defining feature of the new Europe in security terms has been the eastward enlargement of 'Europe', not only in the sense of expanding the European security community or zone of peace, but also in terms of extending the membership of the EU and NATO. This has involved not only the extension of full membership to a swathe of Central and Eastern European states stretching from the Baltic to the Black Sea, but also the development of various partnership and co-operation arrangements with those states remaining outside the EU and/or NATO. The evolution of this enlargement process since the 1990s has resulted in the emergence of a Europe defined not only by an enlarged security community, EU and NATO, but also by a set of distinctive subregions with differing relations with the security community and differing prospects for eventual membership of that community and its institutions. Table 1.1 summarizes this emerging Europe. Contemporary Europe can thus be understood in terms of a set of concentric circles: Western Europe (where the majority of states are members of both the EU and NATO); Central and Eastern Europe (ten states, stretching from the Baltic Sea to the Black Sea, all of whom have joined both the EU and NATO since the late 1990s); the Western Balkans (the former Yugoslav states plus Albania, who are all effectively candidates for EU and NATO membership); the Western former Soviet republics that now lie between the enlarged Western security community and Russia; Russia and Turkey, major powers that are in different ways outside the Western security community; and the Caucasus and Central Asia, on the geographical periphery of the new Europe.

The central drivers behind this enlargement process have been the desire of most of the states of post-communist Europe to integrate themselves with the West, in particular to join the EU and NATO, and the need for the West to find an adequate response to the political, economic and security challenges facing the region. Given their historic vulnerability to larger neighbours and the attractions of the Western security community, it is hardly surprising that many of the states of Central and Eastern Europe, the Balkans and the former Soviet Union have sought close ties with and membership of that community. Inclusion in the Western security community and its central institutions – the EU and NATO – makes a state part of the dominant force in the new Europe and gives it the capacity to contribute to and shape that community's policies towards the rest of Europe and the wider world. More concretely, NATO members gain the protection of the alliance's Article V security guarantee – which commits members to provide all assistance to a fellow member if it is attacked – and the military infrastructure built up to support that commitment. EU membership provides states with the economic benefits associated with access to the Union's internal market and its redistributive economic policies, as well as its common foreign, security and defence policies. In the context of democratization, Central and Eastern European leaders viewed integration with the West as a return to the democratic Europe from which their countries had been separated artificially by the Soviet imposition of communism.

Western governments were initially wary of extending full membership of the EU and NATO to post-communist states, fearing that these states had not made sufficient progress in democratization and economic reforms, that instability might be imported into the EU and NATO, and that both institutions might be weakened by taking in new members. With the new democracies of Central and Eastern Europe pressing for integration with the West, however, it was difficult to deny the principle that the Western security community and its institutions should be open to them. Integration with the EU and NATO, further, was one of the primary means by which the West might stabilize post-communist Europe: just as NATO and the EU had helped to bring peace, prosperity and stability to Western Europe after 1945, it was hoped that the same process might be repeated in the eastern half of the continent after 1989 (Allin, 1995). Against this background, the 1990s saw a gradual process of enlarging Europe through the development of new institutional arrangements (such as NATO's Partnership for Peace (PfP) and the EU's various association and partnership agreements with its eastern neighbours), functional integration, and eventually the extension of full membership of NATO and the EU to Central and Eastern European states (Croft *et al.*, 1999). After much debate about the timing and modalities of enlargement, and the relative merits of the candidate countries, between 1999 and 2007 the group of ten Central and Eastern European states – Bulgaria, the Czech Republic, Estonia, Hungary, Latvia, Lithuania, Poland, Romania, Slovakia and Slovenia – became full members of both the EU and NATO. This process began in 1999 when the Czech Republic, Hungary and Poland joined NATO, reaching its high point in 2004 when most of these states joined both organizations, and concluded in 2007, when Bulgaria and Romania (which had joined NATO in 2004) became members of the EU. Cyprus and Malta also joined the EU in 2004. The borders of the European security community and the EU and NATO thus now stretch from the Baltic States in the north to Romania and Bulgaria on the Black Sea.

TABLE 1.1   *Regions of Europe and membership of European security organizations, 2007*

	EU	NATO	CoE	OSCE	CIS
North America					
Canada		X		X	
USA		X		X	
Western Europe (EU and/or NATO members)					
Austria	X		X	X	
Belgium	X	X	X	X	
Cyprus	X		X	X	
Denmark	X	X	X	X	
Finland	X		X	X	
France	X	X	X	X	
Germany	X	X	X	X	
Greece	X	X	X	X	
Iceland		X	X	X	
Ireland	X		X	X	
Italy	X	X	X	X	
Luxembourg	X	X	X	X	
Malta	X		X	X	
Netherlands	X	X	X	X	
Norway		X	X	X	
Portugal	X	X	X	X	
Spain	X	X	X	X	
Sweden	X		X	X	
UK	X	X	X	X	
Western Europe (non-EU and non-NATO members)					
Andorra			X	X	
Lichtenstein			X	X	
Monaco			X	X	
San Marino			X	X	
Switzerland			X	X	
Central and Eastern Europe (EU and/or NATO members)					
Bulgaria	X	X	X	X	
Czech Republic	X	X	X	X	
Estonia	X	X	X	X	

→

Since all these states have joined both the EU and NATO, the enlargement process has also strongly reinforced the essentially (though not completely) overlapping European memberships and borders of both organizations and their position as twin pillars of the European security community.

→

	EU	NATO	CoE	OSCE	CIS
Hungary	X	X	X	X	
Latvia	X	X	X	X	
Lithuania	X	X	X	X	
Poland	X	X	X	X	
Romania	X	X	X	X	
Slovakia	X	X	X	X	
Slovenia	X	X	X	X	
Western Balkans and Turkey					
Albania			X	X	
Bosnia and Herzegovina			X	X	
Croatia			X	X	
Macedonia			X	X	
Montenegro				X	
Serbia			X	X	
Turkey		X	X	X	
Western Former Soviet Union					
Belarus				X	X
Moldova			X	X	X
Ukraine			X	X	X
Russia				X	X
Caucasus					
Armenia			X	X	X
Azerbaijan			X	X	X
Georgia			X	X	X
Central Asia					
Kazakhstan				X	X
Kyrgyzstan				X	X
Tajikistan				X	X
Turkmenistan				X	X
Uzbekistan				X	X

Notes: EU = European Union; NATO = North Atlantic Treaty Organization; CoE = Council of Europe; OSCE = Organization for Security and Co-operation in Europe; CIS = Commonwealth of Independent States.

There is a strong argument that the processes of EU and NATO enlargement have been central to the stabilization of Central and Eastern Europe since the end of the Cold War (Grabbe, 2006; Cottey, 1999b). Both the EU and NATO made membership conditional on the consolidation of democracy, the normalization of relations with neighbouring states, and progress in economic, administrative and military reforms. This conditionality provided a powerful impetus for states to undertake and entrench reforms. The EU and NATO also provided significant financial support and technical advice to support reforms. Additionally, the process of functional co-operation that began in the 1990s has helped to socialize the Central and Eastern European states towards the norms and standards of the EU and NATO. If there had not been a realistic prospect of EU and NATO membership, the material support both organizations provided, and the experience of co-operation with them, Central and Eastern Europe's post-communist transition might well have been far more troubled than has been the case to date.

The enlargement of the EU and NATO has, however, also created new insider/outsider, inclusion/exclusion dynamics in European security, and given a new centrality to long-standing questions about the definition of Europe and where its borders lie. Such dynamics and debates are hardly new and their cutting edge has usually lain in the east and the south-east of the continent, where Europe meets Asia and the Middle East. The different histories, cultures and developmental paths of Central and Eastern Europe, the Balkans, Russia and Turkey compared to Western Europe have resulted in long-standing debates on the extent to which these countries and regions are European. For four decades after the Second World War, the Cold War division of Europe largely, though never completely, submerged these debates. The end of the Cold War re-opened them. The centrality of the European security community and its institutions – the EU and NATO – to the new Europe have made the question of whether or not one is a member of that community and its institutions, and the nature of one's relations with them, central foreign policy issues for all states. While membership of the European security community and its institutions confers major benefits, exclusion not only denies a state these benefits but also makes it vulnerable to the enormous collective political, economic and military power of the community and a potential subject of its collective external policies. For those European states remaining outside the Western security community and its institutions, whether by choice or by exclusion, the community and its institutions are thus potentially both highly attractive and highly threatening, and an inevitably looming presence. In broad geopolitical terms, the limits of the enlargement of the European security community and the nature of the relationships between that community and those states that remain outside it have become defining questions for the new Europe.

The processes of EU and NATO enlargement inevitably generated parallel dynamics of inclusion and exclusion, with fears of negative consequences for those states remaining outside and the possible emergence of new European dividing lines. Critics of NATO enlargement, in particular, argued that extending a military alliance into Central and Eastern Europe would be viewed as threatening by Moscow, provoke military countermeasures by Russia and in the worst case create a renewed Cold War-style military confrontation (Brown, 1995; Gaddis, 1998). Although less directly threatening in security terms, EU enlargement would involve the extension of the EU's common external trade tariffs, border controls and visa regimes to Central and Eastern European states, thereby disrupting economic, social and political ties with their own eastern and southern neighbours such as Ukraine and Russia. More broadly, the enlargement of the EU and NATO risked isolating those states remaining outside and undermining support in those countries for both domestic reforms and co-operation with the Western security community. In order to counter these dangers, NATO and the EU took a series of steps designed to avoid a new division of Europe, including strengthening institutional ties with these states, in particular Russia, and supporting the new NATO and EU members in building bilateral and subregional co-operation with their eastern and southern neighbours. Although the long-term impact of NATO and EU enlargement remains to be seen, worst case scenarios of a new Cold War-style military confrontation and dramatic setbacks to reform in those states remaining outside NATO and the EU have been avoided.

The enlargement process is also dynamic rather than static, since both the EU and NATO have in principle committed themselves to further enlargement. However, the divergent geostrategic locations and domestic paths of the various regions and countries currently outside the European security community place them in very different political situations in relation to the security community, and the EU and NATO.

The countries of the Western Balkans (the former Yugoslav states, plus Albania) are geographically proximate to the enlarged Western security community; became a de facto Western sphere of influence in the 1990s; are surrounded by the EU and NATO since the recent expansions of both organizations; have since the early 2000s all been recognized as potential candidates for EU and NATO membership; and are at various stages of the path towards that membership. The Yugoslav wars of the 1990s and the ongoing potential for violence, as illustrated by the outbreak of low-level fighting in Kosovo in 2004, however, illustrate that the Western Balkans remains outside the Western security community inasmuch as war remains conceivable within the region. The region's prospects for membership of the EU and NATO are also uncertain: setbacks to reform within states and ongoing unresolved conflicts (in particular, the status of Kosovo, which remains as of 2007 formally part of Serbia but is seeking independence and is effectively a Western protectorate) could delay or derail membership of the EU and/or NATO, while the willingness of NATO and the EU to take in the Western Balkan states remains to be fully tested. Using the model of conditionality and functional integration to help stabilize the Western Balkans thus poses major challenges for the EU and NATO. Former Swedish Prime Minister Carl Bildt (2004), a man much involved in European peacemaking efforts in Yugoslavia in the 1990s, has suggested that 2014, the centenary of the outbreak of the First World War, should be set as a suitably symbolic target date for the admission of the Western Balkans (and Turkey) to the EU. The most likely scenario, however, is that individual Western Balkan states will gradually be integrated into NATO and the EU, depending on their progress with reforms, and joining NATO before they join the EU (because it is, in practice, easier to integrate new members into NATO than the EU). Given their geostrategic position, and unless there is a return to large-scale violence, there is a fairly high likelihood that over the next decade or so the Western Balkan states will join the EU and NATO and gradually be integrated into the European zone of peace.

Lying between Russia and the enlarged NATO and EU, the geostrategic situation of the countries of the Western former Soviet Union – Ukraine, Belarus and Moldova – differs radically from that of the Western Balkans and has led some to describe the region as the 'new Eastern Europe'. The domestic paths of these states further complicate their difficult geostrategic situation. Since the early 1990s, Ukraine has been pulled between Russia and the West, and between the legacy of communism and domestic reform. Ukraine's 2004 'orange revolution' – in which a crisis over presidential elections threatened the survival of democracy but eventually resulted in victory for the pro-Western reformer Viktor Yushchenko – appeared to open up the possibility of domestic reforms and strengthened ties with the West that might eventually put EU and NATO membership on the political agenda. The difficulties of implementing domestic reforms since then and the persistent influence of Yushchenko's pro-Moscow opponents – symbolized by their success in March 2006 parliamentary elections and the appointment of their leader, Viktor Yanukovich, as prime minister – suggest, however, that Ukraine is likely to continue to be pulled in competing directions (Sasse, 2006). Belarus, under its maverick president, Alexander Lukashenko, remains an outpost of old-style communist authoritarianism and a close of ally of Russia, but observers fear that Lukashenko's eventual demise could trigger instability. Moldova's post-communist development has been largely defined by the unresolved conflict with the Russian-backed Transdnistria region in the country's east. There was violence here at the beginning of the 1990s and the region remains outside the control of the Moldovan government, with Russian military forces being deployed in the region despite a commitment by Moscow to withdraw those forces. To date, neither the EU nor NATO has been willing to consider Ukraine, Belarus or Moldova as serious candidates for membership, and in the short-term this is unlikely to change. The ambiguous geostrategic status of the region is likely to pose ongoing dilemmas for the Western former Soviet states and be a source of potential conflict between the Western security community and Russia.

As major European powers in their own right, Russia and Turkey are the two most important outsiders in the new Europe. Both countries are characterized by tensions between a desire to join the European mainstream embodied in the Western security community and arguments that they have distinctive national identities that set them apart from the Western security community. The members of the Western security community also view Russia and Turkey ambiguously, trying to integrate them into that community through various partnership and co-operation arrangements but remaining wary of both states, and in particular of giving them full institutional membership of that community.

The positions of Russia and Turkey in relation to the European security community and the EU and NATO, however, differ in important ways. In the sense of being part of the zone of peace where war is all but inconceivable, Russia is not a full member of the Western security community. Although Russia's relations with the West have improved dramatically since the end of the Cold War, tensions have continued and at points during the Yugoslav conflict of the 1990s could even have brought Russia and NATO into direct military confrontation (most obviously in the 'race for Pristina' during the 1999 Kosovo war, when Russian and NATO troops met head-on at Pristina airport). Although war between Russia and the West is unlikely at present, it is probably not entirely off the map of possibilities for decision-makers in Moscow or Western capitals. Russia, further, is a member of neither the EU nor

NATO. Since the 1990s, both the EU and NATO have developed special partnership relationships with Russia, reflecting its status as a major European power. Although some observers have suggested that making Russia a member of NATO might be a way of bringing it into the Western security community and overcoming the insider/outsider dilemmas associated with NATO enlargement (Baker, 2002), neither Russia nor NATO or the EU appear to have any serious interest in pursuing Russia's full membership. Thus it appears likely that Russia will remain the major outsider beyond the European security community, and the extent to which Russia and that security community will be able to build a viable partnership short of full membership remains uncertain.

In contrast to Russia, Turkey was a Western ally throughout the Cold War and has been a member of NATO since 1952. Turkey has also been recognized as a potential candidate for EU membership since 1963 (when it concluded an association agreement with the then European Economic Community – EEC). In 2004, the EU agreed to open formal membership negotiations with Turkey, beginning in 2005. Both the EU and Turkey, however, are ambiguous about their willingness to move to full membership, and some within the EU are wary of taking in a large, poor Muslim state straddling Europe and the Middle East. Although Turkey has intensified efforts to join the EU since the 1990s, there remain significant forces within Turkey arguing that it should retain its position as an independent power rather than join the EU. Turkey's relations with the larger European security community are also complicated by its relationship with Greece and the unresolved conflict over Cyprus. Greece and Turkey have a long history of conflict and came close to all-out war when Turkey invaded Cyprus in 1974. Although relations between Greece and Turkey have improved significantly since the late 1990s, war between the two states remains conceivable (as illustrated by disputes in the Aegean Sea that brought them to the verge of war in 1996). Despite being a long-standing member of NATO, Turkey's relationship with the European security community and the EU is thus characterized by an unusual mix of both insider and outsider, while the Greco-Turkish relationship also illustrates the limits of the security community as a zone of peace. The issue of whether Turkey will become a full member of the EU will remain a major challenge for both parties and will determine whether Turkey will be fully integrated into the European security community.

While Russia and Turkey are not (yet) fully integrated into the European zone of peace, neither country appears likely to pose the kind of hegemonic threat to European security that great powers have done in the past. Both countries have ambitions to (re-)establish themselves as major European powers, have disputes with many of their neighbours, and have intervened militarily in regions on their periphery (Russia in various parts of the former Soviet Union; Turkey in Cyprus and Iraq). In the Turkish case, while war between Turkey and some its neighbours (primarily Greece, but also conceivably Serbia and Bulgaria) remains possible, military conflict between Turkey and the larger Western or European security community seems extremely unlikely – partly because of Turkey's membership of NATO, but also because there are few, if any, sources of potential military conflict between Turkey and that security community. In the Russian case, despite some resentment of the dominance of the Western security community, Moscow does not appear to have serious ambitions to dominate Europe in the way that hegemonic powers have in the past. Even if this were to change, for the foreseeable future. Russia lacks the material power to mount a hegemonic bid to dominate Europe. Although Russia's 1 million-strong armed forces are the largest in Europe, Russia does not realistically have the military capability to pose a hegemonic threat to European security, nor do its armed forces translate into significant political leverage over the rest of Europe. In economic terms, Russia's gross domestic product (GDP) is much less than those of the European Union or the USA, and its defence expenditure is comparatively smaller. Russia also faces significant domestic political, economic and social challenges that further constrain its external ambitions. In short, while both Russia and Turkey are likely to remain security concerns for their weaker neighbours, neither is likely to pose a continent-wide threat to European security. The real questions for European security are how far they can be integrated into the Western security community, and whether they will be co-operative partners in dealing with security challenges such as proliferation, terrorism and conflicts beyond Europe.

Further to the east and south lie the former Soviet states of the Caucasus and Central Asia. Geography alone means that these states are more distant than other European states from the European security community and in part therefore less important to it. These countries' geostrategic location at the crossroads of Europe, Asia and the Middle East, and between a number of major powers (Russia and China, but also Turkey, Iran and India), and the existence of major oil and gas deposits within the region, however, mean that they are nevertheless of real significance for the European security community.

Following the break-up of the Soviet Union, these states were integrated into European security structures through membership of the Organization for Security and Co-operation in Europe (OSCE), joining NATO's Partnership for Peace (PfP) initiative, the conclusion of Partnership and Co-operation Agreements (PCAs) with the EU, and in the case of the Caucasian states, membership of the Council of Europe. Geography, the existing challenges of enlargement, deference to Russian interests and the authoritarian character of most of the Caucasian and Central Asian regimes, however, has meant that these states have not been viewed as possible candidates for EU or NATO membership. Georgia's 2003 Rose Revolution, however, brought to power reformers committed to integrating their country with the West and pursuing membership of NATO and the EU. NATO and the EU responded by intensifying ties with Georgia, but have (as of early 2007) stopped short of recognizing Georgia formally as a membership candidate – reflecting concern over whether either organization should, even in principle, consider extending its membership to the region.

Europe is being reshaped by the ongoing process of enlarging the European security community and its core institutions, the EU and NATO. Since the late 1990s the EU and NATO have taken in the swathe of Central and Eastern European states from the Baltic Sea to the Black Sea, while creating parallel partnership arrangements with those states remaining outside the two organizations. This process has played an important role in stabilizing Central and Eastern Europe, but has inevitably also created new insider/outsider dynamics. By remaining open in principle to further new members, the EU and NATO have also committed themselves to rather open-ended enlargement processes. The development of enlargement policy and related partnership arrangement with non-members will therefore continue to pose major challenges for the EU and NATO, and continue to reshape the European order over the next ten to twenty years.

Conclusion

This chapter has examined the nature of European security at the beginning of the twenty-first century. Its core argument, and the basis of this book, is that European security has been fundamentally transformed by the emergence of a security community in Europe. Historically, war has been a defining feature of the modern European state system. In this context, the behaviour of states has been shaped by the ever-present risk of war, and Europe's international politics have been driven by the realist logic of balance of power and competing alliances. The emergence of a security community, a zone of peace within which war is inconceivable, in Western Europe since the Second World War has altered this pattern fundamentally. The Cold War to some extent obscured the significance of this development. The risk of a continent-wide East–West war suggested that the old logic of European security remained intact. The end of the Cold War has demonstrated the full depth and significance of the change in European security. In contrast to the predictions of realists, nearly two decades after the end of the Cold War the Western security community remains intact. Furthermore, despite the Yugoslav conflict of the 1990s, that security community is gradually extending into Central and Eastern Europe. Russia and Turkey, however, are not full members of the European security community and their relationships with that community, and the West more generally, remain characterized by an uneasy mix of co-operation and conflict. In the Russian case in particular, war between Russia and the West cannot entirely be ruled out. Just as both Russia and Turkey are ambiguous about whether they are or want to be a full part of Europe or the West, the European security community is ambiguous and divided over whether Russia and Turkey are fully 'European', and whether it wishes to accept either as full members. Notwithstanding these problems, however, the realities of power – in particular the disproportionate imbalance of power between the European security community and Russia and Turkey – means that neither power is likely to pose a hegemonic threat to European security. In short, the Western security community is the defining feature of the new Europe, and the traditional problem of European security – the risk of war among the continent's major powers – is being overcome. As a consequence, international politics within Europe is now being shaped by the possibility of peaceful co-operation between states.

Two further features relating to the existence of the security community also define the new Europe. First, Europe is characterized increasingly by institutionalized security co-operation, in particular in the contexts of the EU and NATO. The national security policies of the members of the security community are becoming integrated into common EU and/or NATO policies towards the rest of Europe and the world. While this process is not unproblematical, and the USA as the world's only superpower to some extent stands apart from it, there is a growing trend towards the convergence and integration of the foreign and security policies of the European members of the security community. Second, the enlargement of the security community and its core institutions is having a powerful dual impact on contemporary Europe. The enlargement of the EU and NATO has helped to extend the zone of peace eastwards and promote stability in Central and Eastern Europe, but it has also created a new inclusion/exclusion dynamic between members and non-members. This has inevitably generated some tensions and problems, but the emergence of hard dividing lines or serious negative repercussions from the enlargement process have so far been avoided. The likelihood that additional Eastern and South-Eastern European states will be integrated into the EU and NATO, but uncertainties as to which states and when, and over the ultimate boundaries of both organizations, however, mean that this is a dynamic process, the long-term outcome of which is uncertain. One of the ongoing security challenges for Europe over the next ten to twenty years will therefore be the management of an open-ended enlargement process and of the continuing relationship between insiders and outsiders.

It is not impossible that history could yet prove realists to be right: a severe political or economic crisis or the reversal of the European integration process could trigger the disintegration of the security community and a return to old patterns of balance of power, competing alliances and great-power war. As of the first decade of the twenty-first century, however, such a development appears highly unlikely: the European and wider Western security community appears to be deeply entrenched, and the circumstances that might give rise to its disintegration are, at most, remote possibilities. The existence of this security community is therefore likely to be the defining feature of the European security landscape for the foreseeable future. This new reality has a number of important implications. First, much of the old agenda of European security, revolving around the management of the balance of power, the role of alliances and military stability *within* Europe is simply no longer relevant. Second, to the extent that the risk of war within Europe has declined, the security agenda is likely to shift increasingly towards global issues, whether in terms of conflicts elsewhere in the world or in terms of potential threats to Europe from challenges such as proliferation and terrorism. Third, the declining salience of traditional political-military security issues within Europe, raises questions about how far non-military problems such as economics, environmental degradation, migration and organized crime should now be seen as central to the security agenda. Fourth, to the extent that the USA is now the world's only truly global superpower and is, in the wake of the September 2001 terrorist attacks, increasingly ready to assert its power unilaterally, American policies will provide an important part of the parameters for European choices in addressing global security issues. In summary, the debate on European security is likely to revolve increasingly around the choices facing European states and institutions in relation to security problems outside Europe. At its root, this will be a debate not simply about specific policy choices but rather about what role European states and the EU as the primary expression of a collective European identity should play in relation to the rest of the world. The next chapter turns to the global challenges that will shape the European security agenda of the early twenty-first century.

Chapter 2

The New Global Security Agenda

This chapter explores the emerging global security agenda of the early twenty-first century. It suggests that the underlying context for the new security agenda is an international order defined by the global dominance of the West and the spread of liberal democracy and market economics – but also by resistance to Western domination, and tensions and instability generated by democratization and market economics. Within this overall context, the new global security agenda is defined by a number of more specific features (United Nations, 2004b; Brown, 2003):

- *New wars*: a shift in patterns of warfare from international wars to internal conflicts that nevertheless have significant regional and international repercussions.
- *Proliferation*: the prospect that a growing range of states, and potentially non-state actors, in particular terrorist groups, may obtain nuclear, biological or chemical weapons of mass destruction.
- *The 'new terrorism'*: the emergence of radical Islamic terrorist groups, in particular Al-Qaeda, engaged in a global struggle against the West, especially the USA, and willing to use terrorist violence on a scale not seen previously.
- *Soft security*: an increasing recognition that non-military problems – poverty and economic instability, environmental change and degradation such as global warming, energy security, mass population movements, diseases such as HIV/AIDS, transnational crime and the protection of critical economic and technological infrastructures – may pose central challenges to human security and cannot be separated from the more traditional security problems of warfare and military security.
- *American hegemony*: the preponderant global power of the USA gives it a central role in defining and responding to the global security agenda and makes American power a defining feature of the international environment for all other states and actors.

The rest of this chapter explores these dimensions of the new global security agenda in more detail. The chapter concludes by suggesting that while there is a loose consensus that the combination of new wars, proliferation, terrorism and soft security constitute a new global security agenda, there is little international agreement on the priority and hierarchy that should be attached to different threats, and even less on how we should respond to these problems. The new global security agenda and the policy challenges it poses are therefore likely to remain highly controversial. The conclusion to this chapter also outlines briefly the implications of the new global security agenda for Europe. Subsequent chapters explore in more detail the challenges posed to Europe by the new global security agenda.

The new international (dis)order

The end of the Cold War in 1989 raised fundamental questions about what form of international order would replace the bipolar super-power conflict that had dominated international politics since the Second World War. Historically, the modern international system has been defined by multipolar balance-of-power politics between the great powers. Some speculated that the end of the Cold War would trigger a return to the type of politics that had existed before the Second World War, with the USA, Europe, Japan, Russia and China competing for power and influence, shifting alliances among these states, and an increasing risk of great-power war. Rather than a return to past patterns, however, what has emerged, or more accurately has been consolidated since the end of the Cold War is a Western-domi-nated international order. In material terms, the major Western centres of power – the USA, Europe and Japan, but also countries such as Australia and Canada – remain the dominant forces in world politics. Economically, these countries provide the majority of the world's production, trade and investment. Militarily, these states have the greatest capacity to project military power beyond their borders. Ideologically, the period since the 1980s has witnessed the global spread of liberal democracy, with democratization in much of Latin America, Central and Eastern Europe, Africa and parts of Asia. Paralleling this has been a similar spread of market economics.

The current Western-dominated international order can also be characterized in core–periphery terms: an order in which the West constitutes the core of the international political and economic system, much of the rest of the world is defined by its relative lack of power and peripheral status, and the core–periphery relationship generates global tensions and conflict (Buzan, 1991b; Goldgeier and McFaul, 1992). Scilla Elworthy and Paul Rogers describe this as the relationship between the minority world (the Euro-atlantic West) and the majority world (the rest of the world where the majority of humanity lives) (Elworthy and Rogers, 2001).

The current Western-dominated international order, however, faces and generates a number of fundamental problems and tensions. Despite the spread of democracy, a number of important states and regions – most importantly China and the Middle East, but also countries such as Cuba, Myanmar (Burma), North Korea and Pakistan – remain holdouts against the global spread of democracy. Similarly, while the Western world has become a 'zone of peace' in which war is extremely unlikely, many other parts of the world – in particular Africa and the Middle East, but also parts of Asia and South America – are 'zones of turmoil', where war, violent internal conflict and political and economic instability are commonplace (Singer and Wildavsky, 1993). The very dominance of Western states and values, further provokes opposition to Western power, values and institutions, whether in the form of radical Islamic groups such as Al-Qaeda; the resistance of Russian nationalists to the Westernization of their country; opposition to the 'imposition' of Western concepts of human rights in Asia; or North Korea and Iran's attempts to develop nuclear weapons. Benjamin Barber thus describes the contemporary world order as 'Jihad versus McWorld', a 'collision between the forces of disintegral tribalism and reactionary fundamentalism . . . and the forces of integrative modernization and aggressive economic and cultural globalization' (Barber, 2003, p. xii; see also Barber, 1992). Similarly, although Samuel Huntington's 'clash of civilizations' thesis posits a world divided between a number of distinct civilizational groups, Huntington (1993, p. 48) nevertheless concludes that 'the paramount axis of world politics will be relations between "the West and the Rest"'.

The tension between the Western-dominated international order and these countervailing tendencies has a number of dimensions. First, resistance to the dominant order sometimes takes a violent form, most obviously in the guise of Islamic terrorism but also in the context of national struggles (such as the Mexican Zapatista movement or Colombia's FARC) and sometimes through the action of so-called 'rogue states' such as North Korea, Syria and Iran. Second, while stable established democracies may have low levels of internal violence and be unlikely to go to war with one another, the transitional process of democratization is usually prolonged, often produces instability both internally and internationally, and is vulnerable to setbacks. Democratization may thus trigger violent conflict within and between states, as in the former Yugoslavia, parts of what used to be the Soviet Union, and Iraq since 2003 (Mansfield and Snyder, 1995; Wimmer, 2003–4). 'Democratization' may also result in what Fareed Zakaria (1997, 2003) describes as 'illiberal democracies' – partial or stalled democratic transitions where leaders or governments are elected, but the weakness of other institutions means that there are no real alternatives to the dominant leader or party, and few constraints on executive power. Post-communist Russia provides a prime example of such a country. Third, the economic dimension of the Western-dominated international order also generates problems (Stiglitz, 2002). While the West has experienced unprecedented economic growth and prosperity since the Second World War, much of the rest of the world has suffered continuing poverty and economic underdevelopment. Similarly, while globalization, trade liberalization and market economic reforms have produced high economic growth rates in some countries since the 1980s, significant parts of the world – in particular, most of Africa and the Middle East – have not benefited from the new globalized economy. Market economic reforms and trade liberalization have created new classes of economic losers, as inefficient industries are put out of business. The liberalization of international financial markets has resulted in economic instability, and triggered major financial and economic crises in East Asia, Russia and Latin America in the late 1990s. These developments have generated widespread resentment of what are viewed as Western-imposed economic reforms, exacerbating more general anti-Western sentiment in much of the world.

A different challenge to the Western-dominated international order, and one that will in the medium term fundamentally alter the core–periphery distribution of power noted above, is the rising economic power of Asia, and the developing world more generally. Since the early 1990s, China, India and a number of other Asian countries have experienced high economic growth rates (averaging somewhere between 5 per cent and 10 per cent per annum). These growth rates are significantly higher than those among the developed Western states, and if they are maintained in the coming decades – which, while not predetermined, is nevertheless likely, given that the Asian and other developing states are at an earlier stage in their economic development than either Europe or the USA – will result in a major shift in global economic, political and military power away from the old West and towards Asia, in particular China and India, and the developing world (Brown, 2000; Hoge, 2004; Mohan, 2006). Signalling this shift, in 2005 the combined output of developed economies accounted for the first time for more than half of world GDP (measured at purchasing-power parity) (Woodall, 2006, p. 3). The extent and implications of this global power shift remain uncertain. China's and India's very large populations and territories, for example, may constrain their ability to convert economic growth into global political or military power. While the rise of Asia (and other potential major powers such as South Africa and Brazil) may involve a shift of power away from the Euro-atlantic region, the extent to which this represents a broader challenge to the Western-dominated international order is also unclear. India, South Africa and Brazil are all democracies. These countries and China are increasingly market-orientated economies integrated into the world economy. All these countries are members of and have largely accepted the norms underpinning the primary international institutions created by the Western powers since the Second World War, such as the United Nations (UN) and the World Trade Organization (WTO). While there is likely to be a growing shift of material power away from the old Euro-atlantic West and this will significantly reshape international politics, central elements of the Western-dominated international order – democracy, capitalism and institutionalized international co-operation along broadly liberal lines – may outlive the dominance of the old West that gave birth to them.

The new wars

For much of the twentieth century, the primary international security concern was the risk of 'total war' – great-power war extending on a continent-wide or global scale (Aron, 1954). As was argued in Chapter 1, the emergence of a security community has radically reduced the likelihood of war among the major Western powers. Some analysts go further, arguing that we are witnessing 'the obsolescence of major war' (Mueller, 1990; see also Kaysen, 1990; Mandelbaum, 1998–9). The decline of major war is attributed to a range of factors. The destructive power of nuclear weapons and the risk of all-out nuclear war has arguably changed the calculus of state behaviour among the major nuclear-armed powers: the destruction likely to be caused by a nuclear war – and the risk that any war among the major powers might escalate into nuclear war – mean that war is no longer a rational means of pursuing state objectives among nuclear weapons states. Even aside from the development of nuclear weapons, the increasing destructiveness of prolonged modern conventional warfare and the vulnerability of industrialized societies to such warfare have arguably reduced the likelihood of war among the major powers. At the same time, the experience of the twentieth century – 'the century of total war' (Aron, 1954) – has resulted in important shifts in normative attitudes to war. Whereas in the nineteenth and early twentieth centuries war was often viewed as a glorious, noble and virtuous activity that strengthened the individual and the nation, today war is widely viewed as an evil, usually justified only in order to prevent a greater evil. How far we should accept 'the obsolescence of major war' thesis remains contentious. War between the USA and China over Taiwan, or between Russia and the major Western powers on the fringes of the former Soviet Union, for example, are not beyond the bounds of possibility. Nevertheless, even these conflicts are probably less likely than great-power war was a century ago. Even if such conflicts were to occur, the competing alliances that resulted in continent-wide and global escalation in 1914 and 1939 are not in place to the same degree today, suggesting that such conflicts might remain limited in scope rather than escalating to become a wider great-power war.

Great-power war is increasingly being replaced by the so-called 'new wars': internal conflicts within states but with significant regional and international dimensions – such as those that have occurred in the former Yugoslavia, Somalia, Rwanda, East Timor, Afghanistan, Colombia, the Caucasus, West Africa and Sudan since the 1990s (Duffield, 2001; Kaldor, 2001). Robert Kaplan (1994) has described the new wars as harbingers of a 'coming anarchy' in which low-level violent conflict and state collapse become the dominant features of global politics. While Kaplan's apocalyptic argument describes the reality in parts of the world (for example, West Africa, on which he draws in particular) it also exaggerates the extent and likely global impact of the new wars. Observers such as Kaplan suggest that there has been a dramatic upsurge in violent internal conflicts since the end of the Cold War. In fact, this is not the case. Between 1990 and 2005, the number of major armed conflicts (defined as conflicts involving more than 1,000 battle-related deaths a year) ongoing at any one time has varied between a high of thirty-one in 1991 and a low of seventeen in 2005, with a trend towards a decreasing number of conflicts (Harbom and Wallensteen, 2006). While new conflicts emerged as a result of the end of the Cold War (in the former Yugoslavia and the Caucasus, for example), others came to an end (as in Central America and Southern Africa) (Wallensteen and Axell, 1993). According to a recent major survey, the number of armed conflicts globally has declined by more than 40 per cent since the early 1990s, the number of armed secessionist conflicts stood at twenty-five in 2004 (the lowest number since the 1970s), and the number of genocides and politicides (attempts to wipe out political opposition groups) also declined significantly after the late 1980s (Human Security Centre, 2005). The vast majority of conflicts in the early twenty-first century are internal. Indeed, the trend towards internal conflicts is not simply a post-Cold War phenomenon but can be traced back to at least 1945. The majority of wars since the Second World War have been internal conflicts, reflecting a pattern of recurrent internal conflict in much of the Third World. The new wars of the 1990s and early twenty-first century are thus an extension of the types of conflict seen in much of the Third World since de-colonization.

The new wars are defined by a number of distinct features. First, there has been a growing shift towards civilians as victims of wars, and a blurring of the boundary between soldiers and civilians. At the beginning of the twentieth century, 85–90 per cent of casualties in wars were military, but by the 1990s 80 per cent of casualties were civilians (Kaldor, 2001, pp. 8, 100). At the same time, there is a growing trend towards the forced displacement of people – 'ethnic cleansing' as it was termed in the Yugoslav conflict – as both a consequence and a means of war. Civilians are often also coerced into taking up arms, or have little alternative but to take up arms in self-defence, thus blurring the boundary between civilians and combatants. As a consequence, most new wars are also 'complex emergencies' or 'humanitarian crises' involving significant numbers of civilian deaths, mass population movements and associated problems of hunger and disease. Second, although not classical international conflicts, the new wars are increasingly regionalized, spreading into neighbouring countries and creating regional nexuses of conflict and instability: combatants, weapons and refugees cross state borders; neighbouring states and ethnic kin become involved; and illicit cross-border economic ties fuel the new wars. The third feature of the new wars is their internationalization through the involvement of the wider international community: foreign troops are deployed as peacekeepers; governments and international organizations supply humanitarian aid and take on conflict resolution and peace-building tasks; non-governmental organizations distribute aid and perform other functions, such as supporting democracy.

The pattern of conflict that has emerged since the 1990s is likely to continue (Nye, 1996). The security community among the major Western powers is deeply entrenched and likely to remain intact unless there is a global political and economic shock equivalent to that of the 1930s. Although war between the Western powers, in particular the USA, and China and Russia is more conceivable, there are powerful forces – in particular, the rising costs of extended war among industrialized states – working against such an outcome. Should such conflicts occur, for example between the USA and China over Taiwan, they are likely to be limited in duration and scope, in contrast to the total wars of the twentieth century. While a number of regions could see more traditional inter-state wars – between Israel and its Arab neighbours; between India and Pakistan; and on the Korean peninsula – experience since 1945 suggests that such conflicts will remain reasonably rare. The most common form of conflict is likely to remain the new internal but regionalized and internationalized wars that have emerged since the mid-1990s. While the numbers of such conflicts may be declining, the difficulty of preventing and resolving them suggests that their incidence is unlikely to subside very quickly. The existence of a core group of states (the Western security community) unlikely themselves to succumb to such conflicts, however, suggests that apocalyptic predictions of a dramatic global upsurge in new wars are also misplaced.

Proliferation: the second nuclear age

For the first four decades of the nuclear age, the risk of all-out nuclear war between the USA and the Soviet Union was central to the global security agenda. The end of the Cold War has dramatically reduced the likelihood of such a conflict, but developments since the early 1990s have triggered increasing concern about the proliferation of nuclear, biological and chemical weapons to a growing range of states and possibly terrorist groups. After the 1990–1 Gulf War it was discovered that Iraq was much closer to developing nuclear weapons than had previously been thought, and might have been in a position to deploy a nuclear arsenal within a few years – a development that might have enabled it to succeed in its invasion and annexation of Kuwait and more broadly altered the balance of power within the Middle East. The break-up of the Soviet Union at the end of 1991 resulted in the dispersal of the superpower's nuclear weapons among its successor states and concern about 'nuclear leakage' – the possibility that nuclear weapons, materials or knowledge might be stolen or sold on the black market. In 1998, India and Pakistan went further, and tested nuclear weapons. Both states have since consolidated their status as nuclear-weapon powers by expanding their nuclear arsenals and delivery systems. North Korea's nuclear ambitions have also been a focus of international concern since the early 1990s: under a 1994 Agreed Framework with the USA, Pyongyang agreed to cease its nuclear weapons programme in return for help in developing civilian nuclear power; the Agreed Framework collapsed in 2003, however, and in October 2006 Pyongyang crossed the nuclear threshold by testing a nuclear weapon. Similarly, there has also been growing concern since the early 1990s that Iran is seeking to develop nuclear weapons. The fact that countries such as Iran, Iraq and North Korea had moved close to developing nuclear weapons despite being signatories of the Nuclear Non-Proliferation Treaty (NPT) and subject to International Atomic Energy Agency (IAEA) inspections of their nuclear facilities, raised serious doubts about the effectiveness of the NPT/IAEA regime in preventing proliferation. In addition, in 2004, a secret black market network in nuclear weapons technology linking Pakistan, Iran, Libya and North Korea was discovered (Traynor *et al.*, 2004). Finally, the September 2001 terrorist attacks on the USA and subsequent revelations of contacts between Al-Qaeda and Taliban leaders and officials associated with Pakistan's nuclear weapons programme raised the possibility that terrorist groups might acquire nuclear weapons.

In combination, these developments suggest that the world may have reached a decisive turning point in nuclear proliferation: India, Pakistan and North Korea have joined the club of nuclear weapon states since the late 1990s, and Iran may follow suit. In this new strategic context, neighbouring states – Japan and South Korea in North East Asia, for example, and Saudi Arabia and Turkey in the Middle East – could also choose to develop nuclear weapons. Colin Gray (1999) has described such a development as the dawning of a 'second nuclear age', in which a much wider range of states will have the ability to threaten to use – or in extremis use – nuclear weapons.

An additional dimension of the proliferation problem is the concern that a range of states or terrorist groups may have acquired chemical or biological weapons. Egypt, Iran, Iraq, Libya, North Korea and Syria are all believed to have (or in Iraq and Libya's cases, have had) active chemical and biological weapons programmes. Although now often grouped together as weapons of mass destruction (WMD), the military threats and proliferation challenges posed by nuclear, chemical and biological weapons differ in important ways (Perkovich, 2004). Nuclear weapons have by far the greatest destructive potential – providing the capacity to destroy entire cities, large industrial or military facilities and large concentrations of armed forces, and kill many thousands, possibly millions, of people – but they require a large and complex infrastructure and are thus particularly difficult to develop. Chemical weapons are easier to develop, and can potentially kill hundreds or thousands of people, but are difficult to disperse over a large area and have hence been viewed more as tactical battlefield weapons or weapons capable of causing terror and disruption but unlikely to cause very large numbers – tens of thousands or more – of casualties. Biological weapons cannot cause the same physical destruction as nuclear weapons, but could if dispersed in populated areas – and because of the infectious nature of the diseases that might be involved – cause many thousands, possibly millions, of deaths. The global diffusion of biotechnology, the relative ease of developing biological weapons compared to nuclear weapons, their potential to cause death on a massive scale and the relatively small amounts of biological material required could make biological weapons the weapon of choice for weak states or terrorist groups, and has thus made them a particular proliferation concern (Chyba and Greninger, 2004). Some analysts, however, argue that the danger of true mass casualty use of biological weapons has been exaggerated (in particular, because of the difficulty of dispersing biological toxins over large areas) and that biological weapons are more likely to be used as more limited battlefield weapons or for terrorist attacks on a more limited scale (Dando, 2005).

The prospect of accelerating WMD proliferation raises major questions about what action can and should be taken to limit the spread of such weapons, and how to respond if proliferation cannot be prevented. An established non-proliferation infrastructure already exists in the form of the NPT, the IAEA, the biological and chemical weapons conventions (which ban the possession and use of these weapons), and related national and multilateral export controls. Developments since the 1990s point to both the substantial limits of traditional approaches to non-proliferation and the difficulty of persuading determined states to abandon their WMD ambitions. Some, particularly in the USA, have argued that only more coercive approaches – diplomatic isolation, economic sanctions and ultimately the threat or use of military force – may persuade states such as Iraq,

Iran and North Korea to abandon their WMD programmes. The 2003 Iraq War illustrated the controversies likely to surround this logic, and ongoing debates over how to respond to Iran and North Korea's nuclear ambitions suggest that these issues will not go away. An alternative logic might suggest that only the more radical approach of moving towards a world free from nuclear weapons or centralized global control of such weapons might persuade states beyond the existing nuclear weapons powers not to develop WMD, but this is an argument that has not yet found much purchase. Beyond this lies the question of how states should respond if proliferation cannot be prevented, for example by preparing to defend themselves against WMD attack (as the USA is now doing with its missile defence plans) or by supporting new nuclear powers to develop stabilizing rather than destabilizing nuclear forces and postures. The inadequacies of the existing non-proliferation regime and the difficulties inherent in the various alternatives to that regime suggest that proliferation will continue to generate controversial policy dilemmas.

The 'new terrorism' and the 'war on terror'

The 11 September 2001 attacks on the USA have pushed terrorism to the top of the global security agenda, made the 'war on terror' the driving force of US foreign policy and in the process reshaped international politics. From a European perspective, terrorism is not a new phenomenon: European states have long experience of terrorism at the national level (the UK in Northern Ireland, Spain in the Basque country, terrorism by extreme left and extreme right groups in various countries) and European citizens and states were among the primary targets of Palestinian terrorism in the 1960s and 1970s. Nevertheless, the threat posed by what has been called the 'new terrorism' is both fundamentally different in nature and significantly greater in magnitude than previous terrorist threats.

The 'new terrorism' had been emerging since the early 1990s (Simon and Benjamin, 2001–2; Burke, 2004). Although other groups such as the Aum Shinrikyo religious cult responsible for the 1995 nerve gas attack on the Tokyo underground and far-right American groups are sometimes seen as part of the phenomenon, the driving force of the 'new terrorism' is the radical Islamism of Al-Qaeda and associated groups. Such groups were responsible for the first attempt to destroy the World Trade Center in New York in 1993, a 1995 attempt to destroy eleven jumbo jets over the Pacific, and the 1998 bombings of US embassies in East Africa, as well as a number of lesser terrorist incidents. The 'new terrorism' differs from most past terrorism in a number of important ways. Much past terrorism was primarily national in that it took place within one country or related to specific national goals, usually independent statehood or reunification with a neighbouring state. The 'new terrorism' is driven by the assumption of an all-embracing global conflict between Islam and its enemies (the West in general and the USA and Israel in particular), and by a broad rejection of the current international order and its norms. Radical Islamic groups see conflicts in the Islamic world – in Palestine, Kashmir, Chechnya, Iraq and elsewhere – as part of this global struggle. The declared goal of Al-Qaeda is to establish an Islamic Caliphate across the Muslim world, expelling foreign forces and overthrowing apostate local regimes in the process. Members of Al-Qaeda and associated groups view themselves as being involved in a struggle against both the 'near enemy' (the current regimes in countries such as Saudi Arabia and Egypt) and the 'far enemy' (the USA and other Western states). The 'new terrorism' is also a global phenomenon in the sense that Al-Qaeda and associated groups have proved themselves capable of initiating attacks in all parts of the world. The nature of Islamic terrorism as a global movement is, however, the subject of debate: up to and immediately after 9/11 some analysts described it as a relatively centralized movement, with the Al-Qaeda leadership exercising a significant degree of political and operational control over groups elsewhere in the world. But after the overthrow of the Taliban and destruction of Al-Qaeda's operating base in Afghanistan in late 2001, analysts suggest that Islamic terrorism as a global phenomenon had become increasingly decentralized and fragmented. The extent to which Al-Qaeda leaders (based primarily in the Afghanistan–Pakistan border region) control or direct Islamic terrorist groups globally, or these groups are largely free-standing, remains the subject of debate. Whatever the case, it is clear that radical Islamic groups have been able to exploit conflicts and grievances in the Muslim world, and that a loose global movement using terrorism as one of its key modus operandi has emerged as a consequence. The term globalized Islamic terrorism is used in this book to refer to this phenomenon. The 'new terrorism' is also defined by an unrestrained attitude to the use of violence. In the past, most terrorists used violence in limited forms to bring attention to their cause, undermine political authorities or provoke repressive responses from their opponents. Thus, whereas past terrorists wanted a lot of people watching rather than a lot of people dead, the new terrorists of Al-Qaeda appear to have abandoned this logic and seek to maximize the death and destruction they cause (Simon and Benjamin, 2000, p. 66). The 'new terrorism' has thus also been described as 'catastrophic terrorism' because it threatens, in particular if terrorist groups obtain WMD, to inflict damage on a far greater scale than previous forms of terrorism (Carter and Perry, 1999, pp. 143–74).

In response to the 9/11 attacks, the Bush Administration declared a 'war on terror', making this a central element of US foreign policy and – given America's predominant global role – world politics more generally. This has had a number of dimensions. Militarily, the USA intervened in Afghanistan in late 2001 to destroy Al-Qaeda's bases in that country and overthrow the Taliban regime that had provided sanctuary for Al-Qaeda. The USA has also undertaken a number of more limited military interventions against terrorist groups and targets, or provided military support to other governments for such operations, in places as diverse as the Philippines, Georgia and Yemen. Politically and institutionally, the 'war on terror' has resulted in a raft of international measures to counter terrorism. This has included the establishment of a UN Counter-Terrorism Committee, intensified intelligence co-operation and new measures to tackle the financing of terrorism, as well as the provision of US economic and military aid to support allies' efforts against terrorism. The 'war on terror' has also resulted in the emergence of a new homeland security agenda, with states taking a wide range of measures to strengthen border controls, provide for the physical security of vulnerable targets (such as nuclear power stations), intensify intelligence and law enforcement efforts directed against terrorist groups, and develop the capacity to respond to terrorist attacks should they occur. These steps have gone furthest in the USA, with the creation of the Department of Homeland Security, but other states have implemented similar measures. The new homeland security agenda has provoked renewed debate on the long-standing question of the appropriate balance between security and freedom, with critics arguing that some measures taken to counter terrorism risk undermining fundamental freedoms, democracy and the rule of law.

The US response to the 9/11 attacks has raised major questions as to how broadly the 'war on terror' should be framed, and what policies are appropriate to counter the terrorist threat. The Bush Administration linked the terrorist threat to the issues of WMD proliferation and 'rogue states' (in particular, the so-called 'axis of evil' of

Iran, Iraq and North Korea), arguing that the risk of terrorists obtaining WMD from such states means that the issues cannot be separated. Critics argue that the USA has dangerously conflated different security challenges, adopted an overly confrontational and militarized approach to counter-terrorism and in so doing has alienated much of global opinion, especially in the Islamic world, while paying too little attention to addressing the root causes and grievances that give rise to terrorism, in particular the Israeli–Palestinian conflict (Howard, 2002; Record, 2003). Whatever the merits of these arguments, there can be little doubt that not only terrorism itself but also international, especially US, responses to terrorism are likely to generate continuing controversies. Although radically different from previous great-power wars, further, the combination of Al-Qaeda and related groups' willingness to use force globally and the centrality of the 'war on terror' to US foreign policy post-9/11 has nevertheless created a type of 'Third World War': a conflict that impinges on virtually all areas of the world and all aspects of global politics (Freedman, 2001).

Soft security

As discussed in Chapter 1, security has traditionally been seen as relating to issues of war and military power. Although some analysts dislike the term soft security, arguing that it implies that such threats are less serious than traditional 'hard' security problems, the term nevertheless encapsulates the idea that there is a range of non-military problems increasingly central to the security agenda. Since the early 1990s, governments and international organizations have increasingly come to accept the argument that non-military problems are central to the security agenda. The EU's first official security strategy document, adopted in December 2003, identified poverty, disease, dependence on transport, energy and information infrastructure, state failure and organized crime as security threats (European Union, 2003a). Similarly, the Bush Administration's 2002 *National Security Strategy* document noted that:

> The events of September 11, 2001, taught us that weak states, like Afghanistan, can pose as great a danger to our national interests as strong states . . . poverty, weak institutions, and corruption can make weak states vulnerable to terrorist networks and drug cartels within their borders. (United States, 2002)

Arguments have also been advanced for the re-conceptualization of security as human security, with an emphasis on the full range of threats to the security and well-being of both human beings and communities, rather than the more traditional focus on the physical security and political independence of states. A number of governments, such as those of Japan and Canada, have formally supported the concept of human security. A UN-sponsored international Commission on Human Security (2003) argued that state security should be supplemented by the concept of human security focused on individuals and communities and aiming to provide not only protection from violent conflict but also basic economic security, health care and education for the populace. In 2004, a high-level panel established by UN Secretary-General Kofi Annan argued that poverty, infectious disease, environmental degradation and transnational organized crime should be viewed as central security challenges alongside warfare, WMD proliferation and terrorism (United Nations, 2004b).

Although this wider interpretation of security is somewhat diffuse, a number of issues are generally seen as central to the emerging soft or human security agenda:

- *Economics*: There is growing recognition of the linkage between economics and security. The EU's 2003 security strategy document argued that:

> In much of the developing world, poverty and disease cause untold suffering and give rise to pressing security concerns. Almost 3 billion people, half the world's population, live on less than 2 Euros a day. 45 million die every year of hunger and malnutrition . . . In many cases, economic failure is linked to political problems and violent conflict. Security is a precondition of development. Conflict not only destroys infrastructure, including social infrastructure; it also encourages criminality, deters investment and makes normal economic activity impossible. A number of countries and regions are caught in a cycle of conflict, insecurity and poverty. (European Union, 2003a)

The nature, meaning and challenges of economic security are, however, far from clear, with conceptions of economic security ranging from problems of dependence on external resources and/or markets, to the interconnected nature of globalized financial markets, and to the problems of underdevelopment and poverty in the Third World (Buzan, 1991a, pp. 230–69; United Nations, 2004b, p. 26).

- *The environment*: there is a growing recognition that environmental change or degradation may pose security threats (Levy, 1995). Environmental degradation may pose a direct threat to human health, well-being and survival, as in cases of severe pollution or industrial accidents such as the 1984 accident at the Union Carbide plant in Bhopal, India, and the 1986 Chernobyl nuclear power station accident in Ukraine. Environmental change or degradation may also cause political instability and violent conflict, by intensifying competition for limited resources (Homer-Dixon, 1991, 1994). Competition for water resources has become part of the Israeli–Arab conflict, and some analysts predict an era of water wars in the Middle East (Gleick, 1993). The most important global environmental security issue, however, is climate change or global warming – the increasing temperature of the earth's atmosphere resulting in significant part from human economic activity. Global warming is likely to have a major impact on humanity in the coming decades, with rising sea levels submerging all or part of some countries, and major changes in weather patterns threatening the well-being and survival of many people and triggering wider economic, social and political changes. According to press reports, a suppressed report for the US Department of Defense argued that climate change may cause major violent conflicts and should be a central US national security concern (Townsend and Harris, 2004). Sir John Houghton (2003), former chief executive of the UK's Meteorological Office and co-chair of the scientific assessment working group of the Intergovernmental Panel on Climate Change (the primary international scientific body assessing climate change), has described global warming as a 'weapon of mass destruction' that already kills more people than terrorism.

- *Energy security*: the issues of reliable access to key energy resources (in particular, oil and gas) and dependence on overseas energy supplies have re-emerged as central elements of the global security agenda post-9/11 (Harris, 2003; Kalicki and Goldwyn, 2005). This issue initially came to prominence in the 1970s after the first major oil crisis and the resulting global economic recession. Rapidly expanding global energy demand and the Middle East's position as both the epicentre of globalized Islamic terrorism and the region with the world's largest concentration of oil resources have, however, pushed the issue of energy security to the fore once more. In parallel with this, Russia's emergence as a major global oil and gas supplier has allowed Moscow to regain some of its previous great-power status, while further complicating its relations with the West.

- *Mass population movements*: Since the mid-1990s, mass population movements have increasingly been viewed as part of the security agenda (Weiner, 1995; Loescher and Milner, 2005). Wars, famines or environmental disasters cause short-term large-scale population movements, creating immediate humanitarian crises, but often also wider social, economic and political instability. Longer-term, large-scale population movements, driven primarily by people's desire to move from poorer parts of the world to richer ones, have also generated concerns about potential threats posed by migration.

- *Disease*: The global HIV/AIDS epidemic has made infectious diseases part of the new security agenda. An estimated 20 million people have died as a result of HIV/AIDS, a further 38 million are estimated to be infected with HIV, and China, India and Russia are predicted to be on the verge of explosive increases in HIV infection (UNAIDS, 2004). Other infectious diseases, in particular malaria, tuberculosis, acute respiratory infections (ARI), diarrhoeal infections and measles, cause the deaths of nearly ten million people each year. HIV/AIDS and other infectious diseases also have wider socio-economic and political repercussions, weakening economies, exacerbating competition for limited resources and undermining states (Elbe, 2003). The 2003 SARS (severe acute respiratory syndrome) outbreak provided a warning of the possible emergence of new diseases (or new strains of existing diseases) that could potentially cause the deaths of many millions of people (Sample, 2003).

- *Crime*: Over the last decade or so the scale of violent and/or organized crime has increased dramatically in a number of countries and regions (Goodson, 2003). In countries such as Colombia and South Africa, for example, the threat of violent crime impinges on the daily lives of the entire population and threatens to destabilize the state, economy and democratic politics. Crime is also a notable feature of the new wars discussed above, with the economies of war zones becoming increasingly dependent on the illegal sale and trafficking of a wide range of goods. Organized criminality has also taken on a growing transnational dimension, with criminal groups, such as Russian mafia, operating across state borders on a large scale. Additionally, transnational organized crime contributes to other security problems such as the illegal trafficking of arms and WMD materials.

- *Critical infrastructure protection*: A further recent security concern is the protection of the key economic and technological infrastructure systems that underpin modern societies, including electricity grids, telecommunications systems, transport networks, water supply systems, and fire and rescue services (Lukasik *et al.*, 2003; Schmitt, 2005). The growing complexity of modern industrial and post-industrial societies has led to arguments that they are increasingly vulnerable to the disruption of such infrastructures, through direct physical attack (whether by states or terrorist groups) or by less direct means (such as poisoning of water supply systems or hacking into computer systems). The centrality of computer systems to critical infrastructures and the advent of the internet age have also led to arguments that societies may be highly vulnerable to cyber-attack or cyber-terrorism, where computer viruses or hacking into computer systems could be used to disrupt critical infrastructures. The extent to which nightmare scenarios – where societies might be thrown into chaos by cyber-attacks and the resulting disruption of critical infrastructures – are realistic is a matter for debate, but governments are now investing significant resources in protecting critical infrastructure systems from cyber and other forms of attack.

While these non-military problems are becoming an increasingly prominent part of the new global security agenda, the broadening of the concept of security is not without problems. The securitization of previously non-security, political, economic and security issues risk producing exaggerated perceptions of the threats posed by such issues and/or overly confrontational or militarized policy responses (Buzan, Waever and de Wilde, 1998, pp. 208–12; Krause and Williams, 1997).

American hegemony

The final feature of the new global security environment is American hegemony. American hegemony is not absolute in the sense that the US power is not limitless and the USA cannot directly control affairs across the globe as previous empires have done, nor can it always easily achieve its objectives. Nevertheless, the global power of the USA is unmatched by any other state or regional group, and is a defining feature of the international environment for all other states. The USA accounts for approximately a third of global economic output and a third to half of global military expenditure, plays a central role in all

major international institutions and has greater global political influence than any other power. Table 2.1 provides a comparison with other
major powers.

America's global predominance is not new but has been accentuated
by the end of the Cold War and the 9/11 attacks. The USA emerged as
a leading global power at the beginning of the twentieth century,
played the decisive role in the two world wars and shaped much of the
post-1945 world order. The twentieth century has thus been described
by some as the American century (Cumings, 1999). The end of the
Cold War and the collapse of the Soviet Union eliminated what had
been the primary potential challenger to the USA, leading many
observers to conclude that the world had entered a unipolar era
(Krauthammer, 1990–1). The 9/11 attacks further reinforced the USA's
dominant global role, leading the Bush Administration to implement a
foreign policy revolution based on the unilateral assertion of American
power (Daalder and Lindsay, 2003).

American hegemony has a number of features. Most importantly,
the USA is the world's only complete global power: only the USA has
the combination of global reach across the full spectrum of power
(Nye, 2002, pp. 1–40). In addition to its hard economic and military
power, the USA has a global network of alliances, bases and intelligence assets built up since 1945, a central role in the key international
institutions (permanent membership of the UN Security Council, an
effective veto over the decisions of the International Monetary Fund
(IMF) and the World Bank, and a leading role in NATO, the G8 and
the World Trade Organization) and the soft power influence of its
democracy, market economics and culture. No other state or group
comes close to matching the USA across the spectrum of power. The
EU's economic power is broadly comparable with (indeed, by some
measures greater than) that of the USA, but the EU lacks America's
global military power and is fragmented politically across its member
states. As was noted earlier, China and India have much larger populations than the USA, and rapidly growing economies, but it will be some
decades, if at all, before they are able to convert their latent power into
global political and military influence. Other potential competitors,
such as Japan and Russia, are even further from being credible chal-
lengers to US dominance.

America's dominance is particularly marked in the military sphere.
US defence spending in 2006 was projected to be between
US$421.1mn and US$513.9mn (depending on the elements that are
included), accounting for almost half (48 per cent) of total global

TABLE 2.1 The global balance of power in the early twenty-first century

Country/ Region	Territory (mn sq km)	Population (mn 2006)	GDP (US$ 2005)	Defence expenditure (US$bn 2005)	Armed forces (active, 000s, 2006)	Nuclear weapons (nuclear arbeads)
USA	9.6	296	11.7tr	495	1 546	5 521
European Union*	4.3	489	13.7tr	244	1 929	–
China	9.6	1 306	1.89tr	99.5	2 255	130
Russia	17.1	143	1.4tr**	59.6***	1 027	5 682
Japan	0.4	127	4.7tr	44.7	260	–
Germany	0.4	82	2.85tr	38.5	285	–
UK	0.2	60	2.23tr	51.1	217	185
France	0.5	61	2.15tr	53.8	256	348
India	3.3	1 080	761bn	22	1 325	50

Notes:

mn = million; 1bn = 1,000mn; 1tr = 1,000,000mn.

* European Union = 27 member states as of 1 January 2007.

** 2004 figures.

Data from: The International Institute for Strategic Studies, *The Military Balance 2006* (Abingdon, Routledge for the IISS, 2006); Stockholm International Peace Research Institute, *SIPRI Yearbook 2006: Armaments, Disarmament and International Security* (Oxford University Press, 2006), table 13A.1, World nuclear forces, by number of deployed warheads, January 2006, p. 640; Central Intelligence Agency, *The World Factbook 2006*, http://www.cia.gov/cia/publications/factbook/.

military spending. The USA's 2005 defence budget was US$507.1bn, compared to US$57.6mn for the UK, the next largest military spender. The US defence budget is larger than the combined budgets of the world's fourteen next-biggest military spenders (Stalenheim *et al.*, 2006, pp. 300–12). Reinforced by six decades of extensive military spending and the development of global military infrastructure since the Second World War, the USA is the only state capable of projecting military power globally on a very large scale. At least in the short-to-medium term, and perhaps in the longer term also, the military gap between the USA and the rest of the world is likely to grow. In response to the 9/11 attacks, the Bush Administration introduced the biggest increase in US defence spending in twenty years, with total spending rising from approximately US$300bn in 2000 to over US$500bn in 2006. Since the early 1990s, the USA has also invested heavily in the Revolution in Military Affairs (RMA – the application of information technology to the armed forces), stretching the military-technological gap between itself and all other states.

Is America's current global predominance likely to last? Many theorists argue that a number of factors inevitably work against prolonged hegemony. In the long-term, changes in technology and modes of economic production result in differential economic growth rates, meaning that no country can permanently sustain the economic power that underpins a leading global role. Hegemony, it is argued, also results in imperial overstretch, as the costs of maintaining global power become unsustainable, forcing retrenchment or collapse (Kennedy, 1988). Realist international relations theorists argue that the existence of a hegemon inevitably provokes the emergence of either a rival challenger or a countervailing coalition (Layne, 1993). Recent developments can be read as supporting these arguments. Economically, the USA is currently running a significant trade deficit and is heavily dependent on foreign inward investment. The problems and costs of trying to stabilize Iraq, as well as fighting a multi-front global war against terrorism, can be seen as signs of imperial overstretch. The broad international opposition to the 2003 Iraq War can be interpreted as the inevitable growth of international opposition to an overweening hegemon.

Predictions of imminent American decline, however, should be treated with caution (Strange, 1987). Observers have at various points in the past – in the 1950s after the Korean War and in the 1970s and 1980s after the Vietnam War – predicted America's imminent decline. These predictions have proved to be misplaced: although the Vietnam syndrome made the USA rather more reluctant to use military force, and its economic dominance was less than it had been in the years immediately after the Second World War, America nevertheless remained the dominant global political, military and economic power. It is also far from clear that the factors usually advanced as causes of a hegemon's decline – the emergence of rival powers, imperial over-stretch and long-term economic change – suggest that the USA is likely to lose its global pre-eminence in the near future. As was noted above, all the potential rivals to US hegemony suffer from weaknesses or constraints that severely limit their capacity to challenge America. Similarly, although China, Russia, India, Europe and Japan to varying degrees express anti-American rhetoric and have sometimes co-operated with one another against the USA, these countries are far from being united into a coherent anti-USA coalition. In addition, compared to many past hegemonic powers – such as Napoleonic France, Nazi Germany or Imperial Japan – the USA has generally acted with strategic restraint in its relations with the other major powers, avoiding threatening directly their survival or core interests (Ikenberry, 2001).

Notwithstanding the problems the USA currently faces in Iraq, the spectre of imperial overstretch may also be exaggerated. Ever since the onset of the Cold War there have been periodic warnings that the USA may not be able to sustain the costs of its global role, yet it has in practice been able to bear these costs. In the area of defence spending, for example, although the USA now accounts for almost half of all global military expenditure, this amounts to only some 4 per cent of American GDP. Compared to the 10–15 per cent or more of GNP that the Soviet Union was estimated to be spending on defence by the 1980s (Cooper, 1998, pp. 243–6) and which arguably contributed significantly to its demise, such expenditure may well be sustainable.

Long-term economic change is more difficult to predict. As discussed earlier, while China and India's economies may in terms of overall size surpass that of the USA in the coming decades, converting economic power into global political and military power is likely to be a long-term process, and Chinese and Indian economic growth rates may slow. Some analysts argue that the combination of a highly productive economy, a strong technological base and an innovative and entrepreneurial culture make the USA well placed to maintain its position at the forefront of the global economy. While China and India may well assert themselves as leading global powers later in the twenty-first century, short of a dramatic economic collapse forcing the USA to abandon its global role there is a strong likelihood that America will remain the pre-eminent, and indeed only truly global, power for at least the next two decades and probably longer.

The post-9/11 debate on America's world role is therefore better understood as a debate over the nature of US engagement with the world rather than a prelude to hegemonic decline. The Bush Administration's foreign policy revolution and the problems the USA faces in Iraq have raised major questions about the extent to which the USA can and should act unilaterally, the extent to which the USA needs the support of allies, and the costs of America's global role. It remains possible that the USA could retreat into isolationism, as it did after the First World War. A more likely scenario, post-Iraq, however, is one of limited retrenchment, as occurred after the Korean and Vietnam wars, rather than complete global withdrawal. US public opinion is broadly supportive of America's global role, the US Congress – although often wary of the constraints of international institutions – has since 1945 shown little appetite for wholesale disengagement from international commitments, and most credible presidential candidates have been similarly committed to maintaining America's global role. The entrenchment of America's global political and military position since the Second World War and its integration with the world economy suggests that a rapid disengagement from its leading global role would be difficult and costly to implement. The most likely scenario in the next two decades or so is that the USA will not only remain the world's dominant power but will also choose to play a leading global role (Gnesotto and Grevi, 2006, pp. 141–54). The more central question, and the real debate on American foreign policy, is about how America should exercise its global power.

Conclusion

Security has classically been viewed as revolving around the problem of inter-state war, and great-power war has been viewed as the most important security problem. At the beginning of the twenty-first century, the likelihood of great-power war is low, and while a return to the total wars of the twentieth century cannot be entirely ruled out, there are good reasons to believe that such a development is reasonably unlikely. Instead, the traditional security problem of inter-state war is being replaced by a set of new security challenges: new internal wars that nevertheless have significant regional and international repercussions; the proliferation of WMD; globalized Islamic terrorism; and non-military soft security challenges. These challenges, further, are linked in important ways: soft security problems such as poverty and environmental degradation may fuel civil wars; internal conflicts may provide a context and recruiting ground for terrorism; most of these challenges have important transnational dimensions – such as the trade in WMD materials and technologies that flow across state borders and are often outside the control of governments.

While there is an emerging international consensus that these problems constitute a new global security agenda and need to be treated holistically (United Nations, 2004b), the priority and hierarchy that should be attached to different threats and the appropriate response to them are deeply controversial. Differing geostrategic situations, political values and socio-economic positions inevitably produce differing assessments of threats and divergent policy responses. International responses to the new global security agenda reflect this basic reality. As the world's only superpower, the USA has become the primary target of globalized Islamic terrorism and is particularly vulnerable to the consequences of proliferation. Post-9/11, it is hardly surprising that terrorism and proliferation are viewed by the USA as *the* central security challenges. Yet, as UN Secretary-General Kofi Annan argued in 2003, 'for many around the globe, poverty, deprivation and civil war remain the highest priority' (United Nations, 2003, p. 3). Similarly, although climate change will have global implications, these will not affect all regions and countries equally: for small Pacific island states facing the prospect of being completely submerged by rising sea levels global warming is the number one security threat, but other states are less vulnerable to the consequences of climate change; and poor states with inadequate socio-economic infrastructures and health care systems are much more vulnerable to the spread of HIV/AIDS than wealthier states.

Similar divisions arise over responses to the new security agenda. The USA's enormous power gives it a greater capacity than other states to act independently and may create a natural inclination towards unilateral approaches to security problems. In contrast, weaker states lack a similar capacity to act unilaterally, are more vulnerable to unilateral action by others and may therefore be predisposed to multilateralism. While few states and peoples are inclined towards absolute pacifism, recent disputes over military intervention indicate that there is little international consensus as to when the use of military force may be necessary and legitimate. Although there is now much discussion about addressing the underlying root causes of security problems such as terrorism, there is little agreement on what this should involve in practice. In the context of globalized Islamic terrorism, for example, some argue that resolving the Israeli–Palestinian conflict is vital to address the deep resentment that gives rise to terrorism. Others argue that the absence of democracy in the Middle East underpins terrorism. In short, while there may an emerging consensus that there is a new global security agenda, the priority that should be attached to different threats and what policies are necessary to address these threats are likely to remain highly controversial.

From a European perspective, the new global security agenda poses a number of challenges. First, while the likelihood of military conflict within Europe is low, the dangers of proliferation and terrorism suggest that the risk of violent attack from outside Europe may be increasing – as the March 2004 and July 2005 terrorist attacks on Madrid and London made starkly clear. Second, even when security problems elsewhere in the world do not directly or immediately threaten Europe in a physical sense, they may nevertheless threaten European interests in indirect ways. New wars in other regions of the world may threaten European citizens and European economic interests. Instability, violent conflict and deep socio-economic problems in other parts of the world, especially those close to Europe such as Africa and the Middle East, may have important long-term repercussions for Europe, by generating pressures for migration to Europe or fuelling problems such as transnational crime that may spill over into Europe. Put simply, it is difficult to avoid the consequences of living next door to poor, unstable and sometimes violent neighbours. Some global problems, such as climate change, will inevitably have important implications for Europe: in the early years of the twenty-first century, many more European citizens have died as a result of extreme weather conditions thought to be caused by global warming than have been killed by terrorism (World Health Organization, 2005). Third, even if global security problems do not have major implications for European interests, violence and suffering elsewhere in the world may create political pressure and arguably a moral duty to act. Given Europe's prosperity and relative security, European governments may face strong political pressure – from European citizens and from elsewhere in the world – to contribute to addressing the security problems of less privileged parts of the world. European states are already among the world's leading contributors to peacekeeping operations and economic development aid, but the scale of the new global security problems suggests that Europe may be called upon to do much more in future.

The dominant role of the USA in shaping and responding to the new global security agenda also raises major questions for Europe. Since the Second World War, Europe – Western Europe during the Cold War, but now the wider Europe of the enlarged EU and NATO – has been a close ally of the USA. The disappearance of the Soviet threat and the post-9/11 revolution in US foreign policy have, however, raised fundamental questions about the future of transatlantic relations. For Europe, these revolve around the issue of how it should relate to the USA in a new era: as a loyal ally, as a critical friend or as a counterweight and competitor? The future of transatlantic relations is examined in more detail in the next chapter.

European responses to the new global security agenda also relate to the wider issue of what role Europe (or perhaps more accurately *Europeans*, since Europe comes in many guises) can and should in play in the world, and indeed of European identity and what it means to be European. A range of possible answers can be envisaged. An insular 'fortress Europe' would involve seeking to minimize vulnerability to the new security challenges by withdrawing inwards and strengthening Europe's borders. The other end of the spectrum would involve asserting Europe as an activist global force, seeking to make it a second superpower alongside the USA. Another alternative might involve emphasizing Europe's distinctive characteristics and comparative advantage by focusing on the application of soft power and non-military security challenges. Since America's pre-eminence inevitably gives it a central role in addressing the new global security agenda, these questions about Europe's global role and identity cannot be separated from the issue of how Europe should relate to the USA. These larger themes of Europe's global role and its relationship with the USA run throughout this book and will be returned to in the concluding chapter.

Chapter 3

Europe and America: The End of an Era?

Early in 2003, hundreds of thousands of European citizens took to the streets of Berlin, Paris, London, Rome, Madrid and other European capitals to protest against the USA's plans for war in Iraq. The demonstrations were among the largest in the continent's history and seemed to symbolize a deepening rift between Europe and the USA. In the run-up to the Iraq War, France and Germany, along with Russia, led opposition to US plans for military action, prompting US Secretary of Defense, Donald Rumsfeld, to disparagingly describe them as 'old Europe' in contrast to the pro-American 'new Europe' to the east (Department of Defense, 2003). The crisis was widely seen as the worst in transatlantic relations since the US–European alliance had emerged in the Second World War (Peterson, 2004). Coming on top of disputes over a wide range of other issues – such as trade, global warming, arms control, the International Criminal Court and the Middle East – the crisis over Iraq seemed to suggest that European and American foreign policies were increasingly diverging, and the post-1945 transatlantic alliance was coming to an end.

This chapter examines transatlantic relations, exploring developments since the end of the Cold War and assessing the future prospects for the US–European relationship in light of competing theoretical perspectives and the wide range of factors bearing on that relationship. It suggests that 9/11 and the Iraq War are likely to mark the end of an era in transatlantic relations, and in particular that the close US–European alliance that emerged after the Second World War is fragmenting. It also argues, however, that the debate on the future of transatlantic relations is too often polarized between those who argue that we are witnessing a fundamental break in US–European relations and those who argue that a close US–European alliance can be maintained. Instead, a more complex and nuanced picture is emerging. The USA is gradually disengaging from Europe as its priorities shift to other regions of the world, and its role in the management of security issues in Europe is likely to decline, but US disengagement from Europe is unlikely to be complete. US–European relations at the beginning of the twenty-first century are characterized by important elements of co-operation, on issues ranging from mutual investment in each other's economies to counter-terrorism, but by equally significant conflicts in other areas, such as global warming or the broader conduct of the US 'war on terror'. The emphasis in US policy towards Europe is also shifting, away from co-operation with NATO and Europe as a whole, and towards bilateral co-operation and ad hoc coalitions of the willing. As will be explored in more detail in the next chapter, Europeans are also divided over relations with the USA, with some seeking to maintain a close alliance with America while others seek to establish the EU as a counterweight to it – suggesting that European policy towards America is likely to continue to be ambivalent. While the close alliance of the post-1945 era may be over, the most likely scenario for transatlantic relations remains one of important common interests but divergent perspectives on how those interests should be pursued, with a mixed pattern of co-operation in some areas, and differences – and occasional, but limited, competition – in others.

The post-Cold War era

The end of the Cold War raised fundamental questions about the post-Second World War alliance between the USA and Western Europe. In the absence of the unifying external threat posed by the Soviet Union, would the long-standing alliance between Europe and America survive? If, as mainstream opinion in both Europe and America argued, a continued alliance was desirable, what was the purpose of that alliance? The first Bush Administration, which was in power as the Cold War ended from 1989 to 1992, sought to maintain the existing bases of the Euro-atlantic alliance. In particular, it played a central role in the diplomacy surrounding German reunification in 1989–90, facilitating the negotiations that saw Germany unified and remaining a member of NATO and the EU on terms that the Soviet Union was willing to accept (Zelikow and Rice, 1995). The Bush Administration also oversaw the first efforts to adapt NATO to a new era, resulting in a new strategic concept for the alliance adopted at its November 1991 Rome summit.

Nevertheless, the end of Cold War triggered doubts about the future of the Euro-atlantic alliance. In response to the fall of the communist regimes in Central and Eastern Europe and the withdrawal of Soviet troops from the region, the Bush Administration initiated a substantial reduction in the US military presence in Europe. More significantly, when the Yugoslav war broke out in the summer of 1991, the Bush Administration signalled that the management of the conflict should be primarily a European concern. Bush's Secretary of State, James Baker infamously argued that the USA had 'no dog in that fight' (Simms, 2002, p. 53). The new strategic concept adopted by NATO at the end of 1991 was to a significant extent still a backward-looking document, premised on the continued existence of a residual Soviet threat (NATO, 1991). Under the 1992 Maastricht Treaty, the new European Union – the successor to the European Community (EC) – was to have a common foreign and security policy (CFSP) 'covering all areas of foreign and security policy', 'including the eventual framing of a common defence policy, which might in time lead to a common defence' (European Union, 1992, Title V, Articles J1 and J4). The CFSP and a possible EU defence role raised the prospect of a more independent Europe, less in need of and less inclined to co-operate with the USA. The first year of the Clinton Administration in 1993 saw continued tensions in transatlantic relations. In contrast to the foreign-policy orientated Atlanticist, George Bush, during the 1992 presidential election campaign Bill Clinton had famously said 'it's the economy, stupid' and promised to 'focus like a laserbeam' on economic issues. Clinton's Secretary of State, Warren Christopher, also indicated that the new Administration planned to pursue an Asia-first policy, emphasizing economic ties with the rapidly growing East (Cox, 1995, p. 75).

The Yugoslav conflict proved the most sensitive issue in transatlantic relations in the early-to-mid 1990s (Silber and Little, 1995; Simms, 2002). Reflecting more general disquiet in Washington, Clinton had criticized the Europeans for failing to take effective action against Serbia and the Bosnian Serbs. On coming to power, the Clinton Administration proposed a policy of 'lift and strike': lifting sanctions and the arms embargo on the Bosnian government and using airstrikes against the Bosnian Serbs. The Europeans countered that such a policy would put their soldiers deployed on the ground as peacekeepers in danger and produce a level killing field rather than the level playing field Clinton desired. Warren Christopher's first visit to Europe as Secretary of State in 1993 resulted in acrimonious disputes over the 'lift and strike' policy and a humiliating back-down by the Clinton Administration.

After these initial disputes, the Clinton Administration sought to reassert America's role in European security affairs, and the 1990s witnessed a remarkable resurgence in transatlantic relations. Richard Holbrooke, one of the leading architects of the Clinton Administration's European policy, argued that America was, and would remain, 'a European power' (Holbrooke, 1995). On all the key European security issues of the 1990s – the Yugoslav conflict, the transformation of NATO, engagement with Central and Eastern Europe, and building a new relationship with Russia – the USA played a central role. On the Yugoslav conflict, the USA gradually gained support for a more robust policy, resulting in NATO's use of airstrikes against the Bosnia Serbs and the Bosnian peace agreement at the end of 1995 – symbolically agreed at a US military airbase in Dayton, Ohio. The USA was equally central in driving NATO's policy during the Kosovo air war of 1999, and the resulting peace agreement. The deployment of US forces as peacekeepers in Bosnia and Kosovo further reinforced America's commitment to European security. The USA also played the leading role in the transformation of NATO, initiating the Partnership for Peace (PfP), the Alliance's enlargement to take in new members from Central and Eastern Europe, the Combined Joint Task Force (CJTF) concept (designed to give NATO the flexibility to mount operations beyond its borders), and brokering a compromise on the vexed issue of European defence co-operation. To the east, the Clinton Administration sought to bring the countries of Central and Eastern Europe into the West by extending NATO membership to them, while at the same time building a co-operative relationship with Russia.

By the late 1990s, the USA had reasserted a central role in European security affairs, and American leadership had been largely welcomed by most European states – suggesting that transatlantic relations were in remarkably good health, given the concerns of the early 1990s. Beneath the surface, however, significant tensions and differences remained. The US Congress, which had come under Republican control in the 1994 Congressional elections, was unsympathetic to the multilateralism supported by most European governments, refusing to ratify and forcing the Clinton Administration to back down on international agreements for a comprehensive nuclear test ban treaty (CTBT), the Kyoto Treaty on global warming and the establishment of the International Criminal Court (ICC). The Congress was also wary of the deployment of US forces on peacekeeping missions, constraining the Clinton Administration's ability to act in the Balkans. And during the 1990s, broader American security thinking was shifting in important ways, in particular towards the new global security concerns of WMD proliferation and the 'new terrorism'. In the late 1990s, the Congressionally appointed bipartisan Hart–Rudman Commission had identified the growing vulnerability of the American homeland to terrorist and WMD attack as central threats to US security (US Commission on National Security in the 21st century, 1999), while the similarly established Rumsfeld Commission had argued that long-range ballistic missile proliferation posed a growing and potentially near-term threat to the USA (Commission to Assess the Ballistic Missile Threat to the United States, 1998).

The Bush Administration, 9/11 and the Iraq War

The victory of George W. Bush in the 2000 US presidential elections prompted renewed concerns about the future of transatlantic relations. During the election campaign, Bush and his advisers had promised to pursue a tougher approach towards Russia and China, raising European fears of confrontation with these two powers (Rice, 2000). The Bush Administration was also more wary than its predecessor of engaging in peacekeeping and nation-building. During the election, Bush's foreign policy adviser, Condoleezza Rice, who subsequently became the President's National Security Advisor, stated that 'We don't need to have the 82nd Airborne [who were at the time deployed in Kosovo] escorting kids to kindergarten' and called for the phased withdrawal of US troops from the Balkans (Gordon, 2000). The Bush Administration was strongly opposed to the CTBT, the ICC and the Kyoto agreement. It was also strongly committed to the deployment of ballistic missile defences – of which most European governments were at best wary. The first months of the Bush Administration, however, did not produce the feared rupture in transatlantic relations. The Bush Administration decided not to pursue the withdrawal of US forces from the Balkans. It also sought continued dialogue, rather than confrontation, with Russia.

The 9/11 terrorist attacks on the USA, however, triggered a new era in US foreign policy and US–European relations. The immediate response to 9/11 seemed to reaffirm the importance and the strength of transatlantic relations. *Le Monde* newspaper famously declared 'We are all Americans now' (Colombani, 2001). The NATO allies invoked the Article 5 security guarantee at the heart of the NATO treaty for the first time in the alliance's history (NATO, 2001). European states supported the US intervention in Afghanistan, with many providing troops. The post–9/11 unity, however, proved to be short-lived. Despite the invocation of the NATO security guarantee and offers of more help from the European allies, the Bush Administration chose to act through an ad hoc coalition rather than NATO in Afghanistan. The Bush Administration's open reluctance to contribute to nation-building in post-Taliban Afghanistan and its apparent disregard for the international laws of war in relation to combatants detained in Afghanistan also prompted concerns in Europe about the direction of US policy.

President Bush's January 2002 state of the union speech signalled a widening of the US war on terror. Bush infamously referred to Iran, Iraq and North Korea as an 'axis of evil' and warned of the dangers of the 'world's most dangerous regimes' obtaining the 'world's most dangerous weapons' (Bush, 2002). Terrorism, WMD proliferation and 'rogue states' were inseparably intertwined in the Bush Administration's thinking. This thinking has underpinned what Daalder and Lindsay (2003) have described as the 'Bush revolution' in American foreign policy. This revolution has had a number of features. The 'war on terror' has become in many ways the driving force behind US foreign policy, fundamentally shaping relations with other states. The fear that terrorist groups might obtain WMD, and dissatisfaction with existing approaches to proliferation, resulted in a new US approach to proliferation with a greater emphasis on coercion and ultimately the use of force as opposed to the more traditional instruments of arms control. US foreign policy has also become more unilateral, with a greater willingness to assert American power and to act with little concern for the views of long-standing allies – as reflected in Defense Secretary Rumsfeld's dictum that 'The mission must determine the coalition, and the coalition must not determine the mission' (Department of Defense, 2002). The events of 9/11 also resulted in what Nicole Gnesotto (2002–3, p. 99) described as an impressive militarization of US foreign policy, with the US increasing its defence expenditure from from US$291.2bn in 2000 to US$535bn in 2006 (International Institute for Strategic Studies, 2000, p. 25; 2006, p. 29), thereby significantly widening the already large gap in military power between itself and all other powers, including its European allies. At the same time, in its 2002 *National Security Strategy*, the Bush Administration made the concept of preventive war a centrepiece of US policy (United States, 2002) – a major, though not unprecedented, break with the dominant view that armed force should be used only in self-defence or in response to an ongoing conflict or humanitarian tragedy. In combination, these developments signalled a dramatic shift in US foreign policy, prompting deep European concerns about an increasingly unilateralist and militarized America with little concern for the views of its long-standing allies or wider international opinion.

Iraq became the lightning rod for diverging American and European perspectives on international security. During the 1990s there had been an uneasy transatlantic consensus on the containment of Iraq through diplomatic isolation, economic sanctions and limited military action in the form of periodic airstrikes by the USA and the UK. In the wake of 9/11, however, the USA was increasingly unwilling to accept the status quo in Iraq (Pollack, 2002). From early 2002, the Bush Administration began to push for a policy of militarily imposed regime change in Iraq. The prospect of a US-led war in Iraq provoked a variety of concerns in Europe (Ortega, 2002; Gordon, 2002): whether the threat posed by Iraq and its WMD ambitions warranted military action; why the existing policy of containment needed to be abandoned; the possible dangers of the precedent set by a preventive war; the potential for destabilization in Iraq and the wider Middle East; and that focusing on Iraq would distract attention from what was widely viewed in Europe as the more important challenge of achieving an Israeli–Palestinian peace settlement.

The US determination to remove Saddam Hussein by force and European opposition to that policy triggered a dramatic crisis in transatlantic relations. A compromise UN Security Council resolution in November 2002 papered over transatlantic differences but left the issue essentially unresolved. As the momentum built towards war, in March 2003 France, Russia (permanent members of the UN Security Council, with the power to veto any Council resolution) and Germany (serving a two-year term as a non-permanent member of the Council) jointly announced that they would oppose any Security Council resolution authorizing the use of force (French Ministry of Foreign Affairs, 2003). Later that month, the USA chose to launch the war in Iraq without Security Council backing. Turkey, a long-standing US ally, refused to allow American forces to use its territory – forcing the USA to abandon plans for a two-front ground offensive from both south and north. As was noted at the beginning of this chapter, massive demonstrations across Europe indicated that European public opinion was largely united in opposition to the war. European governments, however, were divided. Governments in Britain, Italy, Spain, Denmark, the Netherlands, Poland and the other Central and East European states supported the USA, in some cases – in particular, Italy and Spain – in the face of broad public opposition. The polarization of views among the EU's three largest powers – Britain, France and Germany – was particularly stark (although it should be noted that while Germany opposed the Iraq war at the political level, it nevertheless allowed the USA to use its bases in Germany for the deployment of forces to Iraq, and US forces to overfly German territory, reflecting its desire to maintain relations with the USA). While the Iraq crisis was marked by major divisions within Europe, it was nevertheless above all a transatlantic crisis. For the first time since the Second World War, two of America's major European allies were actively opposing the USA on the central security question of the day and as the USA prepared to go to war, while European public opinion was overwhelmingly united against the USA.

The Iraq crisis is likely to cast a shadow over transatlantic relations for some years. The discovery that Iraq's WMD programmes were far less threatening than the US had portrayed them to be, the continuing instability and violence in Iraq since 2003, and the argument that the intervention in Iraq has exacerbated rather than ameliorated the problem of globalized Islamic terrorism have reinforced European views that the US decision to go to war was a major strategic error. European opposition to the Iraq War has led many in the USA to question Europe's value as an ally.

Although arguably the most serious rift in transatlantic relations since the Second World War, the crisis over Iraq has not triggered a complete rupture in the relationship. Despite the differences over Iraq, other important elements of security co-operation have continued. In particular, the USA and Europe have not only maintained but actually deepened co-operation in relation to the wider problem of international terrorism – for example, in intelligence sharing and airline security (Rees, 2006). The EU's first formal security strategy document, developed and adopted in 2003, showed a significant degree of convergence with US security thinking, emphasizing the growing challenge posed by terrorism, proliferation and failed states and calling for a more robust response to these problems (European Union, 2003a). The differences over Iraq also did not significantly spill over into other areas of the transatlantic relationship such as mutual trade and investment, which were largely unaffected by the crisis.

While the Iraq crisis may not have triggered a complete rupture in transatlantic relations, it did reinforce a subtler shift in US policy towards Europe: away from the idea of a broad US–European alliance and towards bilateral ties and ad hoc coalitions of the willing. During the Cold War, the USA placed a high premium on maintaining overall transatlantic unity and developing common approaches towards the Soviet Union. Post-9/11 the USA has taken an increasingly utilitarian attitude towards its European allies – assessing their value primarily on the basis of their willingness and ability to support US policies. At the same time, the USA has become increasingly wary of being constrained by multilateral institutions and alliances. As a consequence, the Bush Administration emphasized bilateral ties with reliable allies such as the UK and Australia. The USA has also sought to build relations with the 'new European' states of Central and Eastern Europe, who have proved more supportive of American policy than many 'old Europe' Western European states. This trend is likely to be reinforced by US plans for the global reorganization of its overseas military presence which envisage a major reduction in forces deployed in Western Europe, especially Germany, and the establishment of new facilities in Central and Eastern Europe, but a greater emphasis in particular on preparations for the rapid deployment of forces into crisis regions rather than the permanent forward-basing of forces (International Institute for Strategic Studies, 2004c). The post-9/11 US response to the problems of terrorism and proliferation has also resulted in the development of new alliance relationships and institutional arrangements (for example, the deployment of US military forces into Central Asia, in particular Uzbekistan and Kyrgyzstan, in the context of the US intervention in Afghanistan). The USA has also established the Proliferation Security Initiative (PSI), a loose framework for co-operation in preventing and interdicting the trafficking of WMD and related materials, bringing together the USA, Western European states, Poland, Turkey and Russia, as well as Australia, Japan and Singapore, and potentially open to other states (Persbo and Davis, 2004; Valencia, 2005). Taken together, these developments indicate a shift away from the relatively fixed US-led alliance pattern of the post-1945 era, of which the US–European alliance was the most central element, towards a much more fluid and flexible set of relationships.

The post-9/11 era has also triggered a limited but strategically significant US disengagement from Europe, in particular from the Balkans (Dassu and Whyte, 2001). When a small NATO peacekeeping force was deployed in Macedonia in 2001 to support the implementation of the peace agreement in that country, the mission was undertaken without US participation, and in 2003 the control of the Macedonia mission was transferred from NATO to the EU. In late 2004, the larger Bosnia peacekeeping mission was similarly transferred from NATO to the EU, with US forces to be withdrawn. In 2000, the

USA had over 11,000 forces deployed in the Balkans, but by 2006 that figure had dropped to 2,000 (International Institute for Strategic Studies, 2000, 2006). Although as of 2004 the larger and more problematic Kosovo peacekeeping mission remained under NATO control with a significant US contribution, the withdrawal of all US troops from the Balkans in coming years is conceivable. With US attention focused on other global security challenges, the EU is becoming the leading external actor in the Balkans, brokering agreements within the region, providing the majority of economic aid and offering eventual membership of the Union to the countries of the region. Supporting the post-communist transition in Russia and the other former Soviet states has also moved down the hierarchy of US priorities post-9/11. US disengagement from Europe is, however, unlikely to be complete, certainly in the short-to-medium term. There is little pressure in the USA for the withdrawal of all American military forces from Europe or the abandonment of NATO, while American foreign-policy-makers continue to view Europe as a region where the USA has significant interests. Nevertheless, gradual US disengagement from Europe seems likely to continue, suggesting that the task of managing security problems and promoting stability on the periphery of the European security community will increasingly fall to European states and the EU.

NATO: transformation and uncertainty

As the central institutional framework for security and defence co-operation between the USA and Europe, these changes in transatlantic relations have major implications for NATO. The end of the Cold War and the disappearance of the 'Soviet threat' removed NATO's raison d'être. As François Heisbourg put it, the question was no longer simply what direction the Alliance should take but whether it could or should survive at all (Heisbourg, 1992). The mainstream view in both Europe and America was that NATO should be maintained, if only as an insurance policy against any residual Soviet/Russian threat, the emergence of an overly powerful Germany or a return to the conflicts of the first half of the twentieth century. What roles NATO could or should play in the new Europe was less clear. At one end of the spectrum, some analysts argued for a minimalist NATO that would act as an insurance policy for worst case scenarios but would not overstretch itself by taking on new tasks (Brown, 1999), while others argued that NATO's potential should be maximized by giving the Alliance a central role in addressing the new security challenges in post-communist Europe (Hunter, 1999). The influential US Senator, Richard Lugar, argued that NATO had to 'go out of area' – that is, take on new security tasks beyond the defence of its members' territories – or risk going out of business (Lugar, 1993).

NATO went through a series of difficult debates on these issues in the 1990s. Most NATO members were initially reluctant to see what had been an alliance for the collective defence of its members' territory take on new military missions beyond its borders, but the Yugoslav conflict drove NATO to adopt new peacekeeping and intervention tasks. The need to engage with the broader security problems of post-communist Europe became one of the key drivers of change within NATO. One innovative response was the Partnership for Peace (PfP), a flexible framework allowing for wide-ranging co-operation with the countries of Central and Eastern Europe. The question of whether to extend full NATO membership to Central and Eastern European states, however, became one of the most controversial issues within NATO in the 1990s. Supporters argued that the security guarantee provided by NATO membership could underpin democratization and reform, just as it arguably had done in Western Europe after the Second World War (Allin, 1995; Asmus *et al.*, 1995). Critics argued that expanding NATO risked provoking a new confrontation with Russia and a new division of Europe (Brown, 1995; Gaddis, 1998). NATO succeeded in squaring this circle by extending membership to some states while offering enhanced co-operation to those remaining outside the alliance, in particular Russia (Asmus, 2004). Poland, the Czech Republic and Hungary joined the Alliance in 1999, followed by Estonia, Latvia, Lithuania, Slovakia, Slovenia, Romania and Bulgaria in 2004, thereby extending NATO's membership across Central and Eastern Europe from the Baltic Sea to the Black Sea. The underlying issue of the limits of NATO's possible enlargement, however, remains unresolved. As of the mid-2000s, Balkan states (in particular, Albania, Bosnia, Croatia and Macedonia) and former Soviet states (in particular, Georgia) are pressing for membership of NATO. Russia remains deeply suspicious of further enlargement of NATO, in particular to countries of the former Soviet Union, fearing encirclement by its old enemy. Some have argued that NATO could resolve its enlargement dilemma by extending membership to Russia (Baker, 2002), but critics argue that Russia is far from a reliable partner and bringing it into NATO would fundamentally undermine the alliance.

The issue of co-operation with Russia was similarly controversial.

Some argued that building a co-operative relationship with the former enemy should be the Alliance's top priority. Critics countered that Russia's future was too uncertain to provide the basis for a sustainable partnership, and close co-operation with Moscow might risk undermining NATO's ability to act. The result was an approach that sought to give Russia 'a voice but not a veto' within NATO (Solana, 1997), embodied in the 1997 NATO–Russia Founding Act and the NATO–Russia Council established in 2002.

NATO has also experienced divisive debates over European defence. Some Europeans, led by the French, argue that Europe needs the capacity to take autonomous military action. In the USA, and to some extent elsewhere in Europe, such proposals are viewed as being fundamentally threatening to NATO. Eventually compromise was reached on the so-called 'Berlin-plus' arrangements, which allow European states to use NATO assets – in particular its military planning and command and control facilities – for operations in which the USA (and other members) do not wish to be involved (NATO, 2006b). By the end of the 1990s NATO had undergone a remarkable transformation, with tens of thousands of troops deployed as peacekeepers in the Balkans, a network of co-operative ties with the countries of post-communist Europe, an expanded membership, and new arrangements for coalitions of the willing from among its members to undertake military operations.

The post-9/11 divisions between Europe and America have, however, called NATO's future into question again. The unwillingness of the USA to engage NATO more directly in its 2001 intervention in Afghanistan raised doubts about the American commitment to the Alliance. The Iraq War provoked what many observers saw as the most serious internal crisis in NATO's history. For the first time in the Alliance's history, two of its leading European members not only sharply criticized American policy on a key security issue but also actively opposed that policy in the UN Security Council. In the run-up to the war, French, German and Belgian reluctance to prepare for the collective defence of fellow NATO member Turkey, lest such a step be seen as supporting US plans for war in Iraq, seemed to call the NATO security guarantee into question – triggering heated disputes and what the US ambassador to NATO called a 'near death experience' for the Alliance (Black, 2003). In the aftermath of the war, France and Germany also resisted US suggestions that NATO might take over the management of the post-war stabilization/peacekeeping operation in Iraq.

More broadly, to the extent that the primary security challenges now emanate from beyond Europe, NATO faces the challenge of responding to these new global security problems or becoming increasingly redundant. NATO has taken some significant steps in this direction. In 2003 the Alliance took over the command and control of the international peacekeeping operation in Afghanistan, its first mission beyond Europe. Since then, NATO has significantly expanded its force in Afghanistan, and the NATO mission in that country is now viewed as a major test of the alliance's future direction (NATO's role in peacekeeping and intervention, including in Afghanistan, is examined in more detail in Chapter 6). At its July 2004 summit in Turkey, NATO agreed to play a role in training Iraq's new security forces and established the Istanbul Co-operation Initiative – similar to the PfP – to promote co-operation with Middle Eastern states. The extent to which NATO takes on broader global security roles is, however, likely to be constrained by a number of factors (Cottey, 2004). The broader divergence of US and European perspectives discussed in this chapter suggests that there may not be sufficient consensus within NATO for the Alliance to develop a wider global role. Even where there may be consensus between America and Europe on global security challenges, NATO will be only one of the institutional frameworks available for addressing such challenges, and not necessarily the first choice of institution. The countries of the Middle East – and other states beyond Europe – may be significantly less receptive to offers of partnership from NATO than the states of post-communist Europe were in the 1990s. With its members already struggling to provide sufficient forces for the peacekeeping mission in Afghanistan, NATO is also likely to face problems of military and institutional overstretch.

As a defence alliance, NATO was the core framework for the collective defence of its members during the Cold War. In this context, it developed a unique and powerful infrastructure of political and military institutions and forward deployed military forces. Since the end of the Cold War this infrastructure has been adapted to new challenges, in particular the deployment of forces beyond NATO's territory. This process remains ongoing, with the establishment since 2002 of a new NATO Response Force (NRF) for rapid deployment in crisis situations. NATO, however, is now only one of an array of frameworks, alongside the UN, the EU, ad hoc coalitions of the willing, and purely national missions, in which its members have deployed military forces over the last decade. Rather than being the core Euro-atlantic defence organization that it once was, NATO is becoming just one of the institutional instruments available to its members when they decide to undertake military action.

Interpreting transatlantic relations

How should we interpret the evolution of transatlantic relations since the end of the Cold War and September 2001, and what does this suggest about their future? Drawing on competing theoretical approaches, analysts suggest a variety of different conclusions. Realists and neo-realists argue that alliances are the products of common external threats or interests. From this perspective, the post-Second World War alliance between the USA and Europe was a product of the Soviet threat to Western Europe and the bipolar world dominated by the two superpowers. Such alliances, however, are not permanent and tend to disintegrate once the threat that gave rise to them ceases to exist (Walt, 1997). The disappearance of the Soviet Union was therefore bound to trigger the break-up of the post-war transatlantic alliance, as the unity imposed by a common external threat dissipated and European and American interests and threat perceptions diverged (Mearsheimer, 1990; Waltz, 1993). For realists and neo-realists, perhaps the only thing that is surprising is that the breakdown of the transatlantic alliance did not come sooner.

An alternative realist perspective has been advanced by Robert Kagan (2002, 2003). Kagan argues that the dramatic differential in power, especially military power, between the USA and Europe, and the different historical experiences of the two are producing increasingly divergent approaches to global security challenges. As the world's only superpower, the USA defines its security and interests in global terms. The USA's hegemonic power inclines it to act unilaterally and to view military force as a key tool of foreign policy. In contrast, Europe's relative weakness – its lack of military power compared to the USA, and the disunity resulting from Europe's decentralized power structure – leads it to support multilateral and non-military approaches to security problems. The post-war European experience of integration also leads Europe to view its post-modern 'paradise' as a model for world order. In contrast, the USA's experience as a global superpower leads it to view global politics primarily in terms of power. Kagan concludes that, while European and American leaders may seek to ameliorate the consequences of their differences, the underlying realities of power and history will produce increasingly divergent perspectives on global security challenges.

In contrast to these realist and neo-realist arguments, liberal and neo-liberal theorists argue that common democratic values, a shared identity and institutional ties will hold Europe and America together. For liberals, states' foreign policy choices are not simply a result of material factors (such as the balance of power or the existence of 'objective' external threats), but rather reflect states' values and political systems. From this perspective, the post-war transatlantic alliance reflected not simply the existence of a perceived external threat but also the common democratic and capitalist heritage of the USA and Europe. Despite the end of the Soviet threat, these common values will continue to provide a key basis for co-operation between the USA and Europe. As the two primary centres of democracy and capitalism in the world, they are therefore natural allies. Notwithstanding the recent transatlantic differences, the USA and Europe have much more in common with each other than they do with any other major centres of power or political forces (such as China, Russia or Islam). In concrete terms, the USA and Europe share a common interest in defending democracy against potential threats (such as globalized Islamic terrorism) and in maintaining the liberal international economic order on which capitalism rests. In the long run, common interests based on common values will reassert themselves (Nye, 2000).

A further variant of the liberal argument suggests that Europe and America share a common identity as the core of the West, forged not only by common values but also by a shared history and cultural heritage (Risse-Kappen, 1996; Sjursen, 2004). This common identity may facilitate continued transatlantic co-operation, since identity shapes states' perceptions of interests and threats. A third strand of liberalism focuses on the role of institutional ties in underpinning long-term co-operation, in particular NATO, but also the formal US–EU relationship established in the 1990s, as well as a multitude of lower-level diplomatic, military and economic ties between the USA and Europe. Here, it is argued that institutionalized ties between states help to maintain long-term co-operation, facilitate compromise, create bureaucratic interests in co-operation and reinforce a sense of common identity (Keohane and Martin, 1995). Together, liberals argue, the combination of shared values, a common identity and institutionalized ties generate a powerful imperative for continued close co-operation between the USA and Europe.

Where does the balance lie between these competing theoretical approaches? The realist argument that the perception of a common threat in the form of the Soviet Union played a central role in the establishment of the post-1945 transatlantic alliance is undoubtedly correct. The disappearance of that threat has removed a significant part of the glue that held the US–European alliance together. The different geostrategic positions of the USA and Europe and the disparity in power, especially military power, between the two has tended to produce different views of the world. The USA views the world from the perspective of a global superpower, with all the attendant risks and responsibilities that go with that status. Europeans tend to view the world from the perspective of a set of middle powers, more conscious of the limits of power and the value of multilateralism. While realists highlight the factors pulling Europe and America apart, the conclusion that these will inevitably produce a long-term split between the two probably stretches the argument too far.

Some weight should be given to the liberal view that common democratic values are likely to produce common perceptions of interests and threats. For all their differences, Europe and America, as noted earlier, still have much more in common with each other than they do with communist China, Islamic radicals or Russian nationalists. There is a strong case that Europe and America share a common long-term interest in maintaining a liberal international economic order, promoting democracy, preventing the emergence of potentially threatening hegemonic powers, countering international terrorism, and containing WMD proliferation. At a minimum, shared democratic values provide an important basis for long-term co-operation. The liberal argument, however, also has shortcomings. While shared values may produce broadly similar world views, they do not necessarily result in more concrete common assessments of threats or how to respond to those threats. Since the 1990s, while there has been a broad transatlantic consensus that proliferation and terrorism are central security challenges, the nature and extent of the threats posed by these problems and how to respond to them have been much more contentious. In addition, while Europe and America share core democratic values, political sociologists have long pointed out that there are also important differences between the two (Lipset, 1990): the USA is more individualistic, more market-orientated and more religious, and Europe is more communitarian, more statist economically and more secular. Since the 1960s, further, American society and politics has shifted to the right, reinforcing the differences between the USA and Europe (Micklethwait and Wooldridge, 2004).

The liberal argument that institutional ties will help to maintain transatlantic co-operation also needs to be subjected to careful analysis. While it probably is the case that institutions can help to maintain co-operation that might dissipate in their absence, countervailing forces – such as changing external forces and changes in members' interests – may pull relationships in other directions. While institutions may have a degree of autonomous influence, their effectiveness as a means of maintaining co-operation nevertheless also depends to a significant degree on the willingness of member states to use them, suggesting that they require deliberate support from their members and may degrade over time if that support declines. As the earlier discussion of NATO illustrates, the current era is likely to provide a severe test for the institutional bases of post-1945 transatlantic relations.

These different theoretical perspectives emphasize the primacy of a particular factor or set of factors – power for realists, values and institutions for liberals – and thus tend towards determinism. A more sophisticated analysis would suggest that the future of transatlantic relations is likely to be determined by the interaction between these factors, rather than any one of them alone. From this perspective, common democratic values are likely to produce important common general interests, but the very different geostrategic positions and power capacities of Europe and America are likely to produce different priorities and different approaches to addressing security challenges. There is thus a strong case that while the USA and Europe share important common interests, their strategic cultures – their broad approaches to foreign and security policy, in particular the use of force – are diverging in important ways. As the world's only superpower, the USA has an inherently global perspective, is used to wielding its hard power, has great capacity to act unilaterally, and balks at the constraints of multilateralism. In contrast, Europe – whether as the EU or as the many states that make up the continent – is often more concerned with developments in its immediate neighbourhood, has less capacity to utilize hard power or act unilaterally, and is more supportive of multilateral institutions. Robert Kagan has summed this up as the difference between a warlike Mars (the USA) and a pacifist Venus (Europe) (Kagan, 2002). Some critics have countered that the real division lies within the USA, between Martian Republicans and Venusian Democrats. While it is true that there are important foreign policy differences between Republicans and Democrats, and the latter's perspectives may generally be closer to those of much of Europe, there nevertheless remains a strong case that the centres of gravity in both domestic politics and foreign policy in the USA and Europe are quite different.

The different theoretical perspectives discussed here also give little space to agency – that is, the freedom of states and political leaders to make significant foreign policy choices, and the impact these choices may have on long-term developments. While states' foreign policies are constrained and shaped by long-term material and social forces, states nevertheless also retain the capacity for independent action and their choices may have an important impact on future patterns of relations. Agency may be particularly important during periods of major international flux, when changed external circumstances enforce changes on states. The post-Cold War and post-9/11 world can be viewed as just such a period of flux in transatlantic relations.

Against this background, James Steinberg (2003) has described the transatlantic relationship of the early twenty-first century as 'an elective partnership' – a relationship which both sides face strategic choices over whether, in what ways and at what cost, they wish to maintain. The USA faces the question of how far it continues to view the Europeans as valued partners, and to what extent it may be willing to compromise in order to maintain European support. In foreign policy terms, the 2004 US presidential election reflected this debate. In its first term, the Bush Administration had pursued a unilateralist strategy, played down the importance of the European allies and shown little willingness to compromise (in particular over Iraq) in order to gain European support. Critics such as Joseph Nye (2002) argue that even with its enormous power the USA cannot achieve many of its core long-term objectives alone and therefore requires the support of allies and partners such as the Europeans. In the 2004 presidential election, George W. Bush offered continuity in foreign policy, whereas the Democratic challenger Senator John Kerry criticized the Bush Administration for squandering post-9/11 international sympathy for the USA and argued for greater attention to be paid to gain the support of international partners, especially America's European allies. President Bush's re-election could be interpreted as a public endorsement of the unilateral assertion of American power; however, the Democratic Party's victory in the 2006 US congressional elections was widely interpreted as a vote against the Bush Administration's foreign policy, in particular the USA's entrapment in Iraq following the 2003 invasion of that country. US foreign policy thus appears pulled in competing directions: the unilateralism and emphasis on hard coercive power of the Bush Administration and an alternative approach placing a greater emphasis on the need for international support and the use of diplomacy and soft power.

Europeans also face strategic choices in their relations with America, in particular between seeking to maintain a close alliance with the USA, and pursuing greater foreign and security policy autonomy. To the extent that the EU is emerging as an independent actor in its own right, it thus faces a choice between positioning itself as a partner and ally of the USA, or acting as a counterweight to American power and policies. As will be explored in more detail in the next chapter, Europeans and the EU are divided on these questions. This intra-European divide is symbolized by the competing perspectives of Britain and France, with the former emphasizing a continued close alliance with the USA and seeking to influence US policy from within that relationship, and the latter seeking to establish Europe as an autonomous force in its own right and influence the USA through the weight of its power. The divisions between and within European countries on relations with the USA suggest that neither the British nor the French view is likely to win out completely. The most likely European strategic choice may therefore be one that combines elements of a continued alliance with the USA with greater European autonomy. Europeans, however, are likely to face important and ongoing choices as to where the balance should lie.

The strategic choices made by the USA and Europe in recent years, and in the future, may also produce path dependencies that shape and constrain transatlantic relations significantly: once certain choices have been made, policies may become entrenched, other actors respond to those choices by making choices of their own, and changes in policy and alternative outcomes become less likely. The Bush Administration's post-9/11 foreign policy and the decision to invade Iraq, in particular, may have an important long-term impact on transatlantic relations. Just as decisions taken in the late 1940s and early 1950s established the framework for a US foreign policy of containment of the Soviet Union that lasted for four decades, so the Bush Administration's 'war on terror' and unilateral assertion of American power may well have established the long-term basis for US foreign policy in the coming decades. The Bush Administration's foreign policy, especially the invasion of Iraq, might also have a powerful, long-term impact on European foreign policies. As was noted at the beginning of this chapter, the Iraq war united much of European public opinion in opposition to the USA. The Iraq war also pushed Germany, which had since 1945 traditionally sought to maintain close ties with both Europe and the

USA, closer to France, and the French vision of an autonomous Europe, provoked a major rupture in relations with another traditional American ally, Turkey, and led Russia to emphasize relations with Europe over those with the USA. The Bush Administration may therefore have in important ways inadvertently shifted the European foreign policy debate towards the view that Europe should assert its autonomy from the USA (Charlemagne, 2004).

Conclusion

The debate on the future prospects for transatlantic relations tends to be polarized between the view that European and America perspectives on international security are diverging and the transatlantic alliance is doomed, and an alternative perspective suggesting that shared democratic values, common interests and institutional ties will provide the basis for a continued long-term partnership. Realism and liberalism provide competing theoretical fuel for this debate. This chapter has suggested that a more subtle and nuanced assessment is needed. Europe and the USA share common democratic values and important broad interests, but European and American threat assessments, priorities and strategic cultures are also diverging in important ways. In the post-9/11 era, US foreign policy priorities have shifted to the new global security challenges of terrorism and proliferation, while a Europe largely at peace is less important to the USA than it was in the twentieth century. The events of 9/11 and relative peace in Europe are producing a partial American disengagement from Europe – as seen by the ongoing reduction of US troop numbers in the Balkans. US alliance relationships are shifting away from the relatively fixed patterns of the Cold War, resulting in a downgrading of the concept of a broad transatlantic alliance and NATO, and a greater emphasis in US policy on bilateral ties and coalitions of willing states. European perspectives on transatlantic relations are also changing. In the absence of an overwhelming external threat, Europe is less dependent on the USA than it was during the Cold War. Europeans are also wary of the direction of post-9/11 American foreign policy, in particular the shift towards unilateralism and the willingness of the USA to use military force. As a consequence, there is increasing pressure for greater European autonomy in foreign, security and defence policy. This drive for increased European, especially EU, autonomy is, however, constrained by differences within Europe on relations with the USA.

The outcome of these trends is a complex pattern of co-operation in some spheres of security, major policy divergences in other areas, and a set of transatlantic relationships – USA–EU, NATO, bilateral and within wider forums such as the United Nations – with a variety of different, overlapping, sometimes complementary and sometimes contradictory dynamics. This pattern does not suggest a complete breakdown in transatlantic relations and the emergence of an era of confrontation between the USA and Europe, but it does indicate that the post-1945 era in which Europe and America were each other's primary partners and default allies has indeed come to an end. For both the USA and Europe, the transatlantic relationship has become 'an elective partnership' – a partnership both sides have greater freedom to pursue (or not) than they did in the post-1945 era, and hence one more dependent on uncertain strategic choices.

Chapter 4

The EU and the Europeanization of European Security

Since the early 1990s, the European Union (EU) has assumed an increasingly prominent role in European security affairs, as well as a growing but more limited role in responding to the new global security agenda. Under the Maastricht Treaty (provisionally agreed in 1991, signed in 1992 and entering into force in 1993), the EU's member states committed themselves to the establishment of a Common Foreign and Security Policy (CFSP) and co-operation in internal security, or what the EU referred to as Justice and Home Affairs (JHA) and now describes as its Area of Freedom, Security and Justice (AFSJ). During the 1990s, the CFSP was given substance through the development of a series of new policies and institutions directed towards the EU's immediate neighbours in Central and Eastern Europe, the Balkans, the former Soviet Union and the Mediterranean. Within this context, the EU has in many ways assumed the central role in efforts to promote stability and security in the wider Europe. At the end of the 1990s, the EU also agreed to establish a common European defence policy, putting in place new political and military institutions for collective military operations. Since then the EU has launched its first, albeit modest, peacekeeping operations, in the Balkans and Africa. Globally, the EU has for some decades played an important role in economic affairs, in particular in international trade negotiations and as a leading provider of development aid. Since the 1990s, however, the EU has also begun to develop a global political and security role, in particular as a leading force behind initiatives such as the International Criminal Court (ICC) and the Kyoto agreement on global warming.

While these developments may be viewed as pointing towards the development of the EU as an increasingly important foreign policy and security actor, the recent history of the CFSP has also been characterized by major failures and setbacks. In the early 1990s, EU member states were deeply divided over the 1990–1 Gulf War and the Yugoslav conflict, preventing the adoption of common policies in both cases

(Salmon, 1992). The Union's inability to bring the bloodshed in the former Yugoslavia to an end, and eventual reliance on the USA and NATO to do so, exposed the gap between rhetoric and reality in EU foreign policy. A decade later, the acrimonious divisions within the EU over the 2003 Iraq War, in particular between the three largest members – Britain, France and Germany – suggested that the Union's ability to forge a truly common foreign and security policy remained, at best, limited.

Assessments of the EU's emerging foreign and security policy and its future prospects vary significantly. More than three decades ago, François Duchene (1972) described the EU's combination of economic power with relative political and military weakness as that of a 'civilian power'. Supporters of a common European foreign and security policy argue that the EU is gradually becoming a more complete power and is likely over time to assume an increasingly prominent foreign and security policy role – in particular within Europe, but also globally. Others argue that the EU is a distinctive and perhaps sui generis power: more than a traditional international organization yet not a centralized nation-state; a power, which because of its internal make-up and in contrast to past great powers, emphasizes norms, co-operation and soft power in its external behaviour (Manners, 2002). Critics argue that the continuing resilience of the nation-states that constitute the EU, and the often divergent foreign policy perspectives of those states, pose insuperable obstacles to a meaningful common foreign and security policy (Gordon, 1997–8).

This chapter explores the EU's efforts to establish a common foreign and security policy, and the Union's emerging role in European and global security. It suggests that as a foreign and security policy actor the EU is, and is likely to remain, more than critics suggest, yet less than its advocates hope: it is likely to assume the dominant role in addressing security challenges on the periphery of the European security community and develop an expanding global role, but it will remain constrained by the central problem of achieving consensus among its member states. Its ability to take on the difficult challenges of immediate crisis management and the use of force are likely to remain limited.

Towards a common foreign and security policy?

The establishment of a common European foreign and security policy has been an ambition of supporters of European integration ever since the process was initiated after the Second World War. Following the establishment of the European Coal and Steel Community in 1951, France, West Germany, Italy, the Netherlands, Belgium and Luxembourg negotiated a European Defence Community (EDC) agreement, which would have established a supranational European military. Concerns over national sovereignty and the rearmament of Germany so soon after the Second World War, however, the led the French National Assembly to vote against the ratification of the EDC Treaty and the project collapsed (Duke, 2000, pp. 12–41). The failure of the EDC consolidated NATO's position as the primary European security institution, while the European integration process took an essentially economic direction. The idea of a European foreign policy re-emerged in the early 1970s and the European political co-operation (EPC) process was established, based around regular meeting of European foreign ministers and efforts to co-ordinate European foreign policies on an intergovernmental basis (Duke, 2000, pp. 42–81). Although EPC gave the then European Community (EC) greater weight in international affairs, NATO and the transatlantic relationship with the USA remained the bedrock of security for Western Europe during the Cold War.

The end of the Cold War generated new momentum behind the idea of a European foreign and security policy. The reunification of Germany in 1989–90 resulted in pressure for closer European integration in order to tie Germany into European structures. As was noted in the previous chapter, the disappearance of the Soviet threat reduced Europe's dependence on the USA for its security, and resulted in a partial US disengagement from Europe. The emergence of new security challenges on Europe's periphery, in particular the Yugoslav conflict, suggested that the EC needed a greater capacity to shape events beyond its borders. The result was the Maastricht Treaty, negotiated in 1990–1 and coming into force in 1993, under which the EC became the European Union, the framework for Economic and Monetary Union (EMU, which subsequently resulted in the introduction of the euro) was put in place, the CFSP was formally established, and JHA co-operation became a central component of the Union. In some ways, the CFSP established under the Maastricht Treaty did not differ greatly from EPC, remaining based on intergovernmental co-operation and consensus decision-making. The political commitment to the CFSP was, however, significantly stronger than EPC, with member states agreeing to 'define and implement a common foreign and security policy . . . covering all aspects of foreign and security policy' (European

Union, 1992, Title V, Art. J.1). The new geostrategic context of the post-Cold War era also meant that the prospects for the implementation of a common foreign and security policy were significantly enhanced.

The Maastricht Treaty set in place the institutional arrangements for the EU's CFSP. Although the Amsterdam Treaty (signed in 1997 and coming into force in 1999) and the Nice Treaty (provisionally agreed in 2000, signed in 2001 and coming into force in 2003) introduced some modifications to these arrangements, they did not fundamentally alter their basis. The central basis of the CFSP is intergovernmental co-operation, with decisions made by the EU's member states on the basis of consensus. This process operates through a series of core EU institutions: the European Council (approximately six-monthly meetings of heads of state and government); the General Affairs and External Relations Council (regular meetings of foreign ministers); the Committee of Permanent Representatives (COREPER – national ambassadors to the EU, based in Brussels); the Political and Security Committee (PSC, better known by its French acronym COPS, established by the Nice Treaty and composed of ambassadorial-level representatives responsible for security and defence policy); and a variety of working groups, again composed of national representatives, responsible for specific policy areas. Since the Amsterdam Treaty this intergovernmental infrastructure has also been supported by a High Representative for the CFSP (a post held by the former Spanish foreign minister and former NATO Secretary-General, Javier Solana) and a Policy Planning and Early Warning Unit, although decisions are still made by the member states themselves.

The development of a common foreign policy is further complicated by institutional divisions within the EU. In contrast to the almost purely intergovernmental CFSP, the economic dimensions of EU foreign policy (trade, commercial agreements and aid – 'external relations' in EU parlance) are subject to different institutional arrangements under which the European Commission plays the central role in developing and implementing policy and decisions are taken on the basis of qualified majority voting rather than consensus. Critics argue that this institutional separation between the more political CFSP and the primarily economic 'external relations' means that the two are often not well co-ordinated and sometimes even run in contradiction to one another – an especially acute problem given that economic leverage is often viewed as one the Union's most important foreign policy tools.

The EU's 2004 Constitutional Treaty included measures designed to address the Union's institutional weaknesses in this area; in particular, proposals to merge the two posts of High Representative and External Affairs Commissioner into the new post of EU Foreign Minister, and to create a new EU External Action Service linking together the General Secretariat of the EU Council, the European Commission and the diplomatic services of the EU's member states (European Union, 2004c, Arts I-28 and III-296). The Constitutional Treaty was rejected by the French and Dutch publics in referenda in summer 2005, but there remains pressure to implement the foreign policy measures included in the Treaty, whether in a revised Constitutional Treaty or independently. Even if these measures are implemented, however, the EU foreign-policy-making process will remained essentially intergovernmental and consensus-based.

The intergovernmental character of the CFSP shapes and constrains the EU's ambitions fundamentally in this area. In essence, the CFSP depends on the EU's member states, especially its largest members, sharing common foreign and security policy objectives and priorities. The difficulty of developing a truly common foreign and security policy becomes clear when one considers the diversity of the EU member states' national foreign and security policy traditions and priorities: two former great powers, Britain a close ally of the USA and France with its Gaullist emphasis on independence from the USA; Germany, a semi-pacifist civilian power since 1945; northern European members, whose immediate foreign policy priorities include Russia and the Baltic Sea region; southern European members, whose immediate foreign policy priorities include the Mediterranean and North Africa; a majority of states who are also NATO members, but four neutral or non-aligned states (Austria, Finland, Ireland and Sweden); and twelve recent members who have joined the EU since 2004 (ten post-communist Central and Eastern European states, plus Cyprus and Malta). Welding the divergent foreign and security policies of twenty-seven – and in the future potentially more – member states into a single common EU policy is an inherently challenging task. As developments since the early 1990s have illustrated, distinctive national foreign and security policies remain deeply entrenched.

At the beginning of the 1990s, the first Gulf War and the Yugoslav conflict cruelly exposed the EU's limitations as a foreign policy actor (Salmon, 1992). In the first Gulf War, the UK strongly supported the US-led military action; France also contributed military forces to the US-led coalition, but pursued a semi-independent diplomatic line; and Germany refused to contribute military forces but provided significant economic aid to the USA, while the other EU members were similarly divided. In the Yugoslav conflict, Germany advocated the early recognition of Slovenian and Croatian independence and the use of military force, but the UK and France opposed diplomatic recognition of Slovenia and Croatia or military action. In both cases a meaningful common EU position was impossible. A decade later, the 2003 Iraq War exposed similar divisions, with the UK again supporting the US-led war, and France and Germany opposing military action. These divisions were mirrored across the EU, with countries such as Spain, Italy and Poland supporting the US-led war, and others such as Sweden, Belgium and Austria opposed to it.

Some have argued that enlargement of the EU, from fifteen to twenty-seven member-states since 2004 and possible future expansion to include the Western Balkan states and Turkey, may significantly complicate the Union's efforts to develop a common foreign policy. For many in the French elite in particular, the strongly Atlanticist leanings of the post-communist Central and Eastern European states risk undermining the EU's ability to develop an autonomous foreign and security policy. These fears were reinforced in the run-up to the Iraq War in early 2003, when the leaders of Poland, the Czech Republic and Hungary joined the UK, Spain, Italy, Denmark and Portugal in signing the 'Letter of the Eight' calling for unity with the USA (Aznar *et al.*, 2003); and ten other Central and Eastern European states (the 'Vilnius Ten') signed an open letter supporting the USA (Vilnius Group, 2003). The French president, Jacques Chirac, responded by accusing the Central and Eastern European states of being 'not very well behaved' and having 'missed a great opportunity to shut up' (Lungescu, 2003). Although enlargement may add to the EU's difficulties in developing a CFSP, however, it is far from clear that it will have a major impact. The EU's new members have shadowed the CFSP since the early 1990s, adopting the vast majority of common EU foreign-policy positions without any problem long before they became EU members. Over the Iraq War, the EU's fundamental problem was not the complicated process of achieving consensus among a larger group of members, but rather the absence of agreement among its three largest members – the UK, France and Germany. Although other EU members may be uncomfortable with a foreign policy dominated by the 'big three', consensus among the UK, France and Germany is a prerequisite for common EU action. When such consensus exists, other member states are more often than not likely to accommodate themselves to that consensus – even in an enlarged Union.

While it is clear that developing a common EU foreign policy is difficult, some argue that the creation of institutions directed towards that
goal and the process of co-operation will in the longer term facilitate
foreign policy convergence among the Union's member states
(Manners and Whitman, 2000; Tonra, 2001). This logic reflects neo-
liberal institutionalist theories of international relations which argue
that institutions help to create and sustain co-operation among states
(Keohane and Martin, 1995). There is some evidence to support this
thesis in relation to EU foreign policy: with regard to a variety of countries, policy issues and international organizations, the EU has gradually built up and maintained common positions, often involving
compromise between the divergent views of member states. The EU
may also have a capacity for learning from its failures: after their initial
divisions over the Yugoslav conflict, EU member states appear to have
realized the importance of maintaining a common front, and since the
mid-1990s the Union has maintained quite a high degree of unity in its
policy towards the Balkans. In the wake of the deep divisions over the
Iraq War, in December 2003 EU members reached agreement on a
formal *European Security Strategy* – an exercise designed deliberately
to overcome the splits over Iraq and reaffirm common EU interests and
goals (European Union, 2003b). While this evidence suggests that there
may be some validity to the neo-liberal institutionalist argument,
building a common foreign policy nevertheless remains at best a slow
and halting process. The experience of the Iraq War suggests that,
while there may be gradual progress towards a common EU foreign
policy, national foreign policy differences remain deeply entrenched
and are likely to re-emerge in crisis situations involving controversial
issues such as the use of force.

The political crisis arising from the rejection of the proposed EU
Constitutional Treaty by the French and Dutch publics in referenda in
summer 2005 highlighted the larger point that the prospects for a
common EU foreign and security policy cannot be separated from the
overall fate of the EU. Some observers viewed the rejection of the
Constitutional Treaty by the French and Dutch publics as reflecting a
deeper crisis of legitimacy for the EU and signalling a likely stalling, or
even a reversal, of the process of European integration. While a wholesale disintegration of existing EU institutions and policies – including
the CFSP – cannot be entirely ruled out, the more likely outcome is a
period of political crisis but continued co-operation within existing
institutional and policy frameworks. Indeed, it may be argued that EU
foreign and security policy co-operation has been affected remarkably

little by the fallout from the crisis over the Constitutional Treaty – indicating that such co-operation is quite robust and not easily derailed.

Euro-atlanticism versus Euro-Gaullism

One of the central foreign policy divisions within the EU is over relations with the USA – what Timothy Garton Ash (2005, p. 58) describes as the clash between Euro-atlanticism and Euro-Gaullism. Euro-atlanticism envisages the EU as one half of a united Euro-atlantic community and a close partner of the USA, influencing America through co-operative engagement and sharing the burden of addressing common security challenges. Euro-Gaullism – named, of course, after the former French president, Charles de Gaulle – envisages the EU as an independent force in world politics and a counterbalance to America's overweening power. Euro-atlanticism and Euro-Gaullism present two radically different strategic visions of the EU's place in the world and its relationship with the USA. The debate between these two strategic visions has been ongoing since 1945, but intensified with the end of the Cold War in 1989–90 and became even more prominent post-9/11 and in the context of the Iraq War.

Euro-atlanticists argue that partnership with the USA is vital to addressing shared security challenges, and that the best way to influence (and sometimes restrain) the USA is from inside such a partnership. However, Euro-Gaullists are of the view that Europe needs to assert distinctive European interest and values, that the USA can only be influenced by an independent and powerful Europe, and that the EU must be the vehicle for achieving both goals. Britain has been the leading advocate of Euro-atlanticism, based on a history of close co-operation with the USA in the two World Wars and the Cold War, and uniquely close military and intelligence ties. France has been the leading proponent of Euro-Gaullism, based on a tradition of foreign-policy independence from the USA. Germany – West Germany after 1945 and the reunited Germany since 1990 – has generally sought to chart a middle course, combining an alliance with the USA with a strong commitment to European integration. Given the British and French positions, this makes Germany the swing country in determining the balance of opinion within Europe. Other EU member states have been similarly divided: Denmark and Portugal have generally been on the Euro-atlanticist side of this debate; Belgium and Luxembourg have sided with the Euro-Gaullists; and the Netherlands, Italy, Spain and

Greece have often followed the German model of seeking to balance the two approaches. Although not members of NATO, the neutral/non-aligned EU states (Austria, Finland, Ireland and Sweden) have supported the development of an EU foreign policy but also value co-operation with the USA. The new Central and Eastern European EU members, grateful for US support and still wary of Russia, are generally committed Euro-atlanticists.

The divisions within Europe over relations with the USA occur not only between countries but also within them. In general, parties and leaders from the right of the political spectrum are closer to the Euro-atlanticist position, while those from the left are more inclined towards Euro-Gaullism. Changes of government can therefore result in significant shifts in national positions – the right-wing government of the Spanish prime minister, José Maria Aznar, was strongly supportive of the US war in Iraq, whereas the left-wing government of José Luis Rodriguez Zapatero, elected after the March 2004 Madrid bombings, withdrew Spanish troops from Iraq. European public opinion has also been divided along similar lines. Although European views of the USA have shifted back and forth since 1945, the overall balance of political forces, both between states and within them, has been such that there has never been a decisive consensus in support of either the Euro-atlanticist or the Euro-Gaullist position.

The debate between Euro-atlanticism and Euro-Gaullism is also shaped by America's foreign policy choices. In the 1990s, Europeans were generally comfortable with the Clinton Administration's liberal internationalist foreign policy leanings and, after initial divisions, welcomed the USA's willingness to engage in the Balkans. After 2000, Europeans were wary of the Bush Administration's more nationalist, unilateralist and militarist approach to foreign policy. As was seen in the previous chapter, the US 'war on terror' and the Iraq war prompted a significant shift in European opinion towards Euro-Gaullism and the articulation of a distinctive European approach to foreign and security policy, based on multilateralism and soft power. The extent to which this heralds a decisive or definitive shift in European policy is, however, open to question. Many European governments and a significant part of European public opinion continue to view partnership with the USA as a central foreign policy goal. Changes of administration in Washington, DC, or other shifts in US policy could also push the balance of European opinion back towards Euro-atlanticism.

Some observers have argued for a middle way between Euro-atlanticism and Euro-Gaullism (Garton Ash, 2005; Howorth, 2003–4). Since neither Euro-atlanticism nor Euro-Gaullism can command a decisive majority within Europe, the best way both to unite Europe and to influence America is around a policy of constructive but critical partnership with the USA. Such an approach would require a historic compromise between Britain and France, with both countries moderating their traditional policies in order to facilitate a common European policy. While the logic of this argument may be sound, the entrenched nature of national foreign policies is likely to make the development of such a policy difficult, and continued European divisions over relations with the USA are probably more likely than a historic compromise between Euro-atlanticism and Euro-Gaullism.

Neighbourhood politics

Relations with countries and regions neighbouring the EU have been central to the Union's foreign and security policy since the early 1990s (Dannreuther, 2004; Bretherton and Vogler, 2006, pp. 137–61). The EU has put in place a set of policies towards the countries of Central and Eastern Europe, the Balkans, the former Soviet Union and the Mediterranean designed to build long-term co-operation with these regions. Implicitly, the EU's objective is to forestall or contain potential security problems arising from challenges such as violent conflict within these states; nationalist and fundamentalist political ideologies; socio-economic discontent; and mass migration. The EU's policies have had a number of dimensions. Institutionally, they have been based on a combination of 'bilateral' ties with individual states, and region-wide (for example, Mediterranean or Balkan) co-operation. Politically, the EU has sought to promote an agenda of good governance, democratization and respect for human rights. Economically, it has provided aid to its various partners while also seeking to promote mutual free trade. The Union has also promoted practical functional co-operation in areas such as environmental protection and transport infrastructure, providing funding to support joint activities in these areas.

After the collapse of communism, the leaders of Central and Eastern Europe's new democracies viewed integration with and membership of the EU as being vital to consolidating democracy, underpinning market economic reforms and securing their independence from Russia. The EU was initially cautious about enlargement, but in 1993 agreed that full membership would be open to these states provided they established stable democracies and functioning market economies, were able to cope with the competitive pressures of the Union's internal market and could meet the obligations of EU membership in terms of the EU's existing rules and laws (the acquis communautaire) – the so-called Copenhagen criteria (named after the location of the 1993 EU summit where they were agreed) (European Union, 1993). Throughout the 1990s, the EU used a combination of political dialogue, economic aid and technical assistance to help the Central and Eastern European states to entrench democracy, reform governmental and administrative structures, undertake difficult market economic reforms and prepare for membership of the Union (Mayhew, 1998). A key element of this process was conditionality: since membership depended on meeting the conditions laid down by the Union, the EU had substantial leverage over the Central and Eastern European states. As discussed in Chapter 1, this process culminated in 2004 with eight Central European states (the Czech Republic, Estonia, Hungary, Latvia, Lithuania, Poland, Slovakia and Slovenia – plus Cyprus and Malta) joining the Union as full members, followed by Bulgaria and Romania in 2007. This eastward enlargement of the Union has been viewed widely as a success story: a powerful example of the ability of the EU to use the magnetic attraction of membership to promote stability and security. Enlargement and the conditionality associated with it has thus been one of the key foreign policy instruments of the Union.

Since the late 1990s, the EU has sought to implement a similar policy towards the Western Balkans (Lehne, 2004). The EU has become the main donor of economic aid to the former Yugoslav republics and Albania, introduced 'bilateral' Stabilization and Association Agreements with these states, agreed in principle that full membership of the Union is open to them and sponsored regional co-operation, in particular through the Stability Pact, which brings together the countries of the region. The EU's challenge in the Balkans is, however, greater than that in Central and Eastern Europe: the wars of the 1990s have left a legacy of unresolved conflicts, weak states and endemic crime and corruption; as a consequence, the problems of conflict resolution and political and economic reform are of a far greater magnitude than in Central and Eastern Europe in the 1990s. Although the EU has been reluctant to set a target date for further enlargement, and the ability of the Union to use its model of integration to extend stability to the Western Balkans remains to be fully tested, the likelihood is that EU membership will be extended to the countries of the Western Balkans over the next decade or so.

In the former Soviet Union, the EU has used a broadly similar model, concluding 'bilateral' Partnership and Co-operation Agreements (PCAs) with the former Soviet republics and providing economic and technical assistance to them. The EU has also sought to build a special strategic partnership with Russia (this will be discussed further in Chapter 5). In contrast to the EU's policies towards Central and Eastern Europe and the Western Balkans, however, the former Soviet republics have not (yet) been considered as candidates for EU membership. As a consequence, the scale of EU political and economic engagement with these states has been significantly less than in Central and Eastern Europe and the Western Balkans, and the EU has had comparably less influence over them. The enlargement of the EU to include the Central and Eastern European states is, however, likely to increase its engagement with the former Soviet Union, since many of the new members directly border the region, and developments in Russia, Ukraine and Belarus are a key concern for the new members – in particular, for Poland.

To the south, in 1995 the EU established the Euro-Mediterranean Partnership (EMP) or 'Barcelona Process' (after the city in which it was launched). The EMP is a broad framework for dialogue and co-operation between the EU and the countries on the southern and eastern shores of the Mediterranean (Algeria, Egypt, Israel, Jordan, Lebanon, Libya, Morocco, Syria, Tunisia and the Palestinian Authority). The aims of the EMP are to foster economic co-operation, including trade liberalization, facilitate practical co-operation (in areas such as environmental protection), and act as a framework for political dialogue (in particular, in relation to human rights). The EU also has bilateral political and economic relations with its Mediterranean partners, and a variety of aid programmes to support co-operation. The 'Barcelona Process' and broader EU policy towards the Mediterranean has, however, been constrained by the authoritarian character of many of the region's regimes and by the Israeli–Palestinian conflict.

In 2004, in the context of enlargement to include the Central and Eastern European states, the EU adopted a new European Neighbourhood Policy (ENP) designed to provide greater support to those neighbouring states likely to remain outside the Union (European Commission, 2004). The ENP thus highlighted the distinction between those states considered as candidates for EU membership (the Western Balkan states and Turkey) and those states not being considered for EU membership and subject to the separate ENP. The ENP covers the EU's Mediterranean partners (Algeria, Egypt, Israel, Jordan, Lebanon, Libya, Morocco, the Palestinian Authority, Syria and Tunisia); the states lying between the enlarged EU and Russia (Belarus, Moldova and Ukraine); and the Caucasian states (Armenia, Azerbaijan and Georgia). The EU's relations with Russia are treated separately. The ENP involves the negotiation of ENP Action Plans between the EU and individual partners, designed to set concrete reform goals for the partner states, and EU financial and technical assistance to help achieve these goals. Although the ENP involved an enhanced political commitment on behalf of the EU and resulted in a limited increase in resources to support the policy, it was in practice an incremental enhancement of the policies the EU had been developing since the 1990s rather than a major shift in policy.

The increasing prominence of the EU's neighbourhood policies reflects the changed nature of security within Europe. In contrast to the Cold War, many of the primary security challenges facing Europe at the beginning of the twenty-first century arise not from direct military threats to European states but rather from the potential consequences of political and socio-economic instability on Europe's periphery. Against this background, it is hardly surprising that governments have turned to a wide range of non-military instruments in an effort to prevent or contain such instability, nor that the multifunctional EU has become one of the central vehicles for such efforts. The EU, however, faces serious problems and constraints in promoting stability and security to its east and south. In Central and Eastern Europe, the EU was working in a receptive environment, where states were already pursuing goals of democratization and economic reform, actively wanted the EU's support, and conflicts within and between states were limited. In the Western Balkans, the former Soviet Union and the Mediterranean, however, the EU faces various combinations of resistance to reform, unresolved or ongoing conflict, authoritarian or semi-authoritarian regimes, and a wariness about external interference. In these circumstances, the EU's ability to shape developments in these regions is often limited. The Union's ability to use the conditionality associated with enlargement as a means of promoting reform also depends on the credibility of eventual EU membership. As was noted above, the EU remains cautious about extending membership to the Western Balkan states, and has yet to consider seriously membership for the former Soviet republics, let alone North African or Middle Eastern states. The 2005 French and Dutch referenda defeats of the proposed EU Constitutional Treaty were also widely viewed in part as a backlash against the Central and Eastern European enlargement, provoking fears that any further enlargement might be derailed (Charlemagne,

2005). In the wake of the French and Dutch referenda, there is increasing opposition within some existing EU members to Turkish membership in particular. The post-enlargement environment thus poses two major challenges for the EU in terms of relations with its neighbours. First, will the EU be able to continue to use enlargement as a key means of stabilizing regions and countries on its periphery, in particular the Western Balkans and Turkey? In the worst case, an end to any further enlargement could have deeply detrimental consequences, fuelling nationalism and authoritarianism in the Western Balkans and turning Turkey away from the West. Second, for those countries unlikely to join the Union (except perhaps in the long term) can the EU develop other policies to help stabilize these states? Relations with neighbouring states and regions to the east and south are thus likely to continue to pose major challenges for the EU.

A global role?

Since the 1960s, the EU has played a major global economic role. This has a number of dimensions: the negotiation of preferential trade relations with former European colonies (the so-called ACP countries – Africa, Caribbean and Pacific); the adoption of common EU policies within the World Trade Organization (WTO) and its predecessor, the General Agreement on Tariffs and Trade (GATT), which made the EU a key force in these negotiations; and the EU and its members' roles as providers of economic development aid, where they have for some decades been the largest aid providers. These policies have made the EU a leading global economic player for some decades (the security dimension and implications of the EU's global economic role, in particular in the area of aid and trade, are examined in Chapter 9).

Since the 1990s, the EU has developed a growing but still limited political and security role beyond Europe. It has, in particular, placed a strong emphasis on the development and strengthening of multilateral international institutions. As the Union's 2003 *European Security Strategy* put it:

> In a world of global threats, global markets and global media, our security and prosperity increasingly depend on an effective multilateral system. The development of a stronger international society, well functioning international institutions and a rule-based international order is our objective. (European Union, 2003a)

The EU's emerging global political and security role has a number of dimensions:

- *'Bilateral' relations*: the EU has sought to develop 'bilateral' relations with a growing range of partners, in particular major powers such as China, India and Japan. While these relations usually have a primarily economic basis, in particular in terms of trade, they are gradually being expanded to include a range of political and security issues, such as human rights and dialogue on specific security crises.
- *Inter-regional co-operation*: the EU has a growing set of inter-regional relationships with other organizations, including in particular the Association of South East Asian Nations (ASEAN), the African Union (AU) and the Latin-American MERCOSUR/MERCOSUL (Mercado Común del Sur/Mercado Comum do Sul, or the Southern Common Market). While these relations again have a strong economic basis, they have also developed an increasing political and security dimension.
- *Global institutions*: the EU has sought to support global institutions such as the United Nations (UN), the international financial institutions (the World Bank and International Monetary Fund) and global arms control regimes (such as the Nuclear Non-Proliferation Treaty and the Biological and Chemical Weapons Conventions), through the adoption of common negotiating positions within these frameworks and the provision of political, technical and financial support for specific activities. Since the early 1990s, the EU has often played a central role in shaping debates within the UN (in particular in the Security Council and the General Assembly) and other global institutions.
- *Conflict prevention and crisis management*: the EU has also engaged in and supported international conflict prevention and crisis management efforts (European Union, 2001). In Africa, in particular, the EU has sought since the 1990s to make conflict prevention and resolution a central element of its policies towards that continent. The EU has also supported conflict prevention and management initiatives undertaken by the UN, regional organizations or ad hoc coalitions of states. In 2005, the EU agreed to provide monitors to help implement the peace agreement in the Aceh region of Indonesia, and in 2006 EU member states made the largest contributions to the expanded UN peacekeeping force in Lebanon following the Israeli–Lebanese war.

Taken together, these developments suggest that the EU is likely to develop a growing global dimension to the CFSP. Nevertheless, the EU also faces serious constraints on its ability to shape and respond to the global security agenda. The general problem of co-ordinating foreign policy among the EU's member states impinges significantly on the EU's global role. While the EU has been supportive of efforts to strengthen and reform the UN, for example, divergent positions on Security Council reform (in particular Germany's demand for permanent seat on the Council, and Italy's opposition to this) precluded the adoption of a common EU approach on this issue in the debate on UN reform in the wake of the 2003 Iraq War. Similarly, the fact that Britain and France are nuclear weapon states and the other EU member states are not has inhibited efforts to develop common positions on nuclear non-proliferation.

While the EU is an economic superpower, it has struggled to translate its economic might into comparable political power. The EU's role in the Middle East highlights this reality. Ever since EPC was established in the 1970s, the EU has sought to play a role in resolving the Israeli–Palestinian conflict; yet throughout this period the USA has been the key external power-broker. Although the EU has been part of the international Quartet (alongside the USA, Russia and the UN) facilitating Israeli–Palestinian peace negotiations since the 1990s, the USA has nevertheless remained the dominant external actor. While the EU is a major trading partner of Israel and the largest provider of economic aid to the Palestinian Authority, it has been unable to use this latent economic power to exercise a decisive influence on the conflict. The USA and the EU's respective roles in the Israeli–Palestinian conflict highlight the contrast between America's combination of a single centralized foreign policy and global political, economic and military power and the EU's decentralized foreign policy, global economic power but more limited political weight and military capacity. Although the EU may well develop an increasing global role, the USA is likely to remain the world's sole superpower for many years to come.

Nevertheless, in some areas of global security – broadly conceived – the EU may play a leading role. The 1997 Kyoto agreement on global warming and the International Criminal Court (ICC), established in 1998, illustrate this dynamic. In both cases, international negotiations began in the mid-1990s among a wide group of states, but the USA, which had initially supported the processes, gradually disengaged and then refused to sign the resulting treaties. In each case, the EU acted as the key driver behind the international negotiations and has been central to subsequent efforts to ratify and implement the agreements. The Kyoto agreement and the ICC also highlight the contrast between the EU's emphasis on multilateralism and the USA's reluctance to be constrained by international agreements. The effectiveness of both the Kyoto agreement and the ICC are, of course, open to question. Nevertheless, they suggest that in at least some areas the EU may act as a key driver behind multilateral efforts to address global security challenges. How far the range of global issues in which the EU plays a leading role will expand remains to be seen.

The military dimension: peacekeeping and beyond?

In 1999, EU leaders reached an historic agreement that the Union should develop a common European security and defence policy (CESDP), declaring that 'the Union must have the capacity for autonomous action, backed up by credible military forces, the means to decide to use them, and a readiness to do so' (European Union, 1999). Given the EU's essentially non-military character up to this point, the decision to give the Union a military role was a major strategic shift in its character as an international actor. The decision reflected a growing awareness that the EU might need the capacity to respond to crises with military means, and concern about Europe's continuing military dependence on the USA – both factors having been sharply illustrated by the Kosovo War in the spring of 1999.

The political commitment to give the EU a military role was backed by decisions to develop new military force structures and new political institutions for the conduct of EU military operations. The EU established the 'Helsinki Headline Goal' of being able by 2003 to deploy a force of 50,000–60,000 troops (approximately one military corps or fifteen brigades), which should be available within sixty days (but include more rapidly deployable elements), sustainable for a year and militarily self-sustaining (in terms of command, control and intelligence, logistics, and air and naval forces). Although this force is sometimes referred to as the 'European rapid reaction force', like NATO it is based on national contributions from member states and is thus not a truly supranational 'European army'. The EU also established new institutions for the management and conduct of military operations: the PSC/COPS discussed above, plus an EU Military Committee (EUMC) composed of the Chiefs of Defence of the EU members, to

provide military advice and recommendations to the PSC, and an EU
Military Staff (EUMS, with approximately seventy staff) to plan and
manage military operations.

. In 2003, the EU undertook its first military mission, deploying a
small force of approximately 400 soldiers to support the implementation of a peace agreement in Macedonia. More substantively, in 2004,
the EU took over responsibility from NATO for the much larger
(7,000-strong) peacekeeping operation in Bosnia. The Balkans was
thus in many ways the incubator of the EU's military role. Since then,
however, the EU has also undertaken or contributed to a number of
peacekeeping and crisis management operations beyond Europe, in
both Africa and Asia.

The EU's role in peacekeeping and intervention is examined in
more detail in Chapter 6, but a number of observations should be
made here. Although the EU has taken on a growing role in peacekeeping and crisis management since the beginning of the 2000s, the
EU's missions to date have been limited in size and have focused on
tasks such as peacekeeping, nation-building and civilian aspects of
crisis management (rather than on combat operations or high-inten-
sity warfare). These softer types of operation thus appear to be areas
in which the EU is likely to develop its primary military role. The EU,
further, has not taken responsibility for the military defence of
member states' territories, which remains the responsibility of NATO
for the majority of EU members who are also NATO members. In
addition, although the EU collectively and its member states individually are taking steps to enhance their capacity to deploy military forces
beyond EU boundaries, this process is moving only slowly, and the
Union's capacity to project military power elsewhere in the world is
likely to remain limited. Furthermore, although one implicit aim of
the CESDP has been to encourage member states to contribute more
to collective European defence efforts and to re-orientate their armed
forces towards power projection beyond the EU, the EU has had in
practice only a limited impact on the development of member states'
armed forces (Forster, 2006, pp. 139–45). The EU's 2004 decision to
create eleven smaller high-readiness battle groups of 1,500 troops
each was thus to some extent a backing away from the earlier
'Helsinki Headline Goal'. While the EU's role in peacekeeping,
nation-building and crisis management may continue to grow in the
future, it remains very far from becoming a military superpower
comparable to the USA.

Internal security: the EU's Area of Freedom, Security and Justice

Since the 1997 Amsterdam Treaty, the EU has been committed formally to establishing itself as an Area of Freedom, Security and Justice (AFSJ), providing security for its citizens from threats such as crime, terrorism and illegal immigration, and developing common policies in response to these challenges (European Union, 1997, Art. K.1). Issues such as crime, terrorism, immigration and border controls have historically been viewed as internal security challenges and the prerogative of the nation-state, yet since the 1980s the EU has developed a rapidly expanding role in what is also referred to as Justice and Home Affairs (JHA). There are two drivers behind this development. First, the process of European integration, in particular the removal of internal border controls between most EU member states under the Schengen Agreement, has driven the demand for common controls over the Union's external borders and collective responses to issues such as immigration, asylum and crime. Second, the changed international security environment has led to increasing concern about the Union's vulnerability to transnational security threats such as organized crime and terrorism.

EU co-operation in JHA can be traced back to 1975 when the 'Trevi Group' was established as a loose framework to facilitate co-operation to deal with cross-border terrorism. Similar groups were then established to address judicial co-operation, customs, immigration and organized crime. Under the 1985 Schengen Agreement, five core members of the EU (France, Germany, the Netherlands, Belgium and Luxembourg) agreed to remove internal border controls between themselves, generating a need for new common external border controls and a system for their management. The majority of the other EU members gradually joined the Schengen regime, as did non-EU members Norway and Iceland. The Central and Eastern European states that have joined the EU since 2004 are also being integrated into the Schengen system. Britain and Ireland have, however, opted out of Schengen and retain their national border controls.

The Maastricht Treaty established JHA as one of the three pillars of the EU (alongside the CFSP and the primarily economic European Community – EC). The Maastricht Treaty also identified nine areas of 'common interest': asylum policy; border controls; immigration policy; drug trafficking; international fraud; judicial co-operation; customs co-operation; police co-operation against terrorism; and police co-operation in relation to organized crime (European Union, 1992, Art.

Box 4.1 Co-operation under the EU's Area of Freedom, Security and Justice

- *Schengen Agreement*: removal of internal border controls among the majority of EU member states; concomitant commitment to harmonize external border controls and develop a common visa policy.
- *Asylum*: EU members are committed to developing a common asylum policy, based on common asylum procedures.
- *Immigration*: EU members are committed to developing a common immigration policy; an Action Plan on Illegal Immigration was adopted in 2002.
- *Terrorism*: an Action Plan on Combating Terrorism was adopted in September 2001 and has been expanded substantially since then; an EU Counter-Terrorism Co-ordinator was appointed in March 2004.
- *Police co-operation*: Europol, established under the 1992 Maastricht Treaty, facilitates police and intelligence co-operation within the EU, in particular in relation to organized crime; a European Police Chiefs Task Force, which first met in 2000, also facilitates co-operation among national police authorities; a European Police College (CEPOL), also established in 2000, undertakes training of national police personnel in support of European police co-operation.
- *Customs co-operation*: EU member states are committed to co-operation in relation to customs, in particular in relation to illegal goods; co-operation includes a Customs Information System and arrangements for mutual customs assistance.
- *Organized crime and drugs*: responding to organized crime and the illegal drugs trade are priorities for the AFSJ; in 2004, the EU adopted a Drugs Strategy and a Drugs Action Plan for the period 2005–8.
- *Criminal justice*: the EU has sought to facilitate co-operation between national judicial systems and the approximation of national legislation; a European Judicial Network (EJN) of national contact points was put in place in 1998, and Eurojust – a central team of magistrates, prosecutors, judges and legal experts to support co-operation – was established in 2001; a Convention on Mutual Assistance in Criminal Matters was concluded in 2000; and a Framework Decision on a European Arrest Warrant – providing for the issuing of arrest warrants on an EU-wide basis – was agreed in 2002.
- *External relations*: the ongoing development of the AFSJ has resulted in growing EU co-operation with other states and their police and judicial authorities, in particular the USA.

Data from: 'Freedom, Security and Justice', Directorate-General for Justice, Freedom and Security of the European Commission website, http://ec.europa.eu/justice_home/fsj/intro/fsj_intro_en.htm (accessed 1 December 2006).

K.1). JHA co-operation became the AFSJ under the Amsterdam Treaty, and the Schengen regime, which had previously been separate from the EU, was formally integrated into the Union. A special European Council (meeting of EU heads of state and government) in Tampere, Finland, in 1999, laid down the agenda for the development of the AFSJ. A further agenda – 'The Hague Programme – was adopted in 2004, detailing objectives for the period 2005–10.

Box 4.1 summarizes co-operation under the EU's AFSJ . As Box 4.1 shows, this co-operation is now very wide-ranging, with many areas that were traditionally the sole preserve of the nation-state becoming to varying degrees Europeanized. Institutionally, co-operation within the AFSJ is a complex hybrid, with some areas remaining purely intergovernmental and thus subject to unanimity, while others are subject to qualified majority voting and involve a significant role for the European Commission. Nevertheless, the transfer of powers to the EU in this area has been limited, and this constrains co-operation. Differences between the legal, judicial and policing systems of the EU's member states also mean that co-operation moves slowly and has to overcome various legal, technical and cultural hurdles. Despite the commitment to develop common EU policies, some key areas – such as immigration policy – remain essentially under national control. The extent to which the EU's collective response to transnational soft security problems such as organized crime, terrorism and illegal immigration has been adequate is thus open to question: while the EU has initiated a wide range of measures since the early 1990s, the implementation of these has moved more slowly, whereas the problems of organized crime, terrorism and illegal immigration are fast-moving and their perpetrators resourceful and innovative, exploiting whatever gaps may exist in the EU's collective defences. Continuing public concern about these problems and their inherently transnational character suggest that the EU will face ongoing pressure to strengthen co-operation in relation to what used to be called internal security but is now an increasingly internationalized challenge. The EU's response to the challenges of terrorism and immigration are examined in more detail in Chapters 8 and 9.

Conclusion

Since the early 1990s, the EU has assumed an increasingly prominent role in responding to security challenges within Europe and to some extent globally. Supporters contend that the EU is emerging as a power-ful foreign and security policy actor, even a new superpower. However, critics maintain that the gap between rhetoric and reality in EU foreign policy remains large; and that there are fundamental obstacles that will prevent the EU from developing a true common foreign and security policy, and severely limit the Union's international impact. The reality is a more complex and mixed picture. The EU's member states have made major progress in co-ordinating their national foreign and secu-rity policies since the early 1990s, in particular with regard to the Union's immediate European neighbourhood, but also in relation to other countries and regions and global issues, as well as in the area of internal security. The EU's economic and political weight and its multi-faceted relations with third countries, furthermore, give it substantial power and influence, particularly in the wider Europe. While there remain important foreign policy differences between the Union's member states and periodic major breakdowns in co-operation (as over the 2003 Iraq War), the larger trend is towards the Europeanization of foreign and security policy within the EU. The arrangements for foreign and security policy co-operation put in place since the early 1990s provide a strong institutional basis for this devel-opment, in particular by maintaining bureaucratic momentum for co-operation.

The nature of the foreign and security policy co-operation process within the Union, however, significantly shapes and constrains the EU as an international actor. Foreign and security policy co-operation within the EU remains essentially *intergovernmental* and largely consensus based. Although there have been proposals for the introduc-tion of qualified majority voting and giving the European Commission a greater say in shaping EU foreign and security policy, member states remain strongly attached to their central role in this area, and for the foreseeable future there appears to be little prospect of such arrange-ments being introduced. The intergovernmental, consensus nature of EU foreign and security policy-making means that the Union is partic-ularly dependent on processes of consensus-building and internal bargaining among its member states. As a consequence, it is hardly surprising that the EU has not proved well-suited to the types of crisis management and response that require rapid decision-making on controversial issues of diplomacy and force – as with the Yugoslav conflict in the 1990s. In contrast, the Union has proved to be far better suited to the longer-term strategic challenge of developing complex multi-faceted political, economic and security relations with other states and regions. Indeed, to the extent that the new security agenda involves a range of complex, multi-faceted political, economic and social issues it may be argued that the EU is particularly well-suited to responding to these challenges.

The rejection of the proposed EU Constitutional Treaty by the French and Dutch publics in 2005 could be interpreted as reflecting a deep political crisis within the EU, presaging an end of momentum towards European integration, possible demands for the repatriation of powers back to member states, and even the eventual collapse of the Union. Were such a development to occur, there can be little doubt that the EU's foreign and security policy ambitions would not survive. While the rejection of the Constitutional Treaty has undoubtedly raised major questions about the future direction of the EU, the more likely scenario for the medium-term development of the Union is of continuing co-operation within existing political and institutional arrangements, combined with incremental development and adaptation of those arrangements – a pattern that historically has been the norm within the EU. Despite the difficulties of developing a common foreign and security policy, there remain powerful pressures for foreign and security policy co-operation among the EU's member states. The primary security threats facing EU member states are external, and the capacity for addressing these threats independently at the national level is limited (even in the case of the larger members of the Union, such as the UK, France and Germany). In the face of common external threats and limited national power, there is a compelling case for developing common European responses to the new security agenda. In this context, the real foreign and security challenge for the EU is not so much that of co-ordinating policy per se, but rather of whether it can mobilize the political will and material resources to develop effective responses to the security challenges of the twenty-first century.

Chapter 5

Russia: Partner or Problem in European Security?

The end of the Cold War, the disintegration of the Soviet Union and the collapse of communism in 1989/90 raised major questions about Russia's place in the world and its relations with the rest of Europe, the West more broadly, and its neighbours in the former Soviet Union. For the forty years or so since the onset of the Cold War, and arguably the seventy-odd years since the 1917 revolution, the Soviet Union/Russia had been the defining external security threat for the West. For the Soviet Union, the combination of ideology and geopolitics made confrontation with the West, especially the USA, the defining feature of its foreign relations. With the demise of the Soviet Union, some observers in both Moscow and Western capitals hoped for the development of a close partnership between Russia and the West, and even that a democratic Russia might become a full part of the West. Within Russia, however, others argued that their country had a distinctive Eurasian identity, specific national interests of its own and must reassert its independence from the West and its influence in the former Soviet Union. In the West, some argued that Russia was still far from a democracy, that Russian and Western interests were likely to collide, and that, in the worst case, the collapse of communism might produce a hyper-nationalist 'Weimar Russia'. In the former Soviet Union, decades and in many cases centuries of close integration between Russia and the other former Soviet republics, plus a history of violent conflict, suggested that dismantling the Soviet empire was likely to be a prolonged, difficult and sometimes bloody process.

This chapter examines the evolution of Russian foreign policy since the collapse of communism, and explores Russia's place in the new European security order of the early twenty-first century. It highlights the way in which post-Cold War Russo-Western relations have swung between co-operation and confrontation, and argues that the relationship between Russia and the West is likely to remain characterized by an uneasy mix of co-operation and tension. It also examines Russia's efforts to re-establish a sphere of influence in the former Soviet Union, but concludes that Moscow's ability to achieve this goal remains limited, and countries such as the Baltic States, Georgia, Moldova and Ukraine are likely to continue to resist Russian hegemonism. Against the background of Russia's recent re-emergence as an 'energy superpower' following its economic collapse in 1998, the chapter additionally explores the Janus-faced nature of Russian power. It suggests that while Russia's large energy resources are allowing it partly to re-establish itself as a major power, the international political power flowing from Russia's energy resources should not be exaggerated, and that Russia remains characterized by major internal problems (an unbalanced economy, population decline, widespread crime and serious public health problems, especially HIV/AIDS) and significant external weaknesses. Russia's impact on the European and global security environment is likely to remain defined by this unusual mix of strength and weakness.

Russia: post-communism and foreign policy

Since 1991, Russia has gone through a period of dramatic turbulence and transition: the failed August 1991 coup against then Soviet President, Mikhail Gorbachev, and the subsequent disintegration of the Soviet Union; violent confrontation between Russian President Boris Yeltsin and his political opponents in 1993; shock-therapy economic reforms which introduced basic market economic structures but impoverished many Russians and created a new elite of super-wealthy oligarchs; a low-level dirty war in Chechnya (which remains unresolved at the time of writing); a dramatic economic collapse in 1998; and, since the late 1990s, a period of relative domestic stability under President Vladimir Putin and the country's (re-)emergence as an 'energy superpower' on the basis of its large gas and oil reserves. In the early and mid-1990s Russia was often interpreted (at least in the West) as country undergoing a transition towards a Western-style democracy and market economy. Since the late 1990s, critics in both Russia and the West have argued that, while stabilizing the situation within Russia, President Putin has established an increasingly authoritarian regime, making the country at best a sham democracy.

The relationship between domestic politics and foreign policy in Russia is complex. During the 1990s, the Russian foreign policy debate was often characterized as one between Westernizers and Eurasians,

the former advocating integration with the West and the latter emphasizing Russia's distinctive place as a Eurasian power. Alexei Arbatov
described the Russian foreign policy spectrum in terms of four groups:
a pro-Western group, whose central goal was to integrate Russia politically and economically into the West; moderate liberals, who, while
supporting democracy and market-orientated economics, argued for a
more pragmatic approach based on Russian national interests;
centrists and moderate conservatives, who emphasized the restoration
of Russian influence in the former Soviet Union and the development
of ties with states such as China, India and Iran; and neo-communists
and nationalists supporting the re-establishment of the Russian empire
and a strongly anti-Western foreign policy (Arbatov, 1993, pp. 8–14;
see also De Nevers, 1994, pp. 23–39).

At the beginning of the 1990s, President Boris Yeltsin, his foreign
minister, Andrei Kozyrev, and key economic reformers (such as Prime
Minister Yegor Gaidar) pursued a strongly pro-Western foreign policy,
winding down the Cold-War military confrontation with the West and
seeking Western financial support for market economic reforms.
Yeltsin's market economic reforms and pro-Western foreign policy,
however, provoked opposition, which coalesced in the Russian Duma
(parliament). Tensions between President Yeltsin and his opponents
came to a head in September 1993: Yeltsin dissolved the Duma, Duma
deputies responded by taking up arms, pro-parliamentary mobs took
to the streets and Russia appeared to be on the verge of civil war or
state collapse. The Russian military, however, supported Yeltsin and
shelled the Duma, forcing the deputies to surrender and restoring
order. Duma elections in December 1993, however, produced strong
support for Yeltsin's communist and nationalist opponents (including
the neo-fascist Liberal Democratic Party, led by the extremist Vladimir
Zhirinovsky – viewed by some as a potential Russian Adolf Hitler).

The rise of opposition to Yeltsin raised fears of a possible red-brown
communist–nationalist coalition, while the severe economic disloca-
tion associated with market reforms generated concern about a potential 'Weimar Russia' that might collapse into extreme nationalism, as
Germany had in the 1930s. In the event, these worst case scenarios did
not come to pass, and Yeltsin won the presidential elections in 1996. In
the face of domestic criticism and disillusionment with Western
support, Yeltsin's early pro-Western foreign policy was significantly
modified and a greater emphasis was placed on the re-establishment of
influence in the former Soviet Union. In 1998, however, the Asian
financial crisis of the previous year spread to Russia, with a massive

exodus of foreign capital triggering a 30 per cent devaluation of the rouble in August 1998, a collapse of the banking system and a 4.6 per cent decline in gross domestic product (GDP) by the end of the year. The 1998 financial collapse symbolized the increasing weakness of post-communist Russia.

At the end of 1999, Yeltsin resigned, with his Prime Minister, Vladimir Putin, taking over as President and then winning the presidential elections in March 2000. Since 2000, Russia has undergone a remarkable recovery, underpinned by its emergence as an 'energy superpower' (Hill, 2002, 2004). Russia has the largest gas reserves in the world and the eighth-largest oil reserves. Rising global demand for oil and gas, rapidly increasing oil and gas prices and the restoration of Russian oil and gas production after their decline in the 1990s produced annual GDP growth rates of 4–7 per cent between 2000 and 2006 (almost all of this growth being accounted for by revenues from gas and oil exports). This economic recovery improved the situation of the Russian people significantly, caused a dramatic increase in the financial resources available to the Russian state, and allowed Russia to pay off the majority of its foreign debt.

Politically, the Putin era has been associated with a return to stability compared to the often chaotic Yeltsin era, but also with a steady drift towards authoritarianism. Although the concentration of power in the hands of the presidency began under Yeltsin, it was consolidated and entrenched under Putin. While Russia retains the formal institutions of democracy, in particular an elected presidency and parliament, the President appoints the government and powerful regional governors, and controls key state institutions such as the military and the security services; the Duma has been neutered as a source of opposition or criticism; the media has become largely a mouthpiece for President Putin; and the courts and the legal system are used to intimidate and silence critics. Russia has thus become at best an 'illiberal democracy' (Zakaria, 1997, 2003) in which basic democratic structures exist but power is concentrated in the hands of the President, there a few counterbalancing forces to constrain presidential power and the freedom to advance alternative views is in practice deeply constrained. Arguably, this amounts to little more than an increasingly authoritarian regime masked as a democracy. It was thus no surprise that Putin won Russia's March 2004 presidential elections with 71 per cent of the vote, nor that the pro-Putin United Russia party gained the largest share of votes in the December 2003 Duma elections.

In terms of foreign policy, Russia under Putin initially shifted between a Eurasian and a Western-orientated foreign policy, but has since the mid-2000s followed an increasingly assertive policy, seeking to re-establish Russia as a great power independent of the West. National security strategy and military doctrine documents adopted in 2000 were based on the assumption of a confrontation between a US-led West and Russia. In response to the 9/11 terrorist attacks, however, Putin adopted a significantly more pro-Western foreign policy, supporting US intervention in Afghanistan, including by acquiescing to the deployment of US troops in the Central Asian former Soviet republics and supplying arms to America's Afghan allies the Northern Alliance (Antonenko, 2001). Putin's turn towards the West appeared to reflect a genuine belief that Russia and the West face a common enemy in Islamic terrorism (with Russia's war in Chechnya one front in this confrontation), but also a more pragmatic assessment of 9/11 as an opportunity for Russia to build political capital with the West and in particular the USA. Since 2001, however, there has been a further foreign policy re-orientation, underpinned by Russia's new energy-driven wealth and self-confidence. Russian foreign policy now emphasizes the re-establishment of Russia as a great power and support for a multipolar (as opposed to US/Western-dominated) world order. Russia opposed the 2003 Iraq War (joining France and Germany in indicating that it would oppose any UN Security Council authorizing the use of force against Iraq), is attempting to reassert its influence in the former Soviet Union, and has strengthened political, economic and military ties with a variety of non-Western states (including China, India, Middle Eastern states and Venezuela). Russia's newfound energy wealth, further, means that it is no longer financially dependent on the West in the way it was in the 1990s, expanding its freedom to manoeuvre in its relations with the West. The impact of Russia's new status as an 'energy superpower' was confirmed in January 2006 when Russia temporarily cut off gas supplies to Ukraine over a pricing dispute, which in turn reduced gas supplies to Western, Central and Eastern Europe (because their gas is supplied via the pipeline that crosses Ukraine). This incident was a sharp illustration of Russia's ability to use its energy power to coerce its former Soviet neighbours, but it also highlighted the EU's dependence on Russian energy (in particular, gas) supplies.

The extent to which Russia's energy-fuelled economic recovery will be maintained in the longer term, and Russia will be able to use this to re-establish itself as a great power are, however, open to question. Russia's economic recovery is almost entirely dependent on gas and oil exports, making it very vulnerable to a fall in prices. Even if gas and oil prices remain relatively high, experts suggest that technical and investment problems mean that Russian gas and oil production cannot easily be expanded and may decline in the coming years. Since oil- and gas-exporting states depend heavily on the markets to which they export, Russia's ability to use the energy weapon as a foreign policy tool may also be limited.

Russia and the West: a troubled partnership

The post-Cold War relationship between Russia and the West has been characterized by an uneasy mix of co-operation and confrontation. As was noted above, following the collapse of Soviet communism there were hopes of a new strategic partnership between Russia and the West, but these were quickly dashed as tensions emerged, in particular over the Yugoslav conflict and NATO's enlargement. This pattern of initial hope of a fundamental breakthrough in relations followed by disillusionment as differences re-emerged was also repeated after the events of 9/11.

A variety of factors explain this pattern of relations and suggest that it is likely to continue into the future. The demise of communism in the Soviet Union removed what had been the key ideological source of tension between Russia and the West since 1917. The withdrawal of Soviet forces from Central and Eastern Europe and the break-up of the Soviet Union ended the geostrategic military threat that the Soviet Union had posed to the West since 1945. In order to reform and modernize its economy, Russia needs Western aid, trade and investment. During the 1990s, the West – individual Western states, Western banks and the International Monetary Fund (IMF) – helped to underpin Russian economic reforms by supplying aid, loans and debt relief, and Russia became to a significant degree dependent on Western economic support. Russia and the West also arguably share basic common interests in addressing key elements of the new global security agenda, such as globalized Islamic terrorism and WMD proliferation.

There are, however, countervailing pressures that generate tensions between Russia and the West. Many in Russia, and especially in the Russian security and military elite, still view the West as a threat. NATO's enlargement into Central and Eastern Europe, its intervention in the former Yugoslavia and the expansion of US influence in the Caucasus and Central Asia have fed into historic Russian fears of encirclement. More broadly, Russia is opposed to the current Western, and especially US, domination of global politics, as indicated by President Putin's emphasis on the alternative of a multipolar world. Similarly, Russia's residual great power status and uncertainty about its long-term future direction make other European states wary of Moscow. More immediately, Russia's efforts to maintain its sphere of influence in the former Soviet Union (see below) have generated tensions not only with the former Soviet republics but also with other European states and the USA. Russia's drift into authoritarianism and its poor human rights record, in particular its military interventions in Chechnya in 1994–6 and 1999–2000 – where the conduct of the Russian military campaigns was brutal – have also generated tensions with the West. In addition, Russia's engagement in the arms and nuclear technology trade has been criticized by the West, especially in the case of Iran, where Russia is a key supplier of the nuclear technology that underpins Tehran's reputed efforts to develop nuclear weapons.

More broadly, if the Western security community discussed in Chapter 1 is the defining feature of contemporary Europe, Russia is not a member of that community. Russia's drift towards authoritarianism means that it does not fully share the core democratic values on which that security community is based. Russia is not a member of that community's key institutions, the EU and NATO, nor does it share the high level of economic interdependence that marks that community. Although unlikely, armed conflict between Russia and the West cannot be ruled out. It is not impossible that Russia could yet become a full member of the Western security community, but such a development would require major domestic political change – a shift towards a more substantive democracy – within Russia. Indeed, since the late 1990s, Russia has been moving further away from, not closer to, the Western security community.

Given this balance of factors, it is hardly surprising that the Russian–Western relationship is pulled in contradictory directions. The global balance of power discussed in Chapter 2, however, means that the relationship between Russia and the West (or even between Russia and the EU) is hardly one of equals. Regardless of the EU's dependence on Russian energy supplies, in terms of broad economic, political and military power, the West remains the dominant partner. Thus, while Russia poses a potential (and in some cases real) threat to its weaker and smaller neighbours, it lacks the power to pose a major strategic threat to the rest of Europe as a whole for the foreseeable future. Renewed military confrontation with the West would also be extremely costly for Russia. For these reasons, while continued tensions between Russia and the West appear to be likely over a range of issues, a full-blown political–military confrontation akin to the Cold War seems unlikely.

Russia and NATO

Since the end of the Cold War, NATO and Russia have sought, but often struggled, to build a new, co-operative relationship. NATO–Russia ties have gradually been institutionalized (Weitz, 2005, pp. 59–73): Russia joined NATO's Partnership for Peace (PfP) in 1994; a NATO–Russia Founding Act on Mutual Relations, Cooperation and Security was signed in 1997, at which point a NATO–Russia Permanent Joint Council (PJC) was established; and in 2002 a new NATO–Russia Council (NRC) replaced the PJC. As a consequence, there is now regular political and military dialogue between NATO and Russia.

Despite these efforts to institutionalize co-operation, NATO–Russian relations remain troubled by a number of factors. The Russian leadership, in particular the military, continue to view NATO as a serious potential, and perhaps actual, threat to Russia's security. Moscow views NATO's enlargement into Central and Eastern Europe as an unnecessary and threatening act in Russia's former sphere of influence. At various points, Russian political and military leaders warned of the emergence of a new 'Cold Peace' between Russia and NATO, and threatened countermeasures in response to the Alliance's enlargement. In practice, however, Russia has generally chosen to learn to live with NATO enlargement. This largely reflects Russia's inability to prevent NATO's enlargement and the high political and economic costs of renewed confrontation with NATO, although there may also be an emerging recognition within Russia that today's NATO is very different from that of the Cold War period.

Intervention in the Yugoslav conflict proved a particular bone of contention between NATO and Russia throughout the 1990s. NATO's intervention was viewed in Moscow as an encroachment into a former Russian sphere of influence, directed against Russia's Slavic kin, the Serbs, and setting a potential precedent for NATO intervention closer to Russia (or even in Russia itself) (Kremenyuk, 2002). In the complex peacemaking efforts in the former Yugoslavia, Russia generally backed the Serbs, while Western sympathies lay primarily with the Bosnian

Muslims, Croats and other non-Serb groups. NATO–Russia relations reached a post-Cold War nadir during NATO's 1999 intervention in Kosovo, when Russia formally broke off relations with NATO and rushed 200 paratroopers from its peacekeeping force in Bosnia to deploy ahead of NATO forces at the airport in Kosovo's capital, Pristina, prompting the commander of NATO forces on the ground, the British General Sir Michael Jackson, to warn of a possible 'Third World War' (quoted in Tran, 1999). In both Bosnia in 1995 and Kosovo in 1999, however, Russia was eventually persuaded to contribute forces to the NATO-led peacekeeping forces.

Since the 1999 Kosovo war, however, Russia's relations with NATO have stabilized. Ties were formally re-established in 2000 and improved further after 9/11, which made countering terrorism a significant new area of co-operation between Russia and NATO. The normalization of NATO–Russia relations may, however, also reflect another factor: the relative decline of NATO. As was discussed in Chapter 3, in the wake of the 9/11 terrorist attacks and the 2003 Iraq War, NATO is now a less central and less cohesive security institution that it was during the Cold War or the 1990s. From this perspective, NATO is probably both less important for, and less of threat to, Russia than was the case in the past. Equally, for Western states, NATO is simply one part of their broader relationship with Russia. The NATO–Russia relationship may thus be only one part of a broader and more complex Russo-Western relationship, rather than the central element of that relationship, which it appeared (or aspired) to be in the 1990s.

Russia and the EU

Like NATO, the EU has sought to develop an institutionalized partnership with Russia. A Partnership and Cooperation Agreement (PCA) between the EU and Russia was signed in 1994, coming into force in 1997. The PCA provides the framework for regular political dialogue with Russia, as well as for economic and trade relations. Since the mid-1990s, the EU–Russia relationship has expanded to include twice-yearly summits of leaders, regular meetings of officials on a wide range of issues, and EU financial and technical assistance to Russia. In 2003, further, the EU and Russia agreed to create four 'common spaces' – in economics; freedom, security and justice; external security; and research and education – although whether these will amount to much more than rhetoric is open to doubt. Nevertheless, since the mid-1990s, Russia and the EU have developing an increasing network of ties and co-operation:

> EU–Russian relations are unique for both parties in terms of the multiplicity of their dimensions. These range from technical trade cooperation, large-scale regional cooperation frameworks such as the Northern Dimension and space cooperation to joint action in combating organised crime and nuclear safety programmes. (Lynch, 2003, p. 63)

Russian views of the EU have been much less negative than those of NATO. The EU is not perceived by Russia to be a military threat, and Moscow has been much less concerned about the EU's eastward enlargement or the Union's emerging defence role than it has about NATO's post-Cold War evolution. To the extent that some of the key challenges facing Russia are economic, the EU is a more important and relevant partner than NATO. The EU is an important market for Russia. Nevertheless, when the Central and Eastern European states joined the EU in 2004, Russia's concern about the consequences of the Union's enlargement intensified. The extension of the EU's Schengen common border and visa regime to the Central and Eastern European states has restricted the ability of Russian citizens to travel to these states, leading Russia to oppose the extension of its PCA to new EU members in 2004 (although Moscow was later forced to back down on this issue). The anomalous status of the Russian exclave of Kaliningrad is also a concern for Moscow. Located between Poland and Lithuania on the Baltic coast, Kaliningrad became surrounded by EU territory when these states joined the Union in 2004. In 2002, Russia and the EU agreed that Russian citizens of Kaliningrad would be issued with a special Facilitated Travel Document (FTD) authorizing transit between Kaliningrad and the rest of the Russian Federation, although the FTD is in effect a visa by another name and essentially a face-saving gesture for Moscow. Russia has also been concerned about the EU's development of ties with other former Soviet republics, especially Ukraine, viewing these as a challenge to Russian influence.

The EU–Russia relationship is also an uneasy one from the Union's perspective. Russia's drift towards authoritarianism, its poor human rights record and the Chechnya conflict make Russian an uncomfortable partner for the EU, although the Union has been cautious in its criticism of Russia on these issues. EU member states are also wary of Russian attempts to reassert its influence in the former Soviet Union.

More broadly, there are major differences of culture and strategic outlook between the EU and Russia. As Daniel Gros of the Brussels think tank, the Centre for European Policy Studies, has put it, 'The EU is really a large bureaucratic machine whereas Russia works on the basis of power politics so there are often difficulties in the relationship between them' (quoted in Smyth, 2006).

Russia's (re-)emergence as an 'energy superpower' is also reshaping its relations with the EU and the West more generally. Western European dependence on Russian energy supplies dates back to the 1970s and 1980s, when expanding energy needs and the desire for détente with the Soviet Union led to the conclusion of oil, and especially gas, supply agreements and the construction of new pipelines. The interruption of gas supplies to Western, Central and Eastern Europe in January 2006 created a new awareness within the EU of the dangers of this dependence. Western dependence on Russia gas and oil and the revenue Russia receives from its gas and oil exports have reduced Western leverage over Russia compared to the 1990s, while Russia's foreign policy freedom of manoeuvre has increased. At the same time, however, the extent to which Russia will be able to use its latent power over the EU or the West may be limited, since revenue from gas and oil exports are central to the Russian economy and the political costs of interrupting supplies to Western, Central and Eastern Europe would be high.

Russia and the former Soviet Union: the 'near abroad'?

In many ways, Russia's relations with the other former Soviet republics are the classical problems of withdrawal from empire: the imperial power's reluctance to lose its empire, the weakness of newly emergent post-colonial states, the continued significance of economic ties developed under the empire, and the potential for violent conflict over borders and ethnic minorities. In the former Soviet case, however, these problems are compounded by geography: proximity means that Russia and the other former Soviet republic are destined to be neighbours.

Historically, there was never a clear dividing line between the Russian state and the Russian empire: 'Until at least the late nineteenth century, Russia was defined not as the land of the Russians but as the territory of the Russian Empire-State' (Melvin, 1995, p. 7), a pattern upon which the Soviet Union built after 1917. Russia has thus struggled to come to terms with the loss of much of its empire-state. This struggle has been further complicated by the Russian diaspora in the former Soviet Union – the approximately 25 million ethnic Russians left in other former Soviet republics by the break-up of the Soviet Union. The largest of these Russian minorities are in Ukraine (8 million), Kazakhstan (4.5 million), Belarus (1.2 million), Latvia (700,000), Uzbekistan (650,000) and Kyrgyzstan (600,000). Russia has set itself up as the defender of the rights of these Russian minorities, but has also used the issue of Russian minority rights to assert influence over the other former Soviet republics. Russian concerns about encirclement and the penetration of other powers into the region have reinforced a consensus in Moscow in favour maintaining a sphere of influence in the former Soviet Union.

The initial vehicle for Russian efforts to maintain a sphere of influence was the Commonwealth of Independent States (CIS), established at the end of 1991. Many of the other former Soviet republics, in particular Ukraine, viewed the CIS as little more than a vehicle for a civilized divorce from the Soviet Union, and while it continues to exist more than a decade after its creation, the CIS has become a largely paper institution. Russia has also sought to build alliances with those states supportive of its dominant role in the region (such as Armenia, Belarus and Kazakhstan), while putting pressure on others (such as Georgia, Moldova and Ukraine), which have pursued greater independence from it. During the 1990s, Russia intervened militarily in conflicts in Moldova, Georgia and Tajikistan, both as a means of maintaining influence in the region and in order to put pressure on these states to accede to Russian demands. A Collective Security Treaty (CST), under which an act of aggression against one signatory is viewed as an act of aggression against all, was signed by a number of CIS states in 1992–3. Ukraine, Moldova and Turkmenistan stayed outside the CST, and Armenia, Georgia and Uzbekistan withdrew from it in 1999 (although Uzbekistan rejoined in 2006). The CST was upgraded to the status of an organization (the CSTO) in 2002–3 and at the time of writing includes Russia, Armenia, Belarus, Kazakhstan, Kyrgyzstan, Tajikistan and Uzbekistan. The former Soviet Union is thus characterized by a patchwork of security arrangements, including the CSTO, bilateral military co-operation arrangements between Russia and various former Soviet states, and multilateral military exercises among varying combinations of states (Willerton and Cockerham, 2003, pp. 193–6).

The attitudes of the other former Soviet states towards Russia have varied significantly. Belarus, which lacks a strong sense of national identity independent of Russia, has been Moscow's most loyal ally in the former Soviet space. Armenia has maintained a strategic alliance with Russia to counter its historical enemies, Azerbaijan and Turkey. The Central Asian states have largely sought to maintain close relations with Russia, with the partial exception of Uzbekistan, which has been torn between asserting itself as a power in its own right within Central Asia and maintaining close ties with Russia. The Baltic States – Estonia, Latvia and Lithuania – refused to join the CIS in 1991, succeeded in consolidating their independence from Russia after this, and joined NATO and the EU in 2004. Azerbaijan, Georgia, Moldova and Ukraine have also sought to distance themselves from Russia. In the late 1990s, Georgia, Ukraine, Uzbekistan, Azerbaijan and Moldova formed the so-called GUUAM group to facilitate co-opera-tion among those states seeking greater autonomy from Russia. Uzbekistan withdrew from the group in 2005, but the other four members upgraded the group in 2006, renaming it the Organization for Democracy and Economic Development – GUAM.

Relations with Russia are linked to domestic politics within the former Soviet states, with internal divisions between those supporting close ties with Russia and those seeking greater independence from Moscow. These divisions also relate to democracy, with authoritarian regimes generally supporting close ties with Russia, and their liberal opponents seeking closer ties with the West. In November 2003, Georgia's 'Rose Revolution' brought to power a new leadership committed to democratization and closer ties with the West. A year later, Ukraine's 'Orange Revolution' followed a similar pattern, and in 2005 Kyrgyzstan's 'Tulip Revolution' saw the overthrow of that coun-try's authoritarian post-communist regime. This series of 'colour revo-lutions' seemed to hint at a wave of political change that might see the overthrow of authoritarian post-communist rulers in most of the post-Soviet space, and alter its geopolitics in the process. Developments since these revolutions have shown, however, that even under new leadership these countries face major challenges in reforming their political systems and economies. Fear of similar revolutions has also led other states to clamp down on dissent, as in Uzbekistan in May 2005, when security forces opened fire on protesters in the city of Andijan, killing many of them.

Since the early 1990s, a variety of factors – the need to respond to conflicts within the region, access to its oil and gas resources, the rise of Islamic movements, opposition to Russian neo-imperialism, and concerns about democracy and human rights – have drawn other external actors, in particular the USA, the EU, China, Turkey and Iran, into the former Soviet space. Some argue that a new great game is emerging in the former Soviet Union, with the major powers competing for influence, just as Russia and the UK did in Central Asia in the nineteenth century. In practice, however, the USA and European states have been very cautious in engaging in the region, reflecting both the limited nature of their interests there, and a desire not to antagonize Russia. China and Iran, further, have largely co-operated rather than competed with Russia in the former Soviet space. In particular, the Shanghai Co-operation Organization (SCO), established in 2001, brings together Russia, China and four Central Asian states (Kazakhatan, Kyrgyzstan, Tajikistan and Uzbekistan). The Shanghai co-operation process began in the late 1990s with the conclusion of arms reduction and military confidence-building agreements, and the SCO now brings its members together on a regular basis, with a focus on security concerns relating to Islamic movements and terrorism. The SCO is also to some extent a counterweight to Western, and in particular US, influence in the region.

At the time of writing, nearly two decades after the break-up of the Soviet Union, the majority of the former Soviet states remain in an ambiguous and uncertain strategic situation. The Baltic States have succeeded in making themselves part of the West, are now full members of the EU and NATO and are far less vulnerable to Russian interference than was the case in the early 1990s. Ukraine, Belarus and Moldova, in contrast, have been described as the 'new Eastern Europe': a group of countries squeezed between the enlarged EU and NATO and an assertive Russia. The combination of Ukraine, Belarus and Moldova's domestic problems and the desire not to antagonize Russia has made the West reluctant to consider these states, above all Ukraine, as potential members of the EU or NATO. The largely authoritarian Caucasian and Central Asian states remain even further from the West, both geographically and politically. Since its 2004 'Rose Revolution', however, Georgia has sought to develop much closer relations with the West, pressing for membership of the EU and NATO. While the West has upgraded Georgia's ties with the EU and NATO, Western governments are likely to remain wary of provoking Russia. The uncertain strategic status of the former Soviet states creates potential for misunderstanding and conflict between Russia and the West. The overthrow of authoritarian leaders, state collapse and/or large-scale internal violence in one or more of the former Soviet states (Belarus or Georgia, for example) could pit Russia and the West against one another, or in the worst case trigger Russo-Western armed conflict. The continuing desire of Russia to maintain its dominant role in the former Soviet space and a West that is pulled between opposing Russian neo-imperialism and the wish to avoid conflict with Russia, nevertheless, suggest that the uncertain strategic status of the former Soviet states is unlikely to be resolved soon.

The security problems of Russian weakness

With the break-up of the Soviet Union, Moscow lost half of its population, 40 per cent of its gross national product (GNP), and a quarter of the territory it once controlled. In absolute GNP terms, Russian fell from third in the world in 1987 to fifteenth by the mid-1990s, behind India, Australia, the Netherlands and South Korea and just ahead of Mexico, Switzerland and Argentina (Graham, 1999b, p. 3). The 1998 economic collapse further exacerbated Russia's decline and internal weaknesses. By the late 1990s, Thomas Graham, Jr, a former US diplomat who served in the American embassy in Moscow, suggested that Russia's decline was so severe that there was a possibility of 'a world without Russia' (Graham, 1999b). The security dimensions of Russian weakness include the following problems:

- *The economy*: the collapse of communism and the transition to a market economy resulted in a major recession within Russia. Russia's GDP contracted by an estimated 40 per cent between 1991 and 1998. The 1998 financial crisis further exacerbated the situation. Many Russians were impoverished, while much of the Soviet-era welfare system was dismantled or downgraded. And, despite the economic recovery since 2000, Russia still faces major economic problems: the economic recovery has been almost entirely fuelled by gas and oil exports, and the rest of the Russian economy remains uncompetitive and in need of major reform and investment. Although the economic situation of the Russian population has improved greatly since 2000, Russia has very high levels of inequality, and significant parts of the population have benefited only marginally from the economic reovery.
- *Governance*: Russia faces major governance problems. Although the situation within Russia stabilized under President Putin, the concentration of power in the hands of the president, the lack of

accountability and transparency in state institutions, and widespread corruption are arguably severely detrimental to both public faith in the Russian state and long-term prospects for sustainable economic development. At the same time, ongoing low-level violence in the North Caucasus and the inability of the Russian government to stabilize the situation there, threatens to turn southern Russia into a semi-permanent arc of instability.

- *Demographic decline*: Russia faces a major problem of demographic decline: its population fell from 149 million in 1992 to 143 million in 2003; Russian fertility rates are below the replacement level of 2.1 children per woman of reproductive age, and mortality rates are high compared to many other states; if current trends continue, Russia's population is expected to decline by over 30 per cent over the next fifty years (World Bank, 2005, p. 3). Russia's demographic decline is likely to cause or exacerbate a number of problems. The proportion of the Russian population of working age will decline, inhibiting the prospects for economic development. Demographic decline will reduce the numbers of men of conscription age and increase the proportion of the military budget that has to be allocated to health care and social problems. Demographic decline also raises the prospect that parts of the Russian Federation, especially in the Far East, may become depopulated, which would exacerbate the governance problems facing the Russian state and result in economic and population penetration, and even territorial claims, from other states (especially China).

- *Health*: although the Soviet Union's health situation had begun to worsen from the 1970s, the sudden transition to a market economy in the 1990s resulted in a dramatic deterioration in the health of the population, and Russia is now one of the few countries in the world where life expectancy is falling. Problems include high rates of death from non-communicable diseases such as heart disease; the return of communicable diseases such as tuberculosis and diphtheria; widespread alcoholism; a high suicide rate; and high levels of traffic and work-related accidents (World Bank, 2005). According to Nicholas Eberstadt (1999, p. 4), 'Russia's heath profile no longer remotely resembles that of a developed country; in fact, it is worse in a variety of respects than those of many Third World countries.' Russia also faces a growing HIV/AIDS problem: the HIV infection rate in Russia is among the fastest-growing in the world; worst-case estimates suggest Russia could reach an HIV infection rate of 20 per cent or higher (International Crisis Group, 2001, p. 3); such a scenario would drastically exacerbate Russia's existing demographic, health, economic and governance crises.

- *Crime*: crime has become a pervasive feature of post-Soviet Russia. The collapse of communism resulted in a dramatic upsurge in crime in Russia, and the emergence of powerful organized criminal groups. By the mid-1990s there were an estimated 5,700 criminal gangs in Russia, with a total of more than 100,000 members (International Institute for Strategic Studies, 1995, p. 25). Violent crime poses a direct threat to the security of Russian citizens: Russia's homicide rate increased rapidly during the 1990s and is now one of the highest in the world; almost 30,000 Russians died as a result of homicide in 1999 (World Bank, 2005, p. 10).

- *Environment*: the Soviet Union's industrial, agricultural and military development from the 1930s through to its collapse was undertaken with almost no regard for the protection of the environment, and consequently caused major environmental problems. Russia and the former Soviet republics will face the legacy of these problems for many decades. Various Russian cities and regions constitute dangerous environmental hotspots which continue to pose serious threats to the health and lives of local people.

- *Military disintegration*: the Russian military is in an ongoing state of decay. With the break-up of the Soviet Union, the Russian military lost many of its bases, large numbers of front-line troops, and much of its latest weaponry. Defence spending has declined dramatically since the 1980s, with the consequence that funds for reorganization and modernization are severely constrained. Many professional soldiers have left the military, draft dodging is widespread, training is limited and much equipment is barely maintained. As a result, the operational effectiveness of the armed forces has been seriously undermined, and the Russian military is increasingly 'de-professionalized' (Herspring, 2002). Regional commanders hire out soldiers as labourers in order to raise funds, and elements within the military are widely believed to be involved in corruption and criminality. The practice of *dedovshchina* – hazing, where senior military personnel beat and brutalize their juniors – is all-pervasive. An estimated 5,000 Russian military personnel die each year as a result accidents, suicides and killings (Galeotti, 2002, p. 155).

The disorder of the Yeltsin era and the 1998 financial collapse pushed concerns about Russian weakness to the fore, raising fears that Russia was becoming a giant failed state, or might even break up completely.

Russia's economic recovery since the late 1990s, its (re-)emergence as an 'energy superpower', and the increasing assertiveness of its foreign policy suggest that Russia may be re-establishing itself as a major power. Russia, furthermore, retains important elements of international power: a large territorial and population base (notwithstanding the latter's decline); an important geostrategic location at the heart of the Eurasian landmass; a large military and a substantial military–industrial base; a large nuclear arsenal; and permanent membership of the UN Security Council and the associated veto over Security Council decisions. Nevertheless, the extent to which Russia is likely to re-establish itself as a great power and the implications of its energy power, should not be exaggerated. Russia's economic recovery is very heavily dependent on gas and oil exports, but its ability to maintain and expand these in the future is open to question, while, as noted earlier, a decline in global gas and oil prices would have a major impact on the Russian economy. Large gas and oil resources can also be a curse as well as a boon, making the economy dependent on those resources, retarding wider economic development and encouraging corrupt, clientelist politics. While Russia has been able to assert influence over its weaker former Soviet neighbours, its ability to do so elsewhere is much more limited. Many of the problems of Russia weakness discussed above – governance, economic development, demographic decline, public health, and corruption – remain and will not necessarily be resolved by Russia's new-found energy wealth. Russia is thus likely to remain characterized by an unusual mix of elements of great power strength and serious internal weaknesses. Some of these weaknesses – demographic decline, public health, a high murder rate, instability in the North Caucasus – will pose major security problems to the Russian state and to Russian citizens. The European Commission's 2000–6 Country Strategy Paper for Russia argued that ' "soft" security threats from Russia are a serious concern for the EU and require continued engagement – nuclear safety, the fight against crime, including drug trafficking and illegal immigration, the spread of disease and environmental pollution' (European Commission, 2001, p. 3); yet the extent to which Russian weakness poses major security challenges for Europe as a whole is less clear. Other former Soviet states are primarily vulnerable to Russia because of their *own* internal weakness, which is often even more severe than Russia's. Elsewhere, neighbouring states are vulnerable to transnational security problems emerging from Russia (as in the case of northern European concerns about disused nuclear reactors from submarines based in Russia's far north), but the potential for Russia's weakness to cause more widespread destabilization or security threats, especially on a pan-European scale, is limited.

Conclusion

The end of the Cold War and the break-up of the Soviet Union opened up major questions about Russia's place in Europe and the wider world. During the 1990s, Russia experienced a period of severe political and economic turbulence and dramatic international decline, culminating in the 1998 financial collapse. Since then, Russia's economy has recovered significantly, its domestic political situation has stabilized and its new status as an 'energy superpower' has allowed it to regain at least some of its lost international power and influence.

At the beginning of the 1990s there were hopes in both Moscow and the West that Russia might become a strategic partner of the West, even a full member of the Western security community. As this chapter has shown, however, the post-Cold War Russo-Western relationship has been defined by an ambiguous mix of co-operation, competition and periodic crises. Russia itself is pulled between the West and its distinctive Eurasian geostrategic identity and interests. From a Western perspective, Russia's drift towards authoritarianism and key elements of its foreign policy preclude it from being viewed as a fully reliable partner, let alone a full member of the Western security community. Both Russia and the West have important interests in maintaining a reasonably co-operative relationship, but real differences remain – over democracy and human rights, the future of the former Soviet space, and on global security issues such as peacekeeping and proliferation. Russia's new-found 'energy superpower' status has, however, altered the balance of the Russo-Western relations that emerged in the 1990s: Russia is now much less susceptible to Western influence, and Moscow's ability to pursue an independent foreign policy has increased as a consequence. The uneasy relationship between Russia and the West is therefore likely to continue for the foreseeable future, and a decisive shift towards either full partnership or outright confrontation is unlikely.

In the former Soviet space, Russia has sought to maintain a dominant role. Russia's residual power, the support of some former Soviet states, the weakness of others and the caution or reluctance of external powers to intervene in the region has allowed Moscow to maintain a leading role there. While other actors – the USA, the EU, China, Turkey and Iran – have gradually expanded their engagement in the region since the early 1990s, they have generally been cautious in doing so, both because of the limited nature of their interests in the region and for fear of antagonizing Russia. While there are elements of competition between these powers in the former Soviet space, there are also important elements of strategic restraint and co-operation – suggesting that images of a new great game being played out in the former Soviet Union are exaggerated. In these circumstances, the former Soviet space is likely to remain in a situation of strategic ambiguity for the foreseeable future, caught between Russia efforts to maintain its dominant role in the region and the reluctance or inability of other external powers to assert a more powerful role. The 'colour revolutions' in Georgia, Ukraine and Kyrgyzstan, and fears of the rise of Islamic movements in Central Asia, further suggest that the region remains vulnerable to potentially violent domestic political upheaval, which could draw Russia and external powers into potentially destabilizing crises or confrontations.

Russia's (re-)emergence as an 'energy superpower' since 2000 has focused attention on the consequences of Russian strength. However, as this chapter has shown, Russia remains characterized by major internal weaknesses – economic and governance problems, demographic decline, public health problems, pervasive criminality, environmental degradation and a decaying military – which will not be addressed easily by its new-found energy wealth. These problems pose significant threats to the security of Russian citizens and to some extent to the long-term stability of the Russian state. Russia is thus likely to be characterized by an unusual mix of great power strength and internal weakness for the foreseeable future.

To what extent has a stable, long-term direction in Russian politics and foreign policy emerged since 2000, and are further significant changes likely? The 2008 presidential elections will provide an important test of Russia's direction: President Putin is precluded by the constitution from standing for a third term, but he is likely to anoint a successor who will, with the full support of the state, be elected as president (although Putin might also maintain a role or even effective control over the levers of power). Given the concentration of power in the hands of the presidency and the weakness of alternative centres of power and opposition political forces, the most likely scenario remains the continuation of the soft authoritarianism that has emerged under Putin. Similarly, in terms of foreign policy, there is a fairly high degree of consensus within Russia in support of efforts to reassert the country's status as a great power and strengthen ties with non-Western states in order to counterbalance Western power. If public discontent were to grow (especially if the economic recovery were to stall), more radical political change – along the lines of the 'colour revolutions' elsewhere in the region – could occur. Russia, however, appears less vulnerable to such a development than the other former Soviet states. Even if Russia maintains its economy recovery, however, the scale of the shift in the balance of power that took place with the end of the Cold War and the break-up of the Soviet Union suggests that it is unlikely ever to regain its superpower status or to pose a hege-momic threat to the rest of Europe, but will remain a significant European and second-order international power.

Chapter 6

The New Interventionism

From the Yugoslav wars of the 1990s, through the international community's failure to halt the Rwandan genocide in 1994, to the overthrow of the Taliban in Afghanistan in 2001 and the US war in Iraq, military intervention has been one of the most controversial security issues of the contemporary era. The patterns of military intervention that have emerged since the 1990s, both in Europe and globally, reflect the new strategic environment explored in Chapters 1 and 2. The emergence of a security community has made war unlikely in much of Europe, while direct military threats to that security community are limited. Beyond the Western security community, however, a variety of factors have contributed to the prevalence of civil wars and failed states (the so-called 'new wars'), while major regional wars remain real possibilities in places such as the Middle East, India-Pakistan and the Korean peninsula, and a major war drawing in great powers, in particular the USA, China and Japan, remains conceivable in East Asia. In this new strategic environment, European states are most likely to use military force not to defend their national territory or in a major European war, but rather to intervene in new wars on Europe's periphery or beyond, or in the context of major conflicts elsewhere in the world.

The new interventionism

The period since the end of the Cold War has witnessed major changes in patterns of international military intervention. Military intervention, of course, is hardly a new feature of international politics: states have intervened militarily in regions beyond their borders and in the internal affairs of other states since at least ancient Greek times. During the Cold War, the two superpowers and their allies intervened militarily to protect allies, uphold client regimes and extend their influence, as well as in various proxy wars. In parallel with this, United Nations (UN) peacekeeping emerged as a very different form of military intervention, with UN forces deployed to monitor and reinforce ceasefires, rather than in combat operations. With the end of the Cold War, the pattern of competitive intervention by the two superpowers came to an end, but in the 1990s the new wars and the humanitarian crises associated with them resulted in a new generation of 'humanitarian interventions'. In Iraqi Kurdistan in 1991, in Somalia in 1992–4, in Bosnia in 1992–5, in Haiti in 1994, in Kosovo in 1999, in East Timor in 1999–2000 and in Sierra Leone in 2000, various combinations of states and international organizations intervened militarily in order to bring an end to or alleviate large-scale human suffering (Wheeler, 2000; Weiss, 2005). The defining features of these interventions were the humanitarian crises that generated them, the fact that they involved intervention in the *internal* affairs of the states concerned (often without the consent of those states' governments) and the use of military force to bring an end to violence or secure other humanitarian objectives such as the delivery of food aid or the return of refugees or internally displaced persons. Humanitarian intervention was not entirely new in international politics, but until the 1990s such interventions had been rare – the exception rather than the norm. Although the intervening states in most cases also had more self-interested reasons for taking action, the initiation of a relatively large number of interventions in which humanitarian concerns arguably played a central part suggested that a new norm and practice of humanitarian military intervention was emerging.

Europe was a crucible of the emerging practice of humanitarian intervention: as discussed in more detail below, the Yugoslav conflict was one of the key test cases that drove the demand for more forceful intervention in humanitarian crises. European states also played a significant role in humanitarian interventions elsewhere in the world: the UK and France in Iraqi Kurdistan in 1991 and the UK in Sierra Leone in 2000, with European states also making contributions to interventions in Somalia, Haiti and East Timor. By the end of the 1990s, the majority of European states – in particular, the Western, Central and Eastern European states constituting the security community that is the core of contemporary Europe – had broadly adopted the concept of humanitarian intervention and, as also discussed below, NATO and the EU were being re-orientated towards this new mission.

The concept and practice of humanitarian intervention, however, remained highly controversial. Humanitarian intervention runs contrary to the basic principles of state sovereignty and non-intervention in states' internal affairs on which the modern international system has been based. State sovereignty and non-intervention are viewed as providing the basis for an international order founded on the mutual recognition of states and a defence against egregious interventions: in the absence of these principles, states would have carte blanche to intervene in other states' affairs. Under the Charter of the United Nations, states agree to 'refrain in their international relations from the threat or use of force against the territorial integrity or political independence of any state' and are only permitted to use force in self-defence or if authorized by the UN Security Council (which has 'primary responsibility for the maintenance of international peace and security' under the Charter) (United Nations, 1945, Arts 2, 51 and 24). Furthermore, the Charter states that 'nothing contained in the present Charter shall authorize the United Nations to intervene in matters which are essentially within the domestic jurisdiction of any state' (United Nations, 1945, Art. 2). While some of the humanitarian interventions of the 1990s were authorized explicitly by the UN Security Council, others, such as NATO's 1999 intervention in Kosovo, were not, or were undertaken on the basis of broad (and contentious) interpretations of pre-existing Security Council resolutions. The legal basis for the emerging practice of humanitarian intervention was thus ambiguous.

The humanitarian interventions of the 1990s were also controversial for other reasons. Many governments, especially in the non-Western world, feared an erosion of the principle of state sovereignty that might result in more widespread interventions in the future, especially if the requirement for UN Security Council authorization was abandoned. Russia and China, for example, feared that the precedent of humanitarian intervention might be turned against them in Chechnya and Tibet. Critics also argued that apparent humanitarian concern was, or might in future be, simply a cover for more self-interested strategic or economic motivations for intervention. Some argued that the military instrument was ill-suited to the humanitarian goals of protecting people and providing them with food and shelter – an argument to some extent vindicated by the US-led intervention in Somalia in 1992–4, which escalated from the initial humanitarian goal of facilitating the delivery of food aid to a fighting war between US forces and Somalian factions and ended with the USA withdrawing its forces. Critics could also point to the lack of consistency in the emerging practice of humanitarian intervention: while the major Western powers were willing to intervene in circumstances where humanitarian goals coincided with other interests, other equally deserving cases saw no intervention – most starkly the 1994 Rwandan genocide, when the international community stood by as an estimated one million people were slaughtered in the space of a few weeks.

Despite these criticisms, the moral case for humanitarian intervention – the argument that the outside world should not simply stand by if large numbers of people are killed in conflicts within states, or if governments perpetrate large-scale violence against their own citizens – was (and remains) compelling. Supporters of humanitarian intervention therefore responded to criticism of the concept by seeking to develop legal, political and ethical principles that might act as a stronger basis for future interventions. The International Commission on Intervention and State Sovereignty (ICISS) developed the concept of the responsibility to protect, which argued that governments have a responsibility to protect their citizens, and that when governments fail or are unable to uphold this duty and massive death or human suffering ensues, the international community has not only a right but also a duty to intervene. Drawing on the long-standing tradition of 'just war' thinking, the ICISS also outlined principles to guide the conduct of interventions (including that military intervention should be a last resort; that it should be proportionate to the humanitarian objective concerned; and that there should be a reasonable prospect of success) (ICISS, 2001). In September 2005, the World Summit of UN Heads of State and Government, called to reach decisions on the future direction of the United Nations, formally adopted the concept of the responsibility to protect, emphasizing that the international community has 'the responsibility . . . to help protect populations from genocide, war crimes, ethnic cleansing and crimes against humanity', and declaring a willingness 'to take collective action . . . should peaceful means be inadequate and national authorities manifestly fail to protect their populations' (United Nations, 2005, para. 139). The UN's adoption of the responsibility to protect concept was a remarkable break with the principle of state sovereignty and indicated at least a degree of international consensus on the issue, although the legal status of the summit declaration was unclear. The reluctance of major external powers to intervene in the ongoingongoing conflict in the Darfur region of Sudan in the mid-2000s, however, illustrated the continuing gap between principles such as the responsibility to protect and the willingness of the international community to intervene in practice.

In parallel with the debate on humanitarian intervention, new types of peacekeeping and post-conflict peace-building missions have also emerged. From the 1980s onwards, the UN undertook a series of major new peacekeeping missions in countries such as Cambodia, El Salvador and Mozambique. In contrast to traditional UN peacekeeping missions, these operations involved not just the monitoring of cease-fires but also a much wider set of tasks in support of peace processes (including mediating political settlements, facilitating elections, de-mobilizing combatants, monitoring human rights, helping to rebuild political and governmental institutions, and economic reconstruction). Many of the humanitarian interventions of the 1990s also resulted in similar follow-on missions designed to promote longer-term stability. These complex, multi-faceted missions have become referred to as post-conflict peace-building, state-building or nation-building operations, and often combine peacebuilding with elements of enforcement (usually under a mandate from the UN Security Council that includes authorization to use military force). These operations also involve complex interaction between a variety of international organizations (the UN, regional organizations such as NATO and the EU, and economic institutions such as the IMF and the World Bank), as well as between the military and civilians components of external intervention. Most of the major interventions under way in the world at the time of writing – the UN's operations in Liberia, Democratic Republic of Congo, Haiti and elsewhere; NATO's operations in Kosovo and Afghanistan; the EU's operation in Bosnia; and even, to some extent, the US-led operation in Iraq – fall into this broad category of post-conflict peace-building or state/nation-building. In recognition of the growing challenge posed by these operations, the September 2005 the World Summit of UN Heads of State and Government decided to create an intergovernmental Peacebuilding Commission to integrate efforts at post-conflict peacebuilding, supported by a Peacebuilding Fund and a peacebuilding office within the UN Secretariat (United Nations, 2005, paras 97–105).

The terrorist attacks of 9/11 and the US-led interventions in Afghanistan and Iraq significantly altered these emerging patterns of intervention. As was discussed in Chapter 2, American foreign and security policy has been re-orientated to what are viewed in the USA as the interlinked challenges of counter-terrorism, counter-proliferation and 'rogue states'. In response to the attacks of 9/11, the USA, joined by a coalition of allies, intervened in Afghanistan in late 2001 to over-throw the Taliban regime (which had been hosting Al-Qaeda's presence in the country), destroy Al-Qaeda's operating base in the country, and kill or capture Al-Qaeda leaders and fighters. On a smaller scale, the USA has supported the governments of other states, such as the

Philippines and Georgia, in taking military action against Islamic 'terrorists'. In January 2007, US air forces intervened in Somalia, attacking Islamic militant groups believed to include those responsible for the bombing of the US embassies in East Africa in 1998.

The new US policy was enshrined in the Bush Administration's September 2002 *National Security Strategy*. Most controversially, the *National Security Strategy* placed a strong emphasis on the need for pre-emptive military action against terrorist groups, WMD proliferation and 'rogue states':

> We must be prepared to stop rogue states and their terrorist clients before they are able to threaten or use weapons of mass destruction against the United States or our allies and friends . . . To forestall or prevent such hostile acts by our adversaries, the United States will, if necessary, act preemptively. (United States, 2002, pp. 14–15)

Pre-emptive military action is not new in international politics, and the USA and other states have long maintained the right to take pre-emptive action in the face of imminent attack. The elevation of pre-emption to a central place in US doctrine, and the extension of the concept to 'taking anticipatory action to defend ourselves, even if uncertainty remains as to the time and place of the enemy's attack' (United States, 2002, p. 15), however, marked a radical break with past policy, implying that pre-emptive military action might become to some extent the norm rather than the exception. Against this background, Iraq became the test case for the new doctrine of pre-emption, with the need to prevent Iraq from developing WMD, and to deal once and for all with the threat posed by Saddam Hussein's regime, providing the rationale for the Iraq War in 2003. Furthermore, in the immediate wake of the overthrow of Saddam Hussein's regime, supporters of the pre-emptive war doctrine argued that Iran, North Korea and Syria might be the next targets for such action. The Bush Administration's second *National Security Strategy*, published in March 2006, reaffirmed the central place of pre-emption in US policy (United States, 2006, p. 23).

The new US doctrine of pre-emption was controversial and problematic for a number of reasons. At its root, the doctrine provoked fears that the USA was aggregating to itself the right to attack and invade any state that it deemed to be a threat. Such fears were compounded by the strongly unilateralist inclinations of the Bush Administration and its willingness to intervene in Iraq without UN

Security Council authorization and in the face of massive global opposition. Although the US doctrine used the language of self-defence and pre-emption, it amounted to a radical extension of the concept of self-defence, and critics argued that it risked becoming an open-ended call for preventive wars against potential threats. Pre-emptive or preventive military action is also highly dependent on accurate intelligence of enemies' capabilities and intentions – and as the Iraqi case made clear, intelligence is rarely that reliable and is subject to group-think and manipulation. In addition, the US adoption of the pre-emptive war doctrine and its implementation in Iraq might be viewed as a precedent by other states, risking descent into a wider generation of pre-emptive or preventive wars.

European attitudes to the changing US policy and the pre-emptive war doctrine have been complex and divided. European states overwhelmingly supported the US intervention in Afghanistan in late 2001, with many contributing military forces. As was seen in Chapters 3 and 4, European governments were deeply divided over the Iraq War but European publics were almost universally (with the partial exception of the UK) opposed to the war. Some European leaders (such as British prime minister, Tony Blair, and Italian prime minister, Silvio Berlusconi) strongly supported the logic behind the pre-emptive war doctrine (Dombrowski and Payne, 2006, 117–18). European governments and publics have, however, generally been wary of the case for the broader adoption of a pre-emptive war doctrine. EU member states were divided on the issue of pre-emptive military action during the drafting of the EU's *European Security Strategy* in 2003. The final version of the *European Security Strategy* stated that 'Our traditional concept of self-defence – up to and including the Cold War – was based on the threat of invasion. With new threats, the first line of defence will often be abroad . . . we should be ready to act before a crisis occurs. Conflict prevention and threat prevention cannot start too early' (European Union, 2003a) – reflecting divisions within the Union on pre-emptive military action but also a preference for non-military preventive action. As will be discussed in Chapter 7, European governments also generally appear wary of possible pre-emptive military action to prevent Iran from developing nuclear weapons.

The extent to which the US experience in Iraq since 2003 will trigger a retreat from the pre-emptive war doctrine remains to be seen. The enormous challenges involved in stabilizing Iraq, the casualties the USA has sustained in the country, and the difficulty of disengaging from Iraq without destabilizing the country further and/or being seen to withdraw defeated, however, suggest that the US government and public may be significantly more cautious about pre-emptive wars, and indeed military intervention more generally, for some time.

While there has been a retreat from the earlier high-profile humanitarian interventions since 9/11, other trends suggest that the demand for peacekeeping and peacebuilding operations, often with significant humanitarian dimensions and including elements of enforcement, is likely to remain high (Cottey and Bikin-kita, 2006). Since the late 1990s there has been a major expansion of UN peacekeeping, with relatively large new missions in the Democratic Republic of Congo, Liberia, Ivory Coast, Haiti, Burundi and Sudan combining elements of traditional peacekeeping, peacebuilding and enforcement. Regional organizations have also developed a growing role in peacekeeping, with NATO taking on the task of nation-building in Afghanistan, the EU initiating operations in the Balkans and elsewhere, and the African Union (AU) adopting a new peacekeeping role with its first missions in Burundi in 2003–4 and Darfur in western Sudan from 2004 (NATO and the EU's roles in peacekeeping and intervention are examined in more detail below). Western states have also sought to support other states and regional organizations in undertaking peacekeeping, with NATO and the EU providing logistical and financial support for the AU's mission in Darfur, and Western states helping to train African peacekeepers. In 2006, further, EU member states agreed provide the core contributions to the expanded UN peacekeeping operation in Lebanon following the Israeli–Lebanese war in July–August 2006. The demand for peacekeeping and intervention is thus likely to remain high, and European states, NATO and the EU are likely to play an important role in responding to this demand.

Intervention within Europe

The Balkans

On 25 and 26 June 1991, Yugoslav federal police and customs officers, supported by 2,000 Yugoslav army troops, moved to take control of land border-crossings and the main airport in the secessionist republic of Slovenia, which had declared its independence on 25 June. On 27 June, Slovenian forces shot down a Yugoslav army helicopter, killing its pilot and a mechanic (Silber and Little, 1995, pp. 169–74). Europe had entered the era of the new wars. For the next decade, European governments, NATO, the EU and the UN struggled with the dilemmas of whether and how to intervene in the wars in the former Yugoslavia, as more than 100,000 people were killed, 3.7 million became refugees or were internally displaced within their countries, and the term 'ethnic cleansing' entered the lexicon.

European governments were initially reluctant to intervene in the Yugoslav conflict: fearing the consequences of the country's disintegration, they sought to hold together the Yugoslav federation (composed of six republics, Bosnia, Croatia, Macedonia, Montenegro, Serbia and Slovenia, plus two autonomous regions of Serbia, Kosovo and Vojvodina). In the autumn of 1991, however, the war spread to Croatia, and in 1992 to Bosnia, where fighting broke out between the Muslim, Serbian and Croatian populations. From this point onwards, there was growing debate about whether to intervene forcefully to end the bloodshed. European governments were, however, wary of being drawn into a complex internal conflict, while the USA viewed the conflict as one that the Europeans should take the lead in managing. A UN peacekeeping force (the UN Protection Force, or UNPROFOR), composed primarily of troops from European countries, was deployed in Croatia and Bosnia. UNPROFOR's mandate, however, was limited to peacekeeping and it was not armed or organized to use force. As the war continued, the UN was increasingly humiliated, with UN Security Council-declared 'safe areas' subject to attacks and UN peacekeepers held hostage. In July 1995, Bosnian Serb forces overran the so-called 'safe area' of Srebrenica, which was in theory being protected by Dutch UN peacekeepers, and massacred 7,000 unarmed Muslim men who had been sheltering there – the largest war crime in Europe since the Second World War.

The failures of the UN and European states led the USA to take on the leading role in responding to the Yugoslav conflict persuading its European allies to support the use of force against the Bosnian Serbs, widely viewed as the primary aggressors in the Bosnian conflict. In August–September 1995, following Bosnian Serb attacks on the Bosnian capital, Sarajevo, NATO launched Operation Deliberate Force, a campaign of sustained airstrikes against Bosnian Serb forces, backed-up by artillery fire from a UK–French–Dutch Rapid Reaction Force, now part of UNPROFOR. Combined with Croatian and Muslim ground offensives, Operation Deliberate Force compelled the Bosnian Serbs to withdraw from territory they had taken earlier in the war, and brought them to the negotiating table. A ceasefire was agreed in October 1995, and in November a peace agreement was signed at a US Air Force base in Dayton, Ohio. An almost 60,000-strong NATO force – the Implementation Force (IFOR), subsequently renamed the Stabilization Force (SFOR) – was deployed. Unlike UNPROFOR, IFOR/SFOR was mandated and equipped to use force to implement the Dayton agreement if necessary.

Three years later, in 1998–9 fighting broke out in Kosovo between the region's predominantly Albanian population and Serbian police and military forces. Recalling their earlier failures in Bosnia, Western leaders determined to act decisively. The USA and European governments sought to broker a settlement between the Kosovar Albanians and the Serb authorities, but warned the Serbs that if they did not accept such a settlement NATO would initiate airstrikes against Serbia. The Serbs rejected the outcome of negotiations at Rambouillet, near Paris, in February–March 1999, and on 24 March NATO launched Operation Allied Force, a campaign of sustained airstrikes against Serbia. NATO's leaders expected that the Serbs would backdown quickly, as they had in Bosnia, but they responded by initiating a large-scale offensive against Kosovo's Albanian population, triggering a massive refugee crisis as 1.5 million Kosovar Albanians fled the Serb offensive. NATO's airstrikes continued throughout April and May, amid growing concern that the Alliance might be forced to mount a ground invasion of Kosovo or risk defeat. In June, however, Serbian leader Slobodan Milosevic capitulated, agreeing to withdraw Serbian military and police forces and the deployment of a NATO peacekeeping force. Like I/SFOR in Bosnia, NATO's 55,000-strong Kosovo Force (KFOR) was mandated and equipped to use force if necessary (Judah, 2000). Two years later, in 2001, amid tensions between Macedonians and Albanians in Macedonia, a much smaller NATO force was deployed to support a peace agreement and to help to disarm Albanian guerrillas. Since then, the NATO peacekeeping forces and wider international peacebuilding efforts have brought relative peace to the Balkans, although the underlying conflicts in Bosnia, Kosovo and Macedonia remain unresolved.

A number of conclusions may be drawn from the international community's interventions in the Balkans since the 1990s. First, the region has become a de facto Western sphere of influence: although Western powers were initially reluctant to intervene in the former Yugoslav, major Western European states, the USA, NATO and the EU nevertheless emerged as the central external brokers in the region.

Second, efforts to end the war in Bosnia in the first half of the 1990s highlighted the limits of diplomacy and peacekeeping in the face of intransigent parties to a conflict, resulting in the subsequent adoption of more forceful approaches. Third, the centrality of the USA and NATO in ending the wars in Bosnia and Kosovo illustrated Europe's dependence on American political leadership and military capacity. As was noted in Chapter 3, however, the 2000s have seen a growing transfer of responsibility for the Balkans from the USA and NATO to the EU, with the EU taking over the peacekeeping mission in Bosnia and likely to take over that in Kosovo in coming years.

The former Soviet Union

A very different pattern of intervention emerged in the former Soviet Union in the 1990s. In the context of conflicts triggered by the breakup of the Soviet Union, Russia intervened militarily in a number of other former Soviet republics, in particular Georgia, Moldova and Tajikistan – see Table 6.1. While Russia's interventions were partly motivated by the wish to end or contain conflicts, they were also driven by the desire to consolidate Russian influence in the region and to put pressure on states, such as Georgia and Moldova, which Moscow feared were moving out of its orbit. In general, other external powers were reluctant to intervene in these conflicts on a significant scale. A number of small UN and Organization for Security and Co-operation in Europe (OSCE) peacekeeping or political missions were, however, deployed to monitor ceasefires and promote political settlements. In 1994 war broke out in Chechnya in Russia's North Caucasus, and Russia used military force against Chechen separatists. A ceasefire was agreed in 1996, leaving Chechnya de facto outside Russian control. In 1999, Russia launched a new military offensive to regain control of Chechnya, which it largely succeeded in doing by the year 2000. Low-level violence has, however, continued since then, also spreading to neighbouring parts of the North Caucasus. The Russian military intervention involved extensive use of airstrikes and artillery, destroyed much of the Chechen capital Grozny and resulted in thousands of deaths. The Russian military has also been accused of committing war crimes in Chechnya. Western critics argued that the Russian intervention in Chechnya bore little resemblance to the peacekeeping operations and humanitarian interventions that had been undertaken elsewhere in the world since the early 1990s.

[Handwritten margin notes: "Note for summary of division troop and stationed involvement are En/US/NATO ..."; "Eur – Mold (Also broke Georgia)"; "– see p143 145"]

TABLE 6.1 Intervention in conflicts in the former Soviet space

Country/Region	Conflict	Russian involvement	Other external involvement
Nagorno-Karabakh, Armenia-Azerbaijan	1988–94 conflict in Azerbaijani region of Nagorno-Karabakh between secessionist Armenians and Azeris; ceasefire since 1994; region remains under control of Karabakh Armenians	Russian backing for Armenia and Karabakh Armenians; 3,500 Russian troops deployed in Armenia as of 2006	OSCE 'Minsk Group' has sought to mediate a political settlement
South Ossetia, Georgia	1990–2 violence between South Ossetians and Georgians; cease-fire since 1992	Russian–Georgian–Ossetian peacekeeping force 1992–; 530 Russian troops deployed in South Ossetia as of 2006	
Abhazia, Georgia	1992–4 violence between Abhaz nationalists and Georgian government forces; ceasefire since 1994	Russian military support for Abhazia 1992–4; Russia peacekeeping force since 1992; 1,600 Russian troops deployed in Abhazia as of 2006; additional 3,000 Russian troops also deployed in Georgia as of 2006	UN Observer Mission in Georgia (UNOMIG) monitoring ceasefire since 1993 (230 military and civilian personnel); civilian OSCE Mission to Georgia 1993–
Transdniestria, Moldova	Violence between Transdniestrian secessionists and Moldovans in 1991–2; ceasefire since 1992; Transdniestrian quasi-state established	Russian 14th army backed Transdniestrian separatist forces in 1991–2; 1,900 Russian troops deployed in Transdniestria as of 2006	OSCE has sought to broker a political settlement and a Russian withdrawal; civilian OSCE Mission to Moldova 1993–

Tajikistan	1992–4 civil war between competing regional and political factions	1992– Russia-led peacekeeping force backed Tajik government and brought war to an end; Russian forces also deployed for border protection purposes; 22,300 Russian troops deployed in Tajikistan as of 2006	UN Mission of Observers in Tajikistan (UNMOT) monitored cease-fire 1994–2000 (80 military obersvers); UN Tajikistan Office of Peacebuilding 2000– (9 civilian personnel)
Ferghana Valley, Uzbekistan–Kyrgyzstan–Tajikistan	The Ferghana Valley is divided between Uzbekistan, Kyrgyzstan and Tajikistan; ongoing tensions between the three ethnic groups, as well as Islamic groups; various violent incidents since 1989	Russian support for Uzbek, Kyrgyz and Tajik governments against Islamic groups	OSCE diplomatic efforts to moderate tensions in the Ferghana Valley
Chechnya/North Caucasus, Russia	1994–6 and 1999– war between Chechen separatists/Islamists and Russian government forces; terrorist attacks by Chechen forces in Chechnya and elsewhere in Russia; terrorism and low-level violence has also spread to other parts of North Caucasus (Dagestan and Ingushetia)	Suppression of Chechen separatists by Russian military	Limited role for OSCE and UN in monitoring conflict

Data from: Pavel K. Baev (1999) 'External Intervention in Secessionist Conflicts in Europe in the 1990s', *European Security*, vol. 8, no. 2, pp. 22–51; Kenneth Weisbrode (2001) *Central Eurasia: Prize or Quicksand? Contending Views of Instability in Karabakh, Ferghana and Afghanistan*, Adelphi Paper No. 338 (Oxford: Oxford University Press for The International Institute for Strategic Studies); and International Institute for Strategic Studies (2006) *The Military Balance 2006* (London: Routledge for The International Institute for Strategic Studies); UN Department of Peacekeeping Operations website: http://www.un.org/Depts/dpko/dpko/; and Organization for Security and Co-operation in Europe, *OSCE Field Operations*: http://www.osce.org/about/13510.html.

Europe and global interventions

In the post-1945 era, European states intervened militarily outside Europe in three different – although sometimes interrelated – contexts. First, European states engaged in neo-imperial interventions in attempts to defeat nationalist movements and retain control of or influence over their empires and colonies (for example, France in Indochina (1945–54), Britain in Kenya (1952–6), France in Algeria (1954–62), and the Anglo-French (and Israeli) 1956 Suez War). As the European empires gained independence and the decline of European power became clearer, however, European military forces were gradually withdrawn from Africa, Asia and the Middle East, and European interventions of this type began to wane. Second, European states deployed forces outside Europe in the context of the Cold War. In the 1950s, Belgium, France, Greece, the Netherlands, Turkey and the UK deployed forces alongside the USA in the Korean War. During the Cold War, however, the priority for Western European governments was to defend Western Europe against the Soviet Union, and European states generally played a declining part in Cold War conflicts beyond Europe, with the USA taking the leading role. European states did not participate in the Vietnam War in the 1960s and 1970s. Third, European states contributed to the new model of UN peacekeeping that emerged after 1945. In particular, the Nordic countries (Denmark, Finland, Norway and Sweden) and some of the other European neutral states (Austria and Ireland) established reputations for contributing to UN peacekeeping operations. The overall picture from 1945 until the end of the Cold War in 1989, however, was one of declining European military involvement outside Europe.

The end of the Cold War, the new interventionism of the 1990s and the 'war on terror' have generated a new debate on the extent and ways in which Europe – in its various guises – should and can play a significant military role beyond Europe. In the first Gulf War in 1990–1, following the Iraqi invasion of Kuwait, the UK contributed 42,000 troops to the US-led coalition, and France 20,000, while quite a large group of European states (Czechoslovakia, Denmark, Greece, Hungary, Italy, the Netherlands, Norway, Poland, Portugal, Spain and Turkey) contributed small numbers of troops, mainly in non-combat roles. The USA, however, contributed the overwhelming majority of the forces, more than half a million military personnel, and the conflict symbolized – the UK and France aside – European reluctance and inability to deploy military forces outside Europe.

European states did, however, play a role in the humanitarian interventions and expansion of UN peacekeeping of the 1990s. The UK and
France contributed to the enforcement of a no-fly zone and the establishment of safe havens in Iraqi Kurdistan in 1991 following the end of
the Gulf War, and a number of other European states also contributed
ground forces. The Netherlands contributed an infantry battalion to
the UN peacekeeping operation in Cambodia 1992–3. Belgium,
France and Italy contributed infantry battalions to the US-led force
that intervened in Somalia in 1992–3. France, Germany, Ireland, Italy,
Norway, Portugal and the UK contributed forces to International
Force East Timor (INTERFET) operation in 1999–2000. In most
cases, however, European forces were deployed only as part of larger
missions, led by either the USA or the UN. France's intervention in
Rwanda in 1994 – Operation Turquoise, which involvement the
deployment of 2,500 French troops to establish protected areas – and
the UK's intervention in Sierra Leone in 2000 – Operation Palliser,
involving the deployment of 1,100 troops to support the Sierra Leone
government against rebels and help to stabilize the country – were
exceptions in which European states played the central role. After
9/11, European countries played a significant role in the US-led interventions in Afghanistan and Iraq. In 2006, European countries agreed
to provide the core of the expanded UN peacekeeping mission in
Lebanon following the Israeli–Lebanese war, with Italy contributing
3,000 troops, France 2,000, Spain 1,000 and a number of other states
smaller numbers (Pirozzi, 2006).

Developments since the early 1990s suggest a number of conclusions about European involvement in peacekeeping and intervention
operations beyond Europe. Although European contributions to such
operations have increased since the early 1990s, European military
involvement beyond Europe remains relatively limited in scale.
European states, further, have in general deployed forces either as part
of US-led operations in which the USA remains the dominant partner,
or as part of UN operations to which European states have been some
of a number of contributors (rather than the leading partners). The
extent to which European states will move beyond this and establish a
more distinctively European contribution to peacekeeping and intervention, and what the nature of that contribution should and will be,
probably depends on the evolution of NATO and the EU as frameworks for collective military intervention, to which this chapter turns
next.

NATO and the EU: global peacekeepers?

NATO

As discussed in Chapter 3, NATO has since the early 1990s been undergoing a transition from being a collective defence alliance based on the defence of its members' territory to becoming a security organization addressing security challenges beyond its members' borders. Peacekeeping and intervention have been central to NATO's post-Cold War transformation. In the 1990s, NATO took on the tasks of peacekeeping and peace-making in the Balkans. Since 9/11, it has take on these tasks beyond Europe – primarily in Afghanistan. NATO's peacekeeping and intervention activities to date are summarized in Table 6.2.

Afghanistan has become the central test of NATO's role as a peacekeeper. Despite the invocation of NATO's Article 5 security guarantee and European willingness to act through NATO, the USA, wary of the constraints of operating through a multilateral alliance, chose to create an ad hoc coalition when it intervened in Afghanistan at the end of 2001. The Bush Administration's reluctance to engage in nation-building resulted in the establishment of a separate UN Security Council-mandated peacekeeping mission, the International Security Assistance Force (ISAF), operating alongside the ongoing US counter-insurgency operation against the remnants of Al-Qaeda and the Taliban. European NATO members provided the majority of forces for the ISAF. In August 2003, NATO assumed command of the ISAF, which had up to that point been operating under an ad hoc command of its members. The first-stage ISAF had 5,000 troops and its mandate was limited to the Afghan capital Kabul and the surrounding region. With ongoing instability across much of Afghanistan, however, the NATO-led ISAF was gradually extended across the whole of the country, to the north and west in 2004–5 and to the more unstable south and east in 2006. The ISAF was also significantly expanded in size, with 32,800 troops under its command by November 2006 (the USA contributed 11,800 of these troops, the UK 6,000, Germany 2,700, Canada 2,500, the Netherlands 2,000, Italy 1,800, and other NATO members smaller numbers) (NATO, 2006d). The 11,800, US troops were brought under ISAF command in 2006, although another 8,000 US troops continued to operate under separate US command arrangements.

The NATO operation in Afghanistan faces a number of major challenges. NATO is, in effect, engaged in two parallel and to some extent contradictory missions in Afghanistan: a counter-insurgency war against Al-Qaeda and Taliban forces in the south and east of the country, and a peacekeeping/nation-building mission designed to provide security for the Afghan people, promote reconciliation between the country's different ethnic and political groups, and facilitate economic reconstruction. Critics argue that the successful stabilization of Afghanistan will require significantly more than the 32,000 troops NATO had deployed by 2006, perhaps a doubling or more of the force. Other critics argue that NATO has focused too much attention on the counter-insurgency element of its operation, to the detriment of the larger challenge of facilitating a long-term political settlement in Afghanistan. As of 2006, the ultimate success or failure of the NATO-led nation-building exercise in Afghanistan remained deeply uncertain. The successful medium-term stabilization of Afghanistan would set a potentially important precedent for similar NATO-led operations elsewhere. A prolonged and debilitating low-level war in Afghanistan or withdrawal in the face of failure will presumably make NATO's members more wary of engaging in such exercises again.

The discussion over NATO's role in Afghanistan reflects a larger debate over NATO's role as a global peacekeeper. The story of the NATO Response Force (NRF) illustrates this debate. In response to the 9/11 attacks, the Alliance agreed in 2002 to establish a new NATO Response Force (NRF) – a 20,000-strong, high-readiness, multinational, combined ground, air and naval force to be deployable within five days (NATO, 2002). The NRF, which became fully operational in November 2005, is based on the principle of 'first force in, first force out' and may be deployed as a stand-alone force or as an initial entry force for a larger operation. The USA, the initial architect of the NRF, viewed it as a force that might be used in counter-terrorist or counter-proliferation operations in line with the pre-emptive war doctrine discussed above. European NATO members were, however, wary of being tied too closely to US counter-terrorism, counter-proliferation and pre-emptive war policies, and emphasized the NRF's potential role in peacekeeping and nation-building. The agreed potential missions of the NRF were therefore defined in a rather open-ended way as: show of force and solidarity to deter aggression; evacuating non-combatants; supporting consequence management in the event of an attack or disaster; providing support in a humanitarian crisis; crisis management, including peacekeeping; counter-terrorism operations; and embargo operations (NATO, 2005).

NATO's role as a peacekeeper is likely to be constrained by a

TABLE 6.2 *NATO peacekeeping and crisis management operations*

Operation	Country/Region	Date	Mission/Role	Force size
Operation Maritime Monitor/Sharp Guard	Adriatic Sea	1992–6	Enforcement of economic sanctions and arms embargo against former Yugoslavia	Naval forces
Operation Deny Flight	Bosnia and Herzegovina	1993–5	Enforcement of no-fly zone and close air support for UN peacekeeping force	Air forces
Operation Deliberate Force	Bosnia and Herzegovina	August–September 1995	Airstrikes and artillery attacks against Bosnia Serb targets to coerce acceptance of a peace agreement	Air and ground forces
Implementation Force (IFOR)/Stabilisation Forces (SFOR)	Bosnia and Herzegovina	1995–2004	Support and enforce Dayton peace agreement	60,000 troops
Operation Allied Force	Kosovo/Serbia-Montenegro	March–June 1999	Airstrikes to halt Serbian attacks on Kosovar Albanians and coerce acceptance of deployment of a NATO ground force	Air and naval forces
Kosovo Force (KFOR)	Kosovo	1999–	Enforce ceasefire and withdrawal of Serbian military and police forces; support maintenance of peace	55,000 troops

Operation	Location	Date	Purpose	Forces
Operations Essential Harvest, Amber Fox and Allied Harmony	Macedonia	2001–3	Disarm Albanian guerrilla groups; protect and support international monitors	3,500 troops
Operation Eagle Assist	United States	October 2001–May 2002	Help protect US airspace post-9/11	Surveillance aircraft
Operation Active Endeavour	Mediterranean Sea	2001–	Monitor and escort vessels for counter-terrorism purposes	Naval forces
Operation Display Deterrence	Turkey	February–April 2003	Deter Iraqi attacks on Turkey	Surveillance aircraft and missile defences
International Security Assistance Force (ISAF)	Afghanistan	2003–	Assist Afghan government in exercising its authority; help create conditions for stabilization and reconstruction	30,000 troops
Distinguished Games	Greece	August–September 2004	Maritime and airspace surveillance during Olympics	Naval and air forces
Pakistan Earthquake Relief Operation	Pakistan	October 2005–February 2006	Deliver relief supplies	1,200 troops; air forces
NATO Assistance to the African Union (AU) in Darfur	Darfur, Sudan	2005–	Provide support to AU peacekeeping mission	Air forces (transport of AU troops)
NATO Training Mission in Iraq	Iraq	2005–	Train Iraqi armed forces and security personnel	Training inside and outside Iraq

Data from: NATO website: http://www.nato.int/.

number of political and military factors. The capacity of European NATO members to project military power beyond their borders remains limited and is growing only slowly. European states are also wary of turning NATO into a 'global policeman' and of being dragged into US-led interventions – such as the Iraq War – over which they may have little control. While the USA has a much greater capacity for military intervention, it is wary of the constraints of working through NATO's multilateral political and military structures, and is often sceptical of the value of European support.

The European Union

As discussed in Chapter 4, the development of a military role since the late 1990s has been a major strategic shift for the EU. Since 2003, the EU has given substance to its ambitions in this area by undertaking a number of peacekeeping and crisis management operations – see Table 6.3. A number of features of the EU's operations to date are notable. They have been relatively small-scale in size, the largest being the 7,000-strong peacekeeping operation in Bosnia. They have also focused largely on post-conflict peacekeeping, stabilization and nation-building, rather than on combat operations or intervention in situations of ongoing violence. Although the EU has undertaken three military missions (in Macedonia, the Democratic Republic of Congo (DRC) and Bosnia), the majority of EU crisis management missions have been civilian, in particular in the areas of policing, security sector reform and justice/rule of law – suggesting that the EU is developing a specialized role in this area. The transfer of the peacekeeping missions in Macedonia and Bosnia from NATO to the EU, and the possibility of a similar transfer of the larger mission in Kosovo in the next few years, suggests an important strategic shift, with the EU taking over as the primary peacekeeper on Europe's immediate periphery. The EU's operations in the DRC, Georgia, Iraq, Sudan and Aceh, however, suggest that it is also likely to play a global role, albeit on a limited scale.

In the military sphere, the EU faces a number of significant limitations. Although the Union's member states collectively possess large armed forces, their ability to deploy these forces overseas for peacekeeping or other intervention operations is generally quite limited. In most cases, only small percentages of European states' armed forces are capable of participating in peacekeeping or intervention operations. The EU and its members also lack the key capabilities necessary for rapid deployment, such as strategic air and sea lift. The development of

TABLE 6.3 *EU peacekeeping and crisis management operations*

Operation	Country	Date	Mission/Role	Force size
EU Police Mission (EUPM) in Bosnia-Herzegovina	Bosnia-Herzegovina	Jan 2003–Dec 2005	Support development of police	472 police; 57 civilians
Operation Concordia	Former Yugoslav Republic of Macedonia	Mar–Dec 2003	Provide security to support peace agreement	357 military
Operation Artemis	Democratic Republic of Congo	June–Sept 2003	Provide stability and security in an area experiencing ongoing fighting, prior to deployment of larger UN peacekeeping force	2,000 military
Operation Proxima	Former Yugoslav Republic of Macedonia	Dec 2003–Dec 2005	Support development of police	200 police
EU Rule of Law Mission to Georgia (EUJUST THEMIS)	Georgia	July 2004– July 2005	Support development and reform of criminal justice system	10 civilians, plus local staff
Operation EUFOR – Althea	Bosnia	Dec 2004–	Ensure compliance with peace agreement and support peace process	7,000 military
EU Police Mission in Kinshasa (DRC) – (EUPOL KINSHASA)	Democratic Republic of Congo	April 2005–	Support development of Congolese police	30 police/civilians

TABLE 6.3 *continued*

Operation	Country	Date	Mission/Role	Force size
EU Advisory and Assistance Mission for Security Reform in the DRC (EUSEC–DRC)	Democratic Republic of Congo	June 2005–June 2006	Advise and assist on security sector reform	8 civilian/police/military
EU Integrated Rule of Law Mission for Iraq (EUJUST LEX)	Iraq	July 2005–July 2006	Training of judiciary, police and penitentiary staff	Training takes place in the EU and in the region; EU liaison office in Baghdad
AMIS EU Supporting Action	Sudan (Darfur)	July 2005–	Advice, assistance, equipment, training and transport for AU Mission in Sudan	Small numbers of advisers and observers
Aceh Monitoring Mission (AMM) – EU jointly with Norway, Switzerland and Association of South East Asian Nation (ASEAN) states (Brunei, Malaysia, Philippines, Singapore and Thailand)	Indonesia (Aceh)	September 2005–	Monitor and support implementation of peace agreement	226 civilians (130 from EU, Norway, Switzerland, 96 from ASEAN states)

Mission	Location	Dates	Purpose	Personnel
EU Border Assistance Mission (BAM) Rafah	Palestinian Territories (Gaza–Rafah border crossing point)	November 2005–November 2006	Monitor border crossing point and support development of Palestinian border control capacity	70 civilian personnel
EU Border Assistance Mission to Moldova and Ukraine	Moldova and Ukraine	Dec 2005–	Support development of Moldovan and Ukrainian border control capacity	69 civilian experts
EU Police Advisory Team (EUPAT)	Macedonia	Dec 2005–June 2006	Support development of Macedonian police	30 police advisers
EU Police Mission in Palestinian Territories (EUPOL COPPS)	Palestinian Territories	June 2006–	Support development of Palestinian police	33 civilian personnel
Operation EUFOR RD Congo	Democratic Republic of Congo (plus Gabon)	July–November 2006	Support UN peacekeeping force during elections	2,000 military (including 'over the horizon' forces in Gabon)

Data from: Gustav Lindstrom, 'On the Ground: ESDP Operations', in Nicole Gnesotto (ed.), *EU Security and Defence Policy: The First Five Years (1999–2004)* (Paris: European Union Institute for Security Studies, 2004), pp.111–29; *European Security and Defence Policy: EU Operations*, EU website: http://ue.eu.int/cms3_applications/solana/index.asp?lang=EN&cmsid=246.

the EU's defence role since the late 1990s has been designed to address these shortcomings. Initial plans centred around the development of a 50,000–60,000-strong reaction force. In 2004, the EU adopted a further goal of developing battle groups of around 1,500 troops to be deployable within fifteen days, with 2–3 battlegroups to be established by 2005 and 7–9 battlegroups by 2007. The EU also agreed in 2004 to develop strategic lift co-ordination, a European airlift command, and the availability of an aircraft carrier by 2008, as well as a European Defence Agency (EDA) to facilitate armaments and procurement cooperation (European Union, 2004). The development of the EU's defence role is, however, ultimately dependent on the Union's member states, and while they are enhancing their armed forces' ability to contribute to peacekeeping and intervention operations this is proving to be a slow process. While the EU increasingly provides part of the context for the reform of member states' armed forces, the experience since the late 1990s suggests that the EU's common European security and defence policy will have at best a limited impact in accelerating the ongoing process of restructuring armed forces for deployment in peacekeeping and intervention operations (Forster, 2006, pp. 139–45, 210–14).

Conclusion

This chapter has explored European responses to the new wars and the new interventionism. In terms of patterns of intervention, a number of trends can be identified. Within Europe, two distinct geostrategic spheres emerged in the 1990s, with very different patterns of intervention. The Balkans was the subject of major military interventions by the leading Western powers and institutions, and in effect became a Western sphere of influence. The failure of European and UN efforts to end the Yugoslav wars in the early 1990s, further, led the USA and NATO to assume the central role in peacemaking in the region. Since the end of the Yugoslav wars, however, responsibility for post-conflict peacebuilding is gradually being transferred to the EU. Assuming that violence does not break out again, this trend is likely to continue. Renewed violence in the region would, however, raise once again the questions of whether Europe, in particular the EU, can halt such bloodshed, and, if not, whether the USA remains willing, or would be forced, to step into the breach. In the former Soviet space, Russia intervened in a number of conflicts in the 1990s as part of its larger strategy of maintaining a dominant role in the region, while other states and international institutions were reluctant to intervene on a significant scale or to challenge Russia. Serious violence or instability in one or more of the former Soviet states would raise renewed questions about how Russia and the wider international community should and would respond, and the extent to which the region will remain a Russian sphere of influence.

Beyond Europe, European states have contributed to a widening range of military operations, but these have usually been as part of either US-led interventions or UN peacekeeping operations. While there have been a number of essentially unilateral national interventions – France in Rwanda in 1994, and the UK in Sierra Leone in 2000 – these have been the exception rather than the norm. The expanding roles of NATO and the EU also suggest that collective Euro-atlantic and European approaches to intervention beyond Europe are beginning to emerge. The limited scale and nature of NATO and EU engagement beyond Europe to date, however, indicate that this is likely to be a slow process.

The debates on intervention since the early 1990s also highlight significant differences between European and US approaches to intervention. First, European states place a strong emphasis on multilateralism and legitimization by international law and/or international organization, as reflected in the fact that virtually all the interventions in which European states have participated since the early 1990s have been authorized and/or undertaken by institutions such as the UN, NATO and/or the EU. Second, European military doctrine and culture diverges from that of America, with the USA placing a strong emphasis on high-end war-fighting operations and European states placing a greater emphasis on mid-range peacekeeping and/or peace enforcement. Third, Europeans have placed a greater emphasis on state-building, post-conflict peacebuilding and non-military aspects of intervention. To the extent that Europe does have a distinctive role to play in international intervention it is likely to be in contributing to tasks such as state-building and post-conflict peacebuilding, rather than in more traditional forms of military intervention.

The European contribution to international intervention will also be constrained by the realities of military capacity. Lord George Robertson, NATO Secretary-General from 1999 to 2004 and British defence secretary before that, repeatedly highlighted the point that the European NATO members had over 1 million regular soldiers and 1 million reserves, yet struggled to deploy 50,000 troops on peacekeeping and intervention operations (Robertson, 2003). O'Hanlon and Singer (2004, p. 84) estimate that whereas the USA has approximately 400,000 troops that could be deployed beyond its borders within 1–3 months and sustained for a year, the rest of NATO's members can muster only 84,000 such troops. Both nationally and collectively within NATO and the EU, European states have been expanding their capacity to contribute to peacekeeping and intervention operations since the early 1990s, but this process is proceeding only slowly. It may also be argued that a more general decline in bellicosity in Europe since the Second World War has made European governments and publics reluctant to invest heavily in defence or intervene militarily elsewhere in the world. Critics, especially in the USA, argue that this has made Europe increasingly incapable of dealing with the new security threats of the post-Cold War and post-9/11 era. To the extent that European bellicosity has declined, however, this may have contributed in an important way to the emergence of the European and wider Western security community discussed in Chapter 1. Given the costs and risks of any large-scale military intervention, further, a cautious attitude to military intervention may be no bad thing – a lesson the USA has arguably learned at high cost in Iraq.

Chapter 7

Proliferation

Since the early 1990s, the threat posed by the proliferation of weapons of mass destruction (WMD) has moved to the centre of the global security agenda. As discussed in Chapter 2, the increasing prominence of proliferation reflects two factors. First, the end of the Cold War dramatically reduced the risk of nuclear war between the USA and Russia, effectively bringing the first part of the nuclear age to an end. Second, India and Pakistan's 1998 nuclear weapons tests, the 2003 Iraq War and the controversy surrounding Iraq's WMD programmes, North Korea's 2006 nuclear test, Iran's ongoing efforts to develop nuclear weapons, and fears, following 9/11, that terrorist groups might obtain WMD, suggested that the world was on the verge of a major new wave of proliferation. This might in particular expand the number of nuclear weapon states significantly, and place nuclear or other WMD in the hands of terrorists.

From the 1960s through to the early 1990s, an international non-proliferation regime was put in place, based around a series of a series of multilateral arms agreements – in particular, the Nuclear Non-Proliferation Treaty (NPT), the Biological and Toxin Weapons Convention (BTWC) and the Chemical Weapons Convention (CWC) – and controls on the export of WMD-related technologies. The emerging wave of proliferation since the 1990s has, however, highlighted the limitations of existing non-proliferation arrangements. Beginning in the 1990s but accelerating under the Bush Administration after 9/11, there has also been a revolution in US non-proliferation policy, shifting it away from the traditional instruments of arms control, export controls and diplomacy and towards political, economic and military coercion (Andreani, 1999–2000; Perkovich, 2003). The USA become increasingly sceptical towards multilateral arms control: the US Senate rejected the Comprehensive Test Ban Treaty (CTBT) in 1999 and the Bush Administration effectively torpedoed a verification protocol for the BTWC and brought the 2005 NPT Review Conference to the point of collapse. The US adoption of the pre-emptive war doctrine in 2002, the 2003 Iraq War and discussion of the possible use of force against

Iran and North Korea signalled a radical new approach to non-proliferation based on coercive diplomacy and the use of force. The extent to which this revolution in US non-proliferation will survive the aftermath of the 2003 US intervention in Iraq remains to be seen.

Europe has thus faced the challenge of responding not only to the problem of proliferation itself but also to a radical and controversial new US non-proliferation policy. This chapter examines European responses to the WMD proliferation threat and the revolution in US non-proliferation policy. As this chapter will show, European governments, while concerned by the proliferation threat, do not view it with the same sense of urgency as does the USA, and remain strongly committed to traditional, multilateral non-proliferation policies and wary of the more coercive approaches advocated by the USA. Nevertheless, in the wake of the 2003 Iraq War, the EU in particular has sought to develop a more proactive role in non-proliferation, adopting a formal *EU Strategy Against Proliferation of Weapons of Mass Destruction* at the end of 2003 and taking the lead, via the Union's three largest members – the UK, France and Germany – in international diplomatic efforts to persuade Iran not to develop nuclear weapons. The difficulties the EU has faced in using its 'soft power' to influence Iran, and the possibility, perhaps even likelihood, that Iran will go on to develop nuclear weapons, however, indicate the serious challenges facing a European non-proliferation policy.

Assessing the proliferation threat: European perspectives

European governments generally accept that WMD proliferation is a major security problem. The EU's 2003 *European Security Strategy* argues that proliferation 'is potentially the greatest threat to our security' (European Union, 2003a). Beyond this, however, the nature, extent and implications of the threat of proliferation are more controversial. Assessing the threat posed by WMD proliferation is deeply problematical because it depends on intelligence information (which may be unreliable, partial or politically biased) but also because it depends on strategic assessments of the consequences of proliferation, which are inevitably political. Bearing in mind these caveats, Table 7.1 summarizes the state of play in terms of WMD proliferation beyond the five established nuclear weapons states (the USA, Russia, China, the UK and France) as of early 2007, indicating states that are believed

TABLE 7.1   *WMD proliferation: the state of play, 2007*

State	Nuclear weapons	Biological weapons	Chemical weapons	Missiles (current)	Missiles (development)
Egypt	–	RP	W	SR	–
India	W	–	D	MR (<2,000)	LR (12,000)
Iran	RP	RP	W	MR	IR
Israel	W	W	W	MR (<1,800)	–
Libya	–	–	D	SR	–
Pakistan	W	–	–	MR (<2,500)	IR (3,000)
North Korea	W?	W	W	MR (<2,500)	LR (>5,500)
Syria	–	RP	W	SR	–

Notes:
Weapons: W = known or suspected weapons or weaponizable agents; RP = known or suspected research programme; D = declared chemical weapons or weapons programme scheduled for destruction in accordance with the terms of the Chemical Weapons Convention.
Missiles: SR = short-range (<1,000km); MR = medium-range (1,000–3,000km); IR = intermediate-range missiles (3,000–5,500km); LR = long-range missiles (>5,500km).
Data from: J. Cirincione, Jon B.Wolfsthal and M. Rajkumar, *Deadly Arsenals: Tracking Weapons of Mass Destruction* (Washington, DC: Carnegie Endowment for International Peace, 2002); J. Cirincione, Jon B.Wolfsthal and M. Rajkumar, *Deadly Arsenals: Nuclear, Biological, and Chemical Threats* (Washington, DC: Carnegie Endowment for International Peace, 2005); International Institute for Strategic Studies, *The Military Balance 2005/2006* (London: Routledge for The International Institute for Strategic Studies, 2005); United States Department of Defense (2001), *Proliferation: Threat and Response*: http://www.defenselink.mil/pubs/ptr20010110.pdf; Michael D. Swaine and Lauren H. Runyon, 'Ballistic Missiles and Missile Defense in Asia', *NBR Analysis*, vol. 13, no. 3 (Seattle, Wash.: National Bureau of Asian Research, 2002): http://www.carnegieendowment.org/files/swainenbr.pdf.

to have nuclear, chemical and/or biological weapons or research programmes, as well as details of the missile systems these states are believed to possess or have under development. Beyond the states listed in Table 7.1, which have been the primary focus of proliferation, there is a larger group of states that do not have WMD programmes as such but have the technological and industrial capacity to develop such weapons – in particular, nuclear weapons – within a relatively short time-frame (a few years, perhaps even months in some cases) if they chose to do so. These include industrialized Western states such as

Germany, Japan and Sweden, but also states such as Saudi Arabia, South Korea, Taiwan, Brazil, Argentina and South Africa (the latter three having had nuclear weapons programmes in the past but abandoned these in the 1980s or 1990s).

From a broad European perspective, the current proliferation landscape poses a number of threats (Krause, 1996; Muller, 2003):

- *Direct attack*: in the worst case, European states might be the subject of WMD attack by states outside Europe. In the short-to-medium term, the only states that might develop WMD and missiles capable of attacking much of Europe are in the Middle East, in particular Iran. Even if Iran and/or other Middle Eastern states develop WMD and missiles capable of reaching much of Europe, the costs of undertaking such attacks (including the possibility of conventional or nuclear retaliation by the USA, the UK or France) probably make such attacks unlikely. Nevertheless, a radical regime – for example, if an Islamic revolution brought to power Al-Qaeda style forces in Saudi Arabia – might be willing to threaten to use, or even in fact use, nuclear weapons against European states in a bid to persuade them to withdraw military forces from the Middle East or cease support for Israel. While a direct WMD attack on Europe (or the threat of such an attack) is probably unlikely in the short-to-medium term, and perhaps also in the longer term, if proliferation widens in the Middle East such a scenario cannot be entirely ruled out.
- *Threats to European armed forces on 'out-of-area' missions*: in a second set of scenarios, European armed forces deployed outside Europe might be the subject of WMD attacks by either states or terrorists, or be threatened with such attacks, in order to deter military action. After the 1990–1 Gulf War many observers concluded that the lesson was 'don't take on the USA unless you have nuclear weapons', a lesson reinforced by the 2003 Iraq War and which probably lies behind North Korea and Iran's pursuit of nuclear weapons. The development of nuclear weapons by Iran and/or North Korea would thus have a potentially very significant impact in terms of deterring US/Western military action against these countries. Indeed, North Korea's ability to threaten massive conventional and possibly nuclear retaliation against South Korea and US forces based there may already preclude US military action against Pyongyang. The use or threatened use of WMD against European forces deployed outside Europe is probably one of the more likely threats if proliferation proceeds.

- *Chemical and biological weapons*: as was noted in Chapter 2, although the term 'weapons of mass destruction' is now widely used, there are important differences between nuclear, chemical and biological weapons (Perkovich, 2004). The destructive power of nuclear weapons gives them unparalleled capacity to destroy large population centres or concentrations of military forces and to kill many thousands (or even millions) of people, making them by far the most serious proliferation concern. Chemical and biological agents, in contrast, are difficult to disperse over large areas, and are more likely to be used for limited battlefield purposes or smaller-scale terrorist attacks.

- *Eroding the WMD taboo*: since the use of nuclear weapons by the USA against Japan in 1945, a powerful taboo against the use of WMD, and in particular nuclear weapons, has emerged, but proliferation increases the long-term risk of the use of such weapons. The 'successful' use of WMD by one or more states – in the sense of allowing that state to achieve its strategic objectives or end a conflict on better terms than might otherwise have been the case – might create significant incentives for other states to acquire WMD and consider their use. Even if European states were not affected directly in first place, erosion of the WMD taboo, and in particular of the international proscription of the use of nuclear weapons, would create a significantly more dangerous international security environment in general, and increase the risk of European states becoming the subject of WMD attack at some point in the future.

- *WMD terrorism*: the 9/11 terrorist attacks have generated significant debate about the prospect of terrorist groups obtaining and using WMD. As will be discussed in Chapter 8, Europe has since 9/11 become one of the main 'fields of *jihad*' for Islamic terrorists, suggesting that, were terrorists to obtain WMD, Europe might be one of their most likely targets. The likelihood and extent of the threat posed by WMD terrorism is, however, controversial. Some, especially in the USA, argue that WMD terrorism, in particular nuclear or biological terrorism, is a very real possibility and would give terrorists the potential to kill, or threaten to kill, millions of people. Senator Richard Lugar, chair of the US Senate Foreign Relations Committee, has argued that 'for the foreseeable future, the United States and other nations will face an existential threat from the intersection of terrorism and weapons of mass destruction' (Lugar, 2005, p. 3). Others argue that there are very serious technical obstacles to true mass casualty terrorism, and that the most likely forms of WMD terrorism are small-scale chemical, biological or radiological attacks such as the 1995 Aum Shinrikyo nerve gas attack on the Tokyo underground and the distribution of anthrax spores in the USA after 9/11 (Frost, 2005; Ruppe, 2005).

Assessments of the threat posed by proliferation also depend to a significant degree on political and strategic context. As the world's only superpower, deeply engaged in all regions of the world, and in particular in the regions of most immediate proliferation concern – the Middle East and North East Asia – the USA is the most likely target of WMD attack and would have its policy options most constrained by the further proliferation of WMD. In contrast, despite the fact that Europe is closer to the Middle East and thus more exposed to direct WMD attack from that region, Europeans do not in general view the proliferation threat to be as immediate or dramatic as the USA does. Leading German non-proliferation expert, Harald Muller, for example, argues that, while proliferation is a 'distinct danger' that is 'increasing incrementally', it 'does not yet pose an immediate threat to the European Union'. (Muller, 2003, p. 97) Similarly, Schmitt, noting that the number of states actively pursuing WMD is limited (essentially to Iran and North Korea in the case of nuclear weapons), concludes that there are 'good reasons to believe that the threat of WMD proliferation is manageable' (Schmitt, 2003, p. 90). Andreani concludes that there is 'considerable asymmetry in the way the issue is characterized on both sides of the Atlantic', reflecting the fact the 'Europe is geographically more exposed than the USA, but strategically considerably less so' (Andreani, 1999–2000, pp. 56–7). The debate surrounding how to respond to Iran's efforts to develop nuclear weapons illustrates these differences: whereas many in the USA view the prospect of a nuclear-armed Iran as serious enough to warrant the use force (Allison, 2006), much European opinion does not view a nuclear-armed Iran as a fundamental threat and argues that the costs of using force against Iran outweigh the risks of its developing nuclear weapons (Grgic, 2004; Woollacott, 2005).

From a European perspective, in the short-to-medium term the proliferation threat may be more limited than the sometimes lurid public debate suggests, essentially to the development of nuclear weapons by North Korea and Iran, and the risk of small-scale chemical or biological weapons attacks by terrorists. Two major caveats should, however, be attached to this assessment. First, although the likelihood of true mass casualty terrorism – involving nuclear or biological weapons – is difficult to assess, the possibility of such attacks should not be excluded and it is a threat of a fundamentally different magnitude from that of more limited, small-scale WMD terrorism. Second, while the Iranian and/or North Korean development of nuclear weapons may in itself mean only a limited threat, if it triggers further proliferation in the Middle East and Asia, a more general breakdown of the non-proliferation regime and, in the worst case, the use of nuclear weapons by one or more states, it will pose a major long-term threat to European and global security.

Arms control

Multilateral arms control has been at the heart of the traditional approach to non-proliferation developed since the Second World War. In general, this has involved two types of arms control regimes: global arms control regimes prohibiting or limiting the possession of entire classes of weapons (the NPT, the BTWC and the CWC); and multilateral export/technology control regimes under which suppliers of the relevant weapons systems and technologies agree common rules constraining the supply of weapons and technologies to other states (the Nuclear Suppliers Group – NSG; the Zangger Committee, which like the NSG seeks to control the export of nuclear materials and technologies; and the Missile Technology Control Regime – MTCR). In general, European states have been strong supporters of these regimes. The EU's December 2003 *European Strategy Against Proliferation of Weapons of Mass Destruction* affirms the 'conviction that a multilateralist approach to security, including disarmament and non-proliferation, provides the best way to maintain international order and hence our commitment to uphold, implement and strengthen the multilateral disarmament and non-proliferation treaties and agreements' (European Union, 2003b). Virtually all European states (EU members, the Balkan states, and Russia and the other former Soviet states) are members of the main multilateral non-proliferation agreements (the only real exceptions are the technology control regimes of which some Balkan and former Soviet states are not members, largely because they are not potential suppliers of the technologies concerned). France and Spain were not signatories initially of the NPT, criticizing the discriminatory basis of the treaty, but Spain later joined, in 1987, and France in 1992.

Since the early 1990s, European states have supported, and to varying degrees led, international efforts to strengthen the various multilateral arms control and non-proliferation agreements. The NPT, having entered into force in 1970, reached the point of a twenty-five-year special review conference in 1995, at which the treaty was extended indefinitely. At the 2000 NPT review conference (the NPT is also subject to regular five-yearly review conferences) signatories endorsed a thirteen-point programme for nuclear arms control and disarmament. During the 1990s, the International Atomic Energy Agency – IAEA, the body charged with verifying states compliance with the NPT – established a strengthened system of 'safeguards' for monitoring states' nuclear facilities and activities. The CWC was signed in 1993 and came into force in 1997. The CTBT was signed in 1996, but at the time of writing has not yet come into force (because not all relevant states have ratified the treaty). European states have also supported negotiations to agree a Fissile-Material Cut-off Treaty (FMCT), which would ban the further production of the fissile material required for nuclear weapons, and a verification protocol for the BTWC, but both sets of negotiations have been stalled since the late 1990s. The negotiations related to these various agreements have been one of the main areas in which the EU has, beginning in the 1980s but especially since the 1990s, sought to develop common policies and assert a collective influence.

European states and institutions, however, face significant obstacles in advancing the multilateral arms control approach to proliferation. The verification mechanisms associated with these arms control regimes are imperfect (as illustrated by Iran's, Iraq's, Libya's and North Korea's progress towards developing nuclear weapons in the 1980s and 1990s despite being signatories of the NPT and subject to IAEA inspections) and strengthening these verification mechanisms has proved difficult. The NPT, BTWC and CWC contain no sanctions or enforcement measures for dealing with states that might violate their commitments not to develop nuclear, biological or chemical weapons under these treaties; and the NPT permits states to withdraw from the treaty (which North Korea did in 2003 and Iran may do in future) and then lawfully develop nuclear weapons. The network of international technology and materials control regimes contains significant holes in terms of the range of technologies and materials covered, and the states that are not members or do not fully enforce its provisions: China has in the past helped Pakistan and North Korea to develop nuclear weapons or missiles; Russia has supplied Iran with civilian nuclear technology; and North Korea and Pakistan have been involved in helping other states to develop nuclear weapons and/or missiles.

Even more fundamentally, there is an undeniable double standard at the heart of the existing non-proliferation regime: while the NPT commits the majority of the world's states not to develop nuclear weapons, it formally recognizes the status of the five established nuclear weapon states. Although the NPT commits the nuclear weapons states to 'to pursue negotiations in good faith on effective measures relating to cessation of the nuclear arms race at an early date and to nuclear disarmament', relatively little progress has been made in this direction since the NPT came into force in 1970. This double standard has led India, Pakistan and Israel to reject the NPT, made many states reluctant to agree tough action against states that attempt to develop nuclear weapons, such as Iran, Iraq and North Korea, and more generally undermined efforts to establish a truly universal non-proliferation regime. Since the UK, France and Russia are three of the five established nuclear weapons states, this double standard has a significant European dimension: although the UK, France and Russia have reduced their nuclear arsenals since the 1990s, none appears likely to abandon their status as a nuclear weapon state. The UK's and France's status as nuclear weapon states also significantly constrain the EU's approach to non-proliferation: while the majority of EU members would support substantial further measures towards nuclear disarmament, the UK and France have been wary of such steps and the EU's position within the NPT negotiations has often been a lowest common denominator dictated by the UK and France. European efforts to support multilateral arms control have also been under-mined by the increasing opposition of the USA to such approaches: while European states, and especially the EU, have supported the CTBT, a verification protocol for the BTWC and the thirteen-point arms control and disarmament programme agreed at the 2000 NPT Review Conference, US opposition has stymied progress in all these areas.

Camille Grand argues that, with the USA increasingly antipathetic to arms control, China committed to modernizing its nuclear arsenal, and Russia determined to maintain the vestiges of its nuclear super-power status, other 'countries, including the Europeans in the first instance, are becoming the main and practically sole defenders of the logic of non-proliferation', and that the EU should play a central role in promoting a multilateral, arms-control-based approach to proliferation (Grand, 2000, pp. 3–5). While the EU has taken significant steps in this direction since the early 1990s, the inherent problems of arms control, the UK and France's status as nuclear weapon states and US opposition are likely to impose significant constraints on the EU's ability to assert leadership in this area.

'Loose nukes' and co-operative threat reduction

The break-up of the Soviet Union at the end of 1991 pushed a new issue to the forefront of the nuclear agenda: the disintegration of a nuclear-armed superpower and the possible loss of control over its WMD arsenal. The Soviet Union was estimated to have over 27,000 nuclear warheads, as well as an extensive chemical and biological weapons programmes and the defence/industrial/scientific infrastructure necessary to support its superpower WMD arsenal (Miller, 1992). In the worst case, the Soviet successor states might lose control over nuclear, biological or chemical weapons, materials, technologies or expertise, and these might become available to other states or terrorist groups – generating fears of so-called 'loose nukes'. In response to this danger, the USA launched the Cooperative Threat Reduction (CTR) programme (also known as the Nunn–Lugar programme, after Senators Sam Nunn and Richard Lugar, its original architects), a major effort to help Russia and the other former Soviet republics reduce and secure control of the previous superpower's WMD arsenal. Between 1992 and 2002, the USA spent nearly US$5billion on CTR activities with Russia and the other former Soviet states; in the 2000s it plans to spend approximately US$1billion annually on CTR (White House, 2002). As of April 2006, US CTR support had contributed to the deactivation of 6,828 nuclear warheads, the destruction of 612 intercontinental ballistic missiles (ICBMs), the elimination of 485 ICBM silos, the destruction of 55 mobile ICBM launchers, the elimination of 155 bombers, the destruction of 885 nuclear air-to-surface missiles (ASMs), the elimination of 436 submarine launched ballistic missile (SLBM) launchers, the elimination of 577 SLBMs, the destruction of 29 ballistic missile submarines, and the sealing of 194 nuclear test tunnels/holes (Defense Threat Reduction Agency, 2006).

Despite Europe's closer proximity to the former Soviet Union, and thus in some ways greater vulnerability to the consequences of WMD diffusion, the USA took the leading role in developing CTR with Russia and the other former Soviet republics during the 1990s. Although various Western European states contributed to specific projects, the overwhelming majority of CTR-type assistance was provided by the USA. Compared to the US$5billion spent by the USA between 1992 and 2002, the EU (that is, EU member states plus the European Commission and EU-funded programmes) spent an estimated €369mn (less than a tenth of the USA's expenditure) (Anthony, 2004, p. 8). Post-9/11, however, there was increased recognition of the continuing dangers posed by WMD-related materials and infrastructure in the former Soviet Union, and growing demands for Western European (and other) states to support CTR efforts. In 2002 the G8 – the Group of Seven industrialized democracies (the UK, Canada, France, Germany, Italy, Japan and the USA), plus Russia – established a Global Partnership Against the Spread of Weapons and Materials of Mass Destruction to 'prevent terrorists, or those who harbour them, from acquiring or developing nuclear, chemical, radiological and biological weapons; missiles; and related materials, equipment and technology' (G8, 2002). In what was dubbed the '10 plus 10 over 10' initiative, the G8 states committed to provide US$20 billion (US$10billion from the USA and US$10billion from the other G8 states) between 2002 and 2012 to support projects under the new Global Partnership. In addition to the European members of the G8, other European states have also made commitments to contribute to the G8 Global Partnership. The G8 Global Partnership involves a major expansion of European involvement in CTR-type activities with Russia and the other former Soviet republics. Fulfilling their G8 pledges for the period 2002–12 will require EU members to increase their funding of CTR-type activities sevenfold compared with the previous decade (Anthony, 2004, p. 7). While European states and the European Commission have provided significant funds within the context of the Global Partnership since 2002, meeting their commitments will require further increases in expenditure.

It is perhaps surprising that European states, and especially the EU, have not played a larger part, and indeed a leadership role, in CTR. European preferences for multilateralism, co-operative engagement and the use of 'soft power' would appear to be particularly well-suited to the area of CTR. The EU's 2003 *European Strategy Against Proliferation of Weapons of Mass Destruction* commits it to 'reinforcing cooperative threat reduction programmes with other countries, targeted at support for disarmament, control and security of sensitive materials, facilities and expertise' (European Union, 2003). There is also emerging discussion of how far the CTR agenda can be extended to other countries beyond the former Soviet Union. Again, however, the USA has played the leading role to date: in 2004, the

USA announced a Global Threat Reduction Initiative (GTRI) aimed at helping to secure, relocate or dispose of nuclear materials globally, and dilute nuclear-weapon-usable, high-enriched uranium to less dangerous low-enriched uranium. While the EU and its member states have increased their contribution to CTR significantly within the context of the G8 Global Partnership, there would nevertheless appear to be significant room for increased European contributions to and leadership of the CTR agenda, both in the former Soviet Union and beyond.

Dealing with tough cases: diplomacy, sanctions and the use of force

Since the early 1990s there has been ongoing debate over how best to respond to proliferation's 'tough cases': the small number of states, such as Iraq, Iran and North Korea, who appear determined to develop WMD, and in particular nuclear weapons. This debate is, in significant part, about the appropriate balance between engagement and coercion (carrots and sticks): to what extent is it possible to engage with states that are seeking to develop WMD and offer them positive incentives not to do so? To what extent is coercion – diplomatic and economic pressure and sanctions, but ultimately military force – a necessary and effective means of preventing states from developing WMD? Since the early 1990s, various combinations of engagement and coercion have been tried, with varying degrees of success and failure. Up to 2003, an essentially coercive approach was imposed on Iraq, combining UN Security Council mandated disarmament, diplomatic isolation, economic sanctions and periodic airstrikes by the USA and the UK. In the context of the US decision to intervene in Iraq in 2003 and subsequent developments (in particular the discovery that Iraq's WMD programmes were much less developed than had been widely believed), the extent to which international strategy towards Iraq up to 2003 had succeeded or failed remains deeply controversial. In the North Korean case, the Clinton Administration negotiated a 1994 agreement under which Pyongyang was to halt its nuclear weapons programme in return for the supply of fuel oil and proliferation-resistant light-water nuclear reactors. The Bush Administration was unsympathetic to this approach and the 1994 agreement collapsed in 2002–3, North Korea withdrew from the NPT in 2003 and tested its first nuclear weapon in 2006. In the Iranian case, the USA has largely sought to isolate Tehran, whereas European states and the EU have sought to engage with Iran (see below). In a different example, an Anglo-American strategy of engagement – offering the normalization of diplomatic and economic relations – was probably central to Libya's 2003 decision to abandon its WMD programmes (although the stick of economic pressure also played its part alongside the carrot of engagement).

The main coercive options are threefold: diplomatic pressure, economic sanctions, and the use of force. Diplomatic measures (condemnations, demarches or the severing of diplomatic relations) may put political pressure on states, but are unlikely in themselves to persuade them to abandon WMD programmes. Economic sanctions bring significant pressure to bear on states, but are usually only effective in the long-term (if at all), are dependent on widespread international support (which often cannot be guaranteed) and may cause significant humanitarian suffering (as in the Iraqi case). The limits of diplomacy and economic sanctions inevitably lead to the discussion of the use of military force as an alternative means of preventing states from developing WMD. The most widely cited precedent is Israel's 1981 airstrike on Iraq's Osirak nuclear reactor, which succeeded in setting back Iraq's nuclear weapons programme by some years. As discussed in Chapter 6, in 2002 the Bush Administration made the pre-emptive use of force to prevent WMD proliferation a central part of US national security strategy, and this logic provided the basis for the US intervention in Iraq in 2003. The pre-emptive use of military force to prevent WMD proliferation is, of course, highly controversial, and the instability in Iraq since 2003 has reinforced the argument that the negative consequences of pre-emptive military action outweigh whatever good may be achieved in terms of ending or setting back states' WMD ambitions. Nevertheless, the inherent limitations of diplomacy and economic sanctions suggest that the pre-emptive use of force is likely to remain on the non-proliferation agenda, especially for the USA.

In responding to proliferation's tough cases, European states have in general preferred to use diplomacy and the incentive of engagement rather than the more coercive strategies of economic sanctions and military force. It would be misleading, however, to translate this preference into Europe-wide opposition to the use of coercive approaches to non-proliferation. European states generally supported the economic sanctions employed against Iraq in the 1990s. While France, Germany and Russia led international opposition to the 2003 Iraq

War, the UK, Spain, Italy and many other European countries supported the USA, including by deploying military forces. Many European states have also joined the US Proliferation Security Initiative (PSI), a loose framework established in 2003 to support the interdiction of WMD or related materials and technologies in transit. As was noted in Chapter 6, the drafting of the EU's *European Security Strategy* in 2003 prompted debate on the pre-emptive use of force, and the open-ended final document reflected the lack of consensus on the issue within the Union. Similarly, the EU's 2003 *European Strategy Against Proliferation of Weapons of Mass Destruction* says little about the possible use of economic sanctions and nothing about the use of force (European Union, 2003b). The pattern since the early 1990s suggests that there are likely to remain significant European divisions over coercive approaches to non-proliferation, and especially the use of force.

European wariness of coercive non-proliferation strategies raised the question of how far Europe, above all the EU, can fashion a credible alternative. In the wake of US intervention in Iraq in 2003, Iran became the central test case of the EU's ability to use its 'soft power' to develop an alternative approach to non-proliferation (Charlemagne, 2006) – see Box 7.1.

An additional important European dimension to the international non-proliferation debate is the position of Russia – a nuclear weapon state, a permanent member of the UN Security Council, a member of the IAEA Board of Governors, a major supplier of nuclear technology, and a country with political and economic ties with Iran and North Korea. While Russia would prefer to avoid nuclear proliferation in the Middle East and North East Asia, it also has other interests in these regions, in particular limiting the expansion of US influence. Since the early 1990s, while Russia has supported diplomatic efforts to dissuade Iran and North Korea from developing nuclear weapons, it has resisted US-led pressure to take a tough line against these states in the IAEA or the UN Security Council. Russia would probably oppose US military action against Iran or North Korea, and use its permanent seat on the Security Council to veto any resolution authorizing such action. Some observers have argued that Russia also has an interest in maintaining the Iranian and North Korean nuclear situations as ongoing crises, since this gives it influence and bargaining counters *vis-à-vis* the USA and the EU. Given these dynamics, Russia is likely to remain a significant actor in dealing with proliferation's tough cases, and to constrain the ability of the USA and the EU to pursue a tougher line towards Iran and North Korea.

Box 7.1   The EU, Iran and nuclear proliferation

Since 2003, the EU has sought to play a leading role in international efforts to prevent Iran from developing nuclear weapons. In October 2003, the foreign ministers of the UK, France and Germany – the EU-3 as they came to be called – negotiated an agreement with Iran under which Tehran agreed to halt its uranium enrichment programme (enriched uranium being the key material necessary for the development of nuclear weapons) in return for European assistance with its civilian nuclear programme and the possibility of improved political and economic ties. In 2004, however, the agreement with the EU began to break down as Iran moved to restart its enrichment activities. In November 2004, Iran announced a further suspension of its enrichment programme, and negotiations continued into 2005. In 2005, however, Iran resumed its enrichment activities once more. In the spring of 2006, negotiations between Iran and the EU-3 broke down again, Iran announced that it had produced enriched uranium, and President Mahmoud Ahmadinejad declared that Iran had joined 'the nuclear club of countries'. Throughout 2006, the EU-3 continued to negotiate with Iran, but Tehran refused to suspend its uranium enrichment.

The repeated breakdown of the EU's negotiations with Iran was a major setback for the Union's efforts to use constructive engagement to promote non-proliferation. In diplomatic and economic terms, the EU lacked sufficient 'carrots or sticks' to induce Iran to abandon its efforts to enrich uranium. The on again/off again character of the negotiations between Iran and the EU-3 also suggested that Tehran was using the talks to buy time and avoid pressure from the International Atomic Energy Agency and the UN Security Council. The negotiations may also have failed, however, because of the absence of US support: the USA was at best lukewarm about the EU's efforts, and without US support the EU could not address some of Iran's key concerns, in particular assurances regarding military action against the country and the normalization of political and economic ties with Washington. Whether the EU's efforts really tested the circumstances under which Iran might abandon its nuclear weapons ambitions is thus open to question. The lesson of the EU's negotiations with Iran may be not so much that engagement does not work per se, but rather than it is unlikely to succeed in the absence of real US support.

Living with proliferation?

Given India and Pakistan's consolidation of their status as nuclear weapon powers, North Korea's 2006 nuclear test and the difficulty of preventing Iran from developing nuclear weapons, it is likely that the world will have to live with a least a limited degree of proliferation. As discussed above, the immediate impact on Europe of proliferation may not be great. Nevertheless, proliferation has already prompted thinking within Europe on two issues: what may be done to deter states from using WMD, and the prospects for defending against WMD attack.

Deterrence, of course, has been the classical rationale for the possession of nuclear weapons. For the USA, the UK, France and NATO as a whole, deterrence of the Soviet Union provided the rationale for nuclear weapons during the Cold War. Since the 1990s, however, there has been a gradual shift in Western thinking on nuclear weapons away from the need to deter Russia and towards the need to maintain nuclear weapons in order to deter WMD attack from elsewhere in the world. The UK's 1998 *Strategic Defence Review* concluded that 'while large nuclear arsenals *and risks of proliferation* remain, our minimum deterrent remains a necessary element of our security' (UK Ministry of Defence, 1998, para. 60 – emphasis added). In announcing the conclusions of a major review of French nuclear strategy in 2001, President Jacques Chirac argued that 'Deterrence must also enable us to deal with the threats to our vital interests that regional powers armed with weapons of mass destruction could pose' (quoted in Yost, 2005, p. 118). Deterrence of WMD attack from outside Europe has also become one of the rationales for NATO's continuing strategy of nuclear deterrence based on the USA's strategic nuclear arsenal and the relatively small numbers of US nuclear weapons that remain forward-deployed in Europe (Yost, 1999, pp. 27–33). In the context of the ongoing development of the EU's defence role, it might be thought that the prospect of WMD proliferation would also have increased interest in the possibility of a 'European' deterrent based around the UK and France's nuclear weapons. However, although the UK and France have engaged in bilateral discussions on nuclear weapons, there has remained little support for the development of a 'European' nuclear deterrent.

The prospect of WMD proliferation and the USA's plans for missile defences have prompted debate on missile defence within Europe. The issue of missile defence – that is, systems capable of intercepting long-range missiles and thereby defending countries against attack with such weapons – is not new: the USA and the Soviet Union explored such systems during the Cold War, but negotiated a bilateral agreement not to deploy them (the 1972 Anti-Ballistic Missile (ABM) Treaty). In 2002, however, President George W. Bush, announced plans for the USA to develop missile defences (withdrawing from the ABM Treaty in the process), with initial deployment beginning in 2004. European governments have been wary of US missile defence plans, but have since the 1990s become involved in missile defences in a number of overlapping areas (DeSutter, 2006).

- *NATO*: NATO members initially agreed to explore missile defences in 1999 and decided in 2004 to proceed with the development of a Theatre Missile Defence (TMD) system designed to protect troops deployed overseas against short- and medium-range ballistic missile attack (NATO, 2006). NATO's Active Layered Theatre Ballistic Missile Defence (ALTBMD) capability will involve member states providing sensors and weapon systems, with NATO collectively providing the battle management, command, control, communications and intelligence (BMC3I) to integrate the components into an overall missile defence system, and has a planned initial operating capability of 2010. In 2002, NATO also initiated a 'NATO Missile Defence feasibility study to examine options for protecting Alliance territory, forces and population centres against the full range of missile threats' (NATO, 2002, para. 4(g)). The study was completed in May 2006 (NATO, 2006), but how far NATO will proceed with the development and deployment of more extensive missile defences remains to be seen.
- *Participation in US missile defences*: a number of European countries have agreed to participate or expressed an interesting in participating in US missile defences. In 2003, the UK agreed to a US request to upgrade the early warning radar system based at Fylingdales, Yorkshire, for missile defence purposes. In 2004, Denmark agreed to a similar upgrading of the early warning radar system at Thule in Greenland. There is also ongoing debate about the possible deployment of US ground-based interceptors in Europe, with a number of the Central and Eastern European states that joined NATO in 1999 and 2004 expressing interest in hosting such interceptors (Traynor, 2005). The closer proximity of such countries to the Middle East and Asia (compared to many Western European states) makes them a more likely location for US interceptor bases, but such proposals have also generated concern in Russia.
- *National and multinational missile defence projects*: A number of European states are involved other multinational missile defence projects. These include the Franco-Italian Surface Air Moyenne Portée/Terre (SAMP/T), the US/German–Italian Medium Extended

Air Defence System (MEADS), and the French–Italian–British Primary Anti-Air Missile System (PAAMS). These existing projects are all short-to-medium-range systems capable only of defence against short-to-medium-range missiles. It remains to be seen how far European states, either individually or collectively, might develop and deploy more extensive and longer-range missile defences similar to those being deployed by the USA.

Critics, including many in Europe, argue that missile defences are, however, deeply problematical (Davis, 2004). Missile defence is technically extremely challenging – akin to trying to hit a speeding bullet in flight – and there are serious doubts about the effectiveness of any systems that might be deployed. Missile defences are also likely to be very (perhaps prohibitively) expensive, especially in the case of systems for the defence of territory and population centres. Critics also argue that missile defences may be destabilizing – for example, by encouraging new arms races with countries such as China or Russia, or contributing to the militarization of outer space. European governments remain sceptical about the overall case for missile defences, and it is probably unlikely that they will move beyond the current pattern of developing limited theatre missile defences and limited involved in US systems towards a more comprehensive Europe-wide missile defence.

Even if European states and NATO or the EU strengthen their deterrent capabilities and deploy missile defences, if WMD (especially nuclear) proliferation proceeds, the changed strategic environment is likely to have a significant impact on European and American attitudes to the deployment of military force overseas. To date, the USA and European countries (in particular the UK and France, Europe's leading military powers) have been able to deploy military forces relatively freely in other parts of the world such as the Middle East because the risk of significant direct retaliation against their territory or major attacks on concentrations of forces deployed overseas has been relatively low. The ability of other states to retaliate with nuclear weapons or to use nuclear weapons against concentrations of US or European forces would radically alter this calculus. If Iran develops nuclear weapons, for example, the possibility of using military force against it will effectively be precluded. In the medium term, therefore, proliferation is likely to significantly curtail the ability of the USA or European states to intervene in other parts of the world, at least against those states that develop nuclear weapons.

Conclusion

This chapter has analysed European assessments of the threat posed by WMD proliferation, and European contributions to international efforts to prevent proliferation. In the USA, proliferation is now viewed, alongside terrorism, as one of the two central security challenges of the early twenty-first century, and the USA has to some degree abandoned its traditional approach to non-proliferation based on arms control and multilateralism in favour of more coercive, unilateral strategies – although it remains to be seen how far this revolution in US non-proliferation policy will be reversed in the wake of the Iraq War. While European governments are seriously concerned by the threat posed by WMD, they do not in general view it with the same sense of an immediate or existential threat that the USA does. European governments, further, continue to view multilateral arms control as the primary vehicle for attempting to prevent proliferation, and have sought – in particular through the EU's common positions in the main arms control negotiations – to strengthen the international non-proliferation regime. European governments are also contributing increasingly to co-operative threat reduction in the former Soviet Union, although the USA remains the leading actor in this area. In terms of proliferation's tough cases – those states that appear determined to develop nuclear weapons, in particular Iran and North Korea – the European preference has been to use diplomacy and soft power rather than the more coercive instruments of economic sanctions and military force. The failure of the EU's efforts to persuade Iran to abandon its apparent nuclear weapons ambitions was thus a major setback to its ambitions to show that its soft-power approach to proliferation could succeed (although it remains possible that Iran may yet be persuaded to halt its apparent march towards nuclear weapons). While the general European preference is for diplomacy and soft power approaches to non-proliferation, Europeans are also divided over the more contentious issues of economic sanctions and military force as tools of non-proliferation. Any US or Israeli use of force against Iran would doubtless bring these divisions to the fore once more.

While the 1990s and the first half of the 2000s have in part illustrated the limitations of arms control and soft power in preventing proliferation, they have also highlighted a deeper problem at the heart of the existing non-proliferation regime: the double standard implicit in the efforts of the five recognized nuclear weapon states to prevent other states from developing WMD while themselves retaining such weapons. So long as the five recognized nuclear weapon states – including three leading European powers, the UK, France and Russia – retain their nuclear arsenals and engage in only modest efforts to reduce those arsenals, it will remain extremely difficult to persuade other states (such as India, Pakistan, Iran or North Korea) not to develop nuclear weapons or to mobilize the sort of international pressure that might compel such states to abandon their nuclear weapons ambitions. Whether more radical progress towards nuclear disarmament is feasible, or would create the circumstances in which proliferators might abandon their nuclear weapons ambitions is a moot point, since none of the five recognized nuclear weapons powers appears inclined to test this logic seriously. In these circumstances, India and Pakistan are likely to further consolidate their status as nuclear weapon powers, and North Korea and Iran may well move down this road. The larger, long-term question is probably whether nuclear (and other WMD) proliferation will remain limited to these countries, or whether a significantly wider group of states will develop such weapons, thereby further increasing the risk that they will be used, or fall into the hands of terrorists. European states – and the USA – are thus likely to have to live with the reality of at least limited nuclear proliferation and, while they may enhance their own deterrent capabilities and deploy missile defences, this reality is likely to fundamentally constrain their ability to use military force against countries such as Iran and North Korea and reshape the strategic calculus in the Middle East and North East Asia.

Chapter 8

The 'New Terrorism' and the 'War on Terror'

The emergence of globalized Islamic terrorism and the US 'war on terror' have had major implications for Europe. As the Madrid and London bombings of March 2004 and July 2005 made clear, Europe is a major target for Islamic terrorism. European vulnerability to Islamic terrorism is multi-faceted and intersects the boundaries of external and internal security. European citizens, embassies, businesses, and military personnel and bases have been the targets of terrorist attacks outside Europe. Terrorists have used European countries as safe havens from which to plan and organize terrorist acts elsewhere in the world (as with the 9/11 attacks on the USA). Terrorist groups from outside Europe have sought to infiltrate Europe in order to undertake terrorist attacks or to foment terrorism. As the London bombings illustrate, elements within Europe's own Islamic populations are also now willing to engage in terrorist acts. European states and international institutions, especially the EU, thus face the multi-faceted challenge of strengthening defences – such as intelligence and border controls – against an external terrorist threat, and responding to what may be a major *internal* terrorist threat from elements within Europe's Islamic population, while trying to address the root causes of both sources of terrorism.

European responses to the 'new terrorism' also take place in the context of (and are thus significantly shaped and constrained by) the US 'war on terror'. As was seen in Chapters 3 and 4, while European governments strongly supported the US-led intervention in Afghanistan after 9/11, many were opposed to the widening of the 'war on terror' to include the invasion of Iraq. Similarly, as discussed below, while European governments are co-operating with the USA on a wide range of lower-profile counter-terrorism measures (in areas such as intelligence, policing and airline security), European governments and populations are increasingly wary of the concept and conduct of the US 'war on terror'.

Europe and terrorism – 'old' and 'new'

Terrorism, of course, is hardly new, and Europe has significant experience of the phenomenon. The term 'terrorism' emerged from 'the terror' of the French Revolution (when revolutionaries used violence and brutality against their enemies) and was subsequently used to describe violence by left-wing and anarchist groups and individuals against the established order in nineteenth- and early-twentieth-century Europe. In the post-1945 era, European states were subject to terrorist campaigns and acts conducted by ethno-national groups within Europe (Irish republicans in the UK, Basque nationalists in Spain, Corsican separatists in France, and Kurdish groups in Turkey); far-left groups (the Baader-Meinhof Gang and the Red Army Faction in Germany, the Red Brigades in Italy, and the Revolutionary Organization 17 November in Greece); and Palestinian groups in the 1960s and 1970s. Indeed, the first hijacking of an Israeli airliner by Palestinian terrorists in 1968, en route from Rome to Tel Aviv, is often seen as the beginning of an 'age of terrorism' (Guelke, 1998, pp. 189–92).

European governments responded to post-1945 terrorism in a variety of different ways, resulting in quite different national policies. Policy responses included intensified intelligence and police action against terrorists; the banning of terrorist groups; the introduction of special judicial courts and procedures to deal with terrorism; political, economic and social measures designed to address the grievances that had given rise to terrorism and undercut support for terrorists; and, in some cases, negotiations (often secret) with terrorists. Some countries emphasized 'tough' policies focusing on legal and security measures directed against terrorists (usually accompanied by a refusal to negotiate with them or to take measures to address their grievances), while others emphasized political, economic and social measures or the possibility of negotiation. Critics, especially in the USA, contended that Europe was soft on terrorism, arguing that negotiation and political, economic and social measures designed to address terrorists grievances amounted to appeasement and would only show that terrorism worked as a means of advancing one's political goals. The French 'sanctuary doctrine' was particularly controversial: up to the 1980s France tried to avoid becoming a subject of foreign terrorist attacks by making French policy and territory neutral in relation to terrorism, effectively allowing terrorist groups to operate from France in return for a commitment by those groups not to undertake attacks within

France (Shapiro and Suzan, 2003, p. 69–73). By the late 1980s and early 1990s, however, terrorism appeared to be a waning force in Europe: far-left terrorist groups had ceased to be active, many of the main ethno-national terrorist campaigns were winding down (with peace processes beginning to emerge in these conflicts) and the earlier internationalization of Palestinian terrorism had dissipated.

Although 9/11 stands as the symbolic moment in the emergence of the 'new terrorism', globalized Islamic terrorism had been developing for a decade or more before this, and Europe was intertwined with this process in a number of important ways. The origins of global Islamic terrorism are contentious, but probably lie in the following factors: the socio-economic and political failures of the authoritarian regimes that rule most of the world's Islamic states; the consequences of Western intervention in the Middle East, where the West has supported exactly those authoritarian regimes; the emergence of radical Islamic leaders and groups in Egypt and Saudi Arabia, who have acted as the religious–ideological vanguard of the movement; and the catalytic role of Afghanistan, where US-backed opposition to the 1979 Soviet invasion brought together many of the forces that subsequently morphed into Al-Qaeda and served as a training camp for some thousands of Islamic militants in the 1990s (Simon and Benjamin, 2001; Burke, 2004). Although the USA is the primary target of global Islamic terrorism, European states and citizens have also been targets since the early 1990s. France, because of its historic role in Algeria and its support for that country's military government (which had abandoned free elections in 1992 when it became clear that Islamists would win), was subject to a series of terrorist attacks by the Algerian Armed Islamic Group (GIA) in 1995, resulting in the deaths of ten people and the wounding of over 150 (Shapiro and Suzan, 2003, pp. 79–81). European governments prevented other planned terrorist attacks by Islamic groups in Europe before 9/11, including on the 1998 football World Cup in France and on Strasbourg Cathedral in 2000 (Shapiro and Suzan, 2003, p. 68). European citizens have also been a target of Islamic terrorism outside Europe: sixty-two people, mainly European and Japanese tourists, were killed in the November 1997 Luxor Massacre in Egypt. Against this background, the March 2004 Madrid bombings were a confirmation that Europe was a prime target for Islamic terrorism.

The March 2004 Madrid bombings were committed by the Moroccan Islamic Combat Group, and the individual terrorists were mostly Moroccans, led by a Tunisian (IISS, 2004, p. 101). Although some of the terrorists were Spanish residents, the Madrid bombings nevertheless suggested that the primary threat was still an external one posed by foreign terrorists that had infiltrated Europe. In contrast, the July 2005 London bombings appeared to signal a new, and in many ways more worrying, threat: the emergence of home-grown Islamic terrorism, combined with suicide attacks (a phenomenon not previously seen in Europe). The London bombings were carried out by four British citizens, three of whom had been born in the UK and the fourth of whom had moved to the UK at the age of two and had lived in the country since then (Home Office, 2006). Two of the London bombers visited Pakistan (and possibly Afghanistan) prior to the bombings, where they may have met and received training from other terrorists, and there is speculation that the London attacks were supported or directed by external terrorist groups (Travis and Norton-Taylor, 2006). Nevertheless, even if the London bombings were supported or masterminded by external Islamic groups, they made it starkly clear that Europe now faces the threat not just of external Islamic terrorism but also of a home-grown European version. The extent and nature of the threat posed by indigenous European Islamic terrorism and the challenges of responding to this are discussed below.

A further element of Europe's interrelationship with Islamic terrorism is the way in which the continent has become a base for radical Islamic individuals and groups seeking to promote their ideology, gain recruits and, in some cases, plan terrorist attacks. Jonathan Stevenson (2004, p. 27) argues that 'liberal asylum laws and standards of religious and commercial freedom have made Europe an effective safe haven as well as a fundraising hub for aspiring terrorists'. The so-called 'Hamburg cell' – a group of the 9/11 conspirators based in Hamburg, Germany – played a central role in the 9/11 attacks (National Commission on Terrorist Attacks Upon the United States, 2004, pp. 160–9). In the wake of the London bombings, commentators in the USA described the British capital as 'Londonistan': a city that had become a haven for radical Islamic preachers fomenting violence against the West, and a recruiting ground for disciples willing to put that doctrine into practice (Younge, 2005; Bergen, 2005). While the UK may be the most severe case of this phenomenon, other Western European countries face similar problems. Although a liberal approach to both asylum seekers and freedom of speech may be partly to blame for the growth of radical Islam in Western Europe, larger geographical and historical factors are at play. Geography alone means that Europe has been and will remain the primary destination in the West for immigrants from the Middle East and North Africa. The historic ties of former imperial powers with Islamic countries also makes them a primary destination for immigration from these states – as in the UK with regard to Pakistan, and France in relation to Algeria. More recently, the Balkan conflicts of the 1990s created a context in which radical Islamists from outside Europe were able to build links with the Muslim communities in Bosnia and Kosovo.

A further interface between Europe and Islamic terrorism has emerged in southern Russia, the Caucasus and Central Asia. The Central Asian 'stans' (Kazakhstan, Kyrgyzstan, Tajikistan, Turkmenistan and Uzbekistan) and Azerbaijan all have predominantly Muslim populations, as do various parts of the Russian north Caucasus. The authoritarian nature of the Central Asian regimes has made Islam one of the primary outlets for political and socio-economic dissent, and resulted in the emergence of radical Islamic groups that sometimes engage in terrorist acts. This problem is most serious in Uzbekistan, where the Islamic Movement of Uzbekistan (IMU) emerged in the late 1990s, is believed to have links with Al-Qaeda, and has engaged in terrorist acts against the ruling regimes and Western targets in Uzbekistan, Kyrgyzstan and Afghanistan (Burgess, 2002). While radical Islam and Islamic terrorism pose a real challenge in Central Asia, the extent of the problem should perhaps not be exaggerated: Central Asian leaders, in particular Uzbek president, Islam Karimov, use the fear of Islamic radicalism as a means of shoring up their authoritarian regimes; and Kyrgyzstan's 2005 'Tulip Revolution' indicated that even if these regimes are overthrown they are not necessarily likely to be replaced by fundamentalist Islamic forces.

It is in the Russian north Caucasus, in particular Chechnya, however, that Islamic terrorism has really come to the fore in the former Soviet Union. Starting in the mid-1990s and escalating from the late 1990s, Russia has been subject to a series of major terrorist attacks, primarily in Chechnya and neighbouring parts of the north Caucasus, but also elsewhere in the Russian Federation. These attacks included a hostage crisis in a Moscow cinema in October 2002, in which 120 hostages and forty terrorists were killed during a rescue attempt, and reached their nadir with the September 2004 school hostage crisis in Beslan, North Ossetia, which resulted in the deaths of over 300 civilians, many of them children. Many Russians thus view themselves as one of the frontlines in the global conflict with Islamic terrorism. The context and nature of the terrorist threat facing Russia are, however, controversial. The Chechen conflict can be viewed in part as a classical example of an ethno-national group using terrorism against a more powerful central government, but Chechen and other north Caucasian radicals have also developed links with and been supported by Islamic terrorists the Middle East. Chechnya therefore appears to be a situation where 'old'- and 'new'-style terrorism have fused. Russia's brutal interventions in Chechnya in the 1990s, further-more, can only have contributed to the rise of Chechen terrorism. Western governments have thus been torn between supporting Russia as an ally in the global struggle against Islamic terrorism, and criticism of Moscow for its failed interventions and human rights abuses in Chechnya.

Europe and the US 'war on terror'

Although the immediate European response to 9/11 was one of near-universal sympathy and support for the USA, since late 2001 Europeans have become increasingly wary, and to varying degrees openly critical, of the nature and conduct of the US 'war on terror'. Gilles Andreani neatly summarizes European concerns over the US 'war on terror' as 'good cause, wrong concept' (Andreani, 2004). Similarly, the British academic, Adam Roberts, has argued that 'There is a need to articulate what might be called a British (or, more ambitiously, a European) perspective on terrorism and counter-terrorism – one that is more historically informed, encompassing certain elements distinctive from the US doctrine' (Roberts, 2005, p. 101). Although the US 'war' on terror is partly rhetorical, many Europeans believe that it nevertheless signals an approach to counter-terrorism that defines the problem too simplistically in terms of good and evil, searches for an impossible total defeat of terrorism, and places too much emphasis on military force as a central instrument of counter-terrorism (Howard, 2002; Muller, 2003; Andreani, 2004; Roberts 2005).

For many in Europe, the Iraq War provided the clearest example of the dangers of the broadening the US 'war on terror' and of conflating terrorism, WMD proliferation and 'rogue states' into a single great threat. European opponents of the Iraq War argued that it would be a major distraction from the more central task of countering Al-Qaeda and associated Islamic terrorist groups, polarize opinion in the Middle East against the USA and the West, and thereby act as a recruiting sergeant for Islamic terrorism. The logic of this argument has been reinforced by developments since 2003. In 2005, the US Central

Intelligence Agency (CIA) concluded that Iraq was providing a training ground for terrorists, similar to the role of Afghanistan in the rise of Al-Qaeda in the 1980s and 1990s, and that terrorists trained in Iraq might go on to destabilize other countries such as Saudi Arabia and Jordan (Jehl, 2005). British officials and intelligence agencies believe that Iraq has become 'a dominant issue for a range of extremist groups and individuals in the UK and Europe' (Evans, 2005) and was a 'contributory factor' behind the 2005 London bombings (Norton-Taylor, 2006). European states' involvement in Iraq alongside the USA may also have made them prime targets for Islamic terrorism. It was hardly coincidental that two of the countries that were the strongest supporters of the US intervention in Iraq – Spain and the UK –were subsequently subject to major terrorist attacks. Overall, developments since 2003 have reinforced the widespread European view of the Iraq War as a dangerous widening of the US 'war on terror'. A June 2005 survey, for example, found that most people in eight European states (the UK, France, Germany, the Netherlands, Poland, Russia, Spain and Turkey) believed that the world was more dangerous rather than safer as a consequence of Saddam Hussein's removal from power (Pew Global Attitudes Project, 2005, p. 27).

Europeans are also concerned about the extent to which the 'war on terror' may be leading the USA to cast aside international human rights commitments. The decision of the USA to define Al-Qaeda/Taliban prisoners captured in Afghanistan as 'enemy combatants' rather than 'prisoners of war' (thereby ensuring that they are not legally subject to the protections of the Geneva Conventions), the detainment of these prisoners at the USA military base at Guantanamo Bay in Cuba, and the decision to try some of these prisoners before secret military tribunals left these prisoners in a legal limbo and created the impression of an American government trying to avoid both international and domestic law. Accusations by some of the Guantanamo Bay prisoners of human rights abuses and the 2004 scandal surrounding human rights abuses against prisoners held in the Abu Ghraib prison in Iraq reinforced the perception of the USA being willing to disregard international human rights standards. Reports that Guantanamo Bay and the Bagram airbase in Afghanistan were part of a larger network of secret prisons where the USA and its allies were holding prisoners, and increasing US use of 'extraordinary rendition' – where suspected terrorists are captured covertly in third countries by US intelligence or security agencies and secretly transferred out of those countries – further reinforced perceptions that the USA was operating outside the bounds of international law. For many Europeans, these elements of America's 'war on terror' not only represent a serious challenge to global human rights norms, but are also likely to be counter-productive in addressing terrorism, since they reinforce the perception in the non-Western world of a hypocritical USA (and wider West, including Europe) willing to abuse human rights and flout international law in its anti-terrorist campaign. In May 2006, the UK's Attorney General, Lord Goldsmith, the British government's most senior legal official, described the Guantanamo Bay prison as a 'symbol of injustice' and called for it to be closed (Smith, 2006).

These legal and human rights dimensions of the US 'war on terror' have also had a number of more specific European dimensions. In a number of cases, European citizens have been held at Guantanamo Bay or other similar US facilities and/or been the subject of 'extraordinary renditions'; European governments have then faced pressure to secure the release of these prisoners, putting those governments in something of a political quandary, since whether these citizens are terrorists is often highly uncertain, the circumstances surrounding their detention are opaque, and governments have been reluctant to confront the USA. In some cases, European governments have persuaded the USA to release such prisoners, but in others these European citizens remain under US detention. Europe has also become involved in the controversy surrounding the US practice of 'extraordinary rendition'. Since 2001, a number of cases of the USA capturing individuals in European countries and transferring those individuals out of these countries have surfaced, causing political scandals in Italy and Sweden in particular (Simpson, 2005). The civilian aircraft the USA uses for rendition flights also appear to have stopped regularly at airports in a number of European states, thereby at least indirectly implicating European states in the 'extraordinary rendition' process. The Council of Europe and the European Parliament have initiated investigations into the issue.

It would be misleading to suggest that European and American approaches to counter-terrorism have diverged completely or that there is no longer a basis for transatlantic co-operation in this area. As is discussed below, Europe and the USA continue to co-operate on many aspects of counter-terrorism, especially in relation to intelligence, policing and internal security. Nevertheless, Europeans are deeply wary of central aspects of the US 'war on terror'.

Counter-terrorism I: the homeland security agenda

The events of 9/11 have led to the emergence of a new homeland security agenda in the USA, the centrepieces of this being the PATRIOT Act, passed by Congress in October 2001, which extends the powers of the US government to counter terrorism, and the creation of a new Department of Homeland Security, bringing together US government offices and agencies dealing with borders, immigration, transportation security, and emergency preparedness and response. European governments and the EU have introduced similar legal, governmental and operational counter-terrorism measures. This has included strengthening internal security policies in relation to terrorism, passing new legislation to deal with terrorism, and increasing the powers of and resources available to police and domestic intelligence services. Many of these steps might traditionally have been labelled internal security measures – that is legal, policing and intelligence policies directed against terrorist threats from within the territory of the state concerned. Governments have also, however, taken other steps that fall beyond the scope of traditional internal security measures: strengthening immigration and border controls; enhancing airport, airline and port security; devoting more resources to external intelligence services with regard to terrorism; and increasing international counter-terrorism co-operation (in areas such as the financing of terrorism, intelligence and extradition). The new homeland security agenda has thus resulted in an increasing blurring of the distinction between internal and external security, and the internationalization of what were traditionally national internal security policies.

At the national level, most European states have introduced a variety of new homeland security measures since September 2001 (van de Linde *et al.*, 2002; Foreign and Commonwealth Office, 2005). This has included increased resources for intelligence, policing, and immigration and border controls; intensified surveillance of groups or individuals believed to be terrorists, or supporting or encouraging terrorism; and, in some cases, major new legislation. European law-enforcement also became 'noticeably more inclined to arrest and detain suspects', with authorities in Belgium, Bosnia-Herzegovina, France, Germany, Italy, the Netherlands, Spain and the UK arresting over 200 suspected Al-Qaeda terrorists between 11 September 2001 and February 2003 (Stevenson, 2004, pp. 54 and 27). In the British case, the government introduced two major new pieces of counter-terrorism legislation after

Box 8.1   EU counter-terrorism measures post-9/11

- *Action Plan on Combating Terrorism*: adopted after the 9/11 attacks in September 2001 to guide EU policy; subsequently revised and expanded.
- *Counter-Terrorism Co-ordinator*: the position of EU Counter-Terrorism Co-ordinator was established after the March 2004 Madrid bombings.
- *European Arrest Warrant*: introduced in 2002; facilitates arrest across the EU of persons indicted in another member state for terrorism (or other serious crimes).
- *Mutual recognition of judicial orders* to freeze and confiscate assets.
- *Common definition of terrorist offences*: agreed EU list of terrorist individuals, groups and entities established; minimum sentences for terrorist offences agreed; criminalization of direction of, support of and incitement to terrorism.
- *Eurojust*: EU judicial agency established to improve co-ordination between member states' magistrates and prosecutors.
- *Europol*: EU police office established to facilitate co-operation in relation to serious crime, including terrorism.
- *European Agency for Management of the External Borders*: established to ensure a high and uniform level of control and surveillance on the EU's external frontiers; operational from May 2005.
- *Passports*: minimum security standards and biometric identifiers introduced for passports and other travel documents issued by member states.
- *Schengen Information System (SIS)*: system for exchange of information on persons wanted in relation to cross-border crimes.
- *Visa Information System (VIS)*: system for exchange of data regarding visa applications and applicants.
- *EURODAC*: European Automated Fingerprints Identification System for asylum applicants and illegal immigrants; operational from 2003.
- *Customs controls*: new legislation strengthening customs controls.

→

9/11 and the July 2005 London bombings: the Anti-Terrorism, Crime and Security Act 2001, and the Terrorism Act 2006 (Home Office, n.d.). The Anti-Terrorism, Crime and Security Act 2001 introduced new measures to cut off terrorist funding; enable government departments to collect and share information required for countering terrorism; streamline relevant immigration procedures; ensure the security of the nuclear and aviation industries; improve security of dangerous substances that might be targeted or used by terrorists; and extend police powers. The Terrorism Act 2006 introduced new criminal

➜

- *Airport/aircraft and harbour/shipping security*: new Energy and Transport Security Directorate established within the European Commission; new European Commission inspectorate monitoring security measures across the EU.
- *Lost/stolen passports*: began delivering information on lost and stolen passports to an International Database managed by Interpol.
- *Freezing of terrorist finances*: ordered freezing of all funds and assets belonging to those suspected of terrorism or of financing terrorism.
- *New anti-money laundering directive*: extended existing anti-money laundering defences to cover financing of terrorism; includes structured rules for movement of cash and wired transfers.
- *Exchange of information on suspicious financial transactions*: intensified exchange of information between member states on suspicious financial transactions.
- *Response measures in event of terrorist attacks*: mechanism established to facilitate and support civil protection assistance in event of major disasters, including terrorist attacks; rapid alert system established to provide early warning of nuclear, radiological, biological or chemical (NRBC) attacks; enhanced programme for EU preparedness and response to NRBC attack.

Data from: European Union, *European Union Factsheet: The Fight Against Terrorism* (Brussels, European Union, 2005), EU website: http://www.consilium.europa.eu/uedocs/cmsUpload/3Counterterrorfinal170605.pdf (accessed 28 May 2006); 'Meeting of the Heads and State or Government of the European Union and the President of the European Commission, Ghent, 19 October 2001, "Road Map" of All the Measures and Initiatives to be Implemented Under the Action Plan Decided on by the European Council on 21 September 2001', in Maartje Rutten (2002) *From Nice to Laeken – European Defence: Core Documents, Vol. II* (Paris: Institute for Security Studies European Union), pp. 164–85; European Union , *EU Action Plan on Combating Terrorism*, 5771/1/06 REV 1 (Brussels: Council of the European Union, 2006), http://register.consilium.eu.int/pdf/en/06/st05/st05771-re01.en06.pdf (accessed 3 May 2006).

offences relating to terrorism (acts preparatory to terrorism; encouragement of terrorism, including its glorification; dissemination of terrorist publications; and terrorist training); introduced warrants to enable the police to search any property owned or controlled by a terrorist suspect; extended police powers to detain suspects after arrest for up to 28 days; and increased the powers of the government to proscribe groups (including those which glorify terrorism). A number of the measures introduced by the British government proved controversial, in particular new powers to detain individuals and to proscribe groups (Fenwick, 2002). The House of Lords ruled that so-called Part 4 powers under the Anti-Terrorism, Crime and Security Act 2001 were incompatible with the UK's civil liberties commitments under the European Convention on Human Rights, and discriminatory because they applied only to foreign nationals, forcing the government to introduce new legislation (the Prevention of Terrorism Act 2005), which established a system of control orders (under which individuals might have their movements restricted or have other prohibitions imposed on them).

In the wake of the 9/11 attacks and the Madrid bombings, the EU also took a series of counter-terrorism measures, including the establishment of a rolling action plan to combat terrorism. and the appointment of a Counter-Terrorism Co-ordinator – see Box 8.1. Many of the EU's counter-terrorism policy initiatives after 9/11 built upon the co-operation established in the 1990s in the framework of the Union's Area of Freedom, Security and Justice (AFSJ). As discussed in Chapter 4, the EU's policies in this area remain primarily intergovernmental and are characterized by a complex institutional infrastructure, with member states participating to differing degrees in various areas of the AFSJ. The EU's counter-terrorism policies reflect this pattern: although the Union has agreed an extensive and in some ways impressive range of counter-terrorism measures, the implementation of most of these depends on individual member states. Critics point out that member states have been slow to implement some of the key measures that have been agreed, the EU's Counter-Terrorism Co-ordinator has no power to force member states to implement their commitments or to propose EU-wide measures, and states are reluctant to share intelligence information on an EU-wide basis (Keohane, 2005; Wilkinson, 2005, pp. 29–37, 49).

Not withstanding European concerns about the US 'war on terror', the EU has also developed intensive counter-terrorism co-operation with the USA since 9/11 – see Box 8.2 (see also Rees, 2006). While the principle of counter-terrorism co-operation with the USA has received broad support within the EU, some of the centrepiece measures proposed or agreed have proved to be controversial within Europe. An EU–US agreement on extradition procedures was held up by concerns that persons extradited to and tried in the USA might be subject to the death penalty, and the agreement was only approved by the EU in 2003 on condition that EU member states retained the right to make extradition conditional on US agreement that the death penalty would not be imposed. The transfer of personal name records (PNR) data held by

---

Box 8.2   US–EU counter-terrorism co-operation post-9/11

- *EU–US Agreement on Extradition*: facilitates extradition between the USA and the EU through an alleviation of legalization and certification requirements and the speeding up of extradition processes; adopted at the June 2003 EU–US Summit.
- *EU–US Agreement on Mutual Legal Assistance*: gives law enforcement agencies access to bank accounts in the EU and the USA for investigations of serious crimes, including terrorism, organized crime and financial crime; allows for Joint Investigative Teams; adopted at the June 2003 EU–US Summit.
- *Transfer of personal name records (PNR) data*: transfer of PNR data held by European airlines to US Customs and Border Protection (CBP); introduced on a provisional basis in 2002; US–EU agreement approved by EU Council of Ministers in May 2004.
- *High-Level Policy Dialogue on Border and Transport Security*: policy dialogue between the EU and the USA, in particular the European Commission and the Department of Homeland Security, established in 2004.
- *Europol–US co-operation*: December 2001 agreement on exchange of strategic and technical information; December 2002 agreement on exchange of personal data.
- *Eurojust–US co-operation*: contacts have been established between Eurojust and the USA in relation to investigation and prosecution of terrorists.

Data from: European Union, *European Union Factsheet: The Fight Against Terrorism* (Brussels, European Union, 2005), EU website: http://www.consilium.europa.eu/uedocs/cmsUpload/3Counterterrorfinal170605.pdf (accessed 28 May 2006); European Union, *European Union Factsheet: Extradition and Mutual Legal Assistance* (Brussels: General Secretariat of the Council of the European Union, 2003), EU website: http://ec.europa.eu/comm/external_relations/us/sum06_03/extra.pdf.

European airlines to the USA has been viewed by critics within Europe as an infringement of people's civil liberties, and the legality of a 2004 US–EU agreement on the transfer of PNR data was called into question by the European Court of Justice in 2006 (Sturcke, 2006). Some in the USA continue to view Europe, and in particular the EU, as being overly concerned with civil liberties and soft in its approach to terrorism.

The debate surrounding these various homeland security measures at the national, EU and transatlantic levels reflects the long-standing tension between security and liberty in responding to terrorism. For liberal democracies, with their basis in the principles of individual rights and limits on the power of the state, striking the appropriate balance between security and liberty in responding to terrorism remains difficult and often deeply contentious (Wilkinson, 2000). Even after the initial post-9/11 measures taken by European governments and the EU, some critics argued that Europe was taking too soft an approach towards terrorism and was overly concerned with protecting individual rights. In the wake of the Madrid and London bombings, however, European governments began to take a tougher approach. The German government, for example, was reported to have initiated 'an aggressive anti-terrorism strategy', including a major counter-terrorism raid in January 2005 involving 700 police and resulting in twenty-two arrests (Whitlock and Smiley, 2005). The UK's Terrorism Act 2006, with its introduction of a new offence of glorifying terrorism and increased government powers to proscribe groups, was also an implicit recognition that before July 2005 the UK had allowed groups and individuals that might promote terrorism to operate with too great a degree of freedom. Civil liberties and human rights groups have, however, argued that measures taken by European governments and the EU risk undermining basic freedoms (Bunyan, 2005; Human Rights Watch, 2005). While 9/11 and the Madrid and London bombings have shifted the parameters of this debate, the fundamental tension between security and liberty in counter-terrorism remains, and European governments and the EU are likely to face further controversies over the issue.

Europe's Islamic population: an internal terrorist threat?

The London bombings made clear that Islamic terrorism poses not only an external threat to Europe but also an internal one of terrorist attack by citizens (or other long-term residents) of European states. Combined with a rapidly growing European Muslim population and intensifying socio-cultural tensions between Muslims and majority populations in European countries, the emergence of European jihadi terrorism has prompted growing concerns over an increasingly troubled relationship between Europe and its Islamic minority. Some observers have even warned of the possible emergence of a 'Eurabia': an anti-Western Islamic-dominated Europe more like the contemporary Middle East than the modern Europe that was hitherto known (*The Economist*, 2006a and 2006b).

Table 8.1 summarizes the number of Muslims in Europe. As can be

TABLE 8.1   *Europe's Muslim population*

Region/Country/ Grouping	Number of Muslims (mn, 2003)	Percentage of total population (2003)
EU-15[1]	15.2	4%
Other Western Europe[2]	0.4	3.2%
New EU Members[3]	0.3	0.4%
EU-25[4]	15.5	3.4%
Balkans[5]	7.36	13.4%
Turkey	67.1	99%

Notes: 1. 15 EU members up to 2004; 2. Iceland, Liechtenstein, Norway and Switzerland; 3. 10 states that joined EU in 2004; 4. Post-2004, 25 member states of EU; 5. Albania, Bosnia, Bulgaria, Croatia, Macedonia, Romania and Serbia-Montenegro.

Data from: Timothy M. Savage, 'Europe and Islam: Crescent Waxing, Cultures Clashing', *The Washington Quarterly*, vol. 27, no. 3, 2004, pp. 25–50.

seen from the table, there are over 15 million Muslims in the EU, predominantly in Western Europe. The largest Muslim populations within the EU are in France (5 million), Germany (4 million), the UK (1.6 million), Spain (1 million), Italy (1 million) and the Netherlands (886,000) (Savage, 2004, p. 32). The Balkans (excluding Turkey) have a Muslim population of about 7 million, with Albania being a majority Muslim country; Muslims are the largest religious group (about 40 per cent of the population) in Bosnia; and there are substantial Muslim minorities in Bulgaria, Macedonia and Serbia. Turkey, with its population of nearly 70 million, is, of course, a predominantly Islamic country, with Muslims estimated to make up 99 per cent of its population. Russia has a significant Muslim minority, primarily in the north Caucasus region. Elsewhere in the former Soviet Union, Azerbaijan and the Central Asian states (Kazakhstan, Kyrgyzstan, Tajikistan, Turkmenistan and Uzbekistan) are predominantly Muslim countries.

Europe's Muslim population, especially that in the EU, is predicted to grow significantly in the next few decades, in absolute terms but also as a proportion of the total EU population. Some projections suggest that Muslims could make up a quarter of France's population by 2025, and possibly even a majority in France and elsewhere in Western Europe by 2050 (Savage, 2004, p. 28; Sendagorta, 2005, p. 69). These trends reflect a number of factors: low birth rates and projected population decline among the general European population, a relatively high population growth rate among the Muslim population and likely future Muslim immigration into Western Europe.

Relations between Europe's long-standing population and its Islamic minorities are complicated by problems of economic marginalization, ghettoization and socio-cultural conflict. In general, Muslims within the EU are economically worse-off than non-Muslims, and concentrated in urban centres, often located within the most disadvantaged neighbourhoods of large cities. Incipient, if not overt, racism in Europe's majority population often results in immigrants, refugees, asylum seekers, Muslims and non-whites being conflated in the popular consciousness into a threatening 'other'. There are also real tensions between 'European' liberalism and secularism and (some) Islamic attitudes to freedom of speech, individual freedom, gender and sexuality. Whether through exclusion by the majority population, choice by the Islamic population or as a consequence of other socio-economic trends, Muslims have to varying degrees come to form separate, parallel communities within European societies rather than integrating fully into those societies. In recent years, these various dynamics have resulted in, but also been reinforced by, a series of controversial incidents: the French government's 2003 decision to ban Muslim women from wearing headscarves in schools, the murder of the Dutch filmmaker Theo van Gogh by a Muslim extremist in 2004, violent disturbances in predominantly immigrant areas of France in late 2005, and the publication of cartoons depicting the Prophet Muhammad as a terrorist by a Danish newspaper in 2006.

Against this background, it is hardly surprising that many within Europe's Islamic population are alienated from the society in which they live, nor perhaps that some turn to violence. Analysts argue that conflicts and Western interventions in the Islamic world have played a catalytic role in radicalizing elements within the European Islamic community: French support for the abandonment of democracy in Algeria after the Islamic Salvation Front (FIS) won elections in that country in 1992 played an important role in the Islamic terrorism that France faced in the 1990s; the conflicts in Palestine, Kashmir and Chechnya have become lightning rods for Islamic discontent; and the Spanish and British governments' support for the US intervention in Iraq was arguably an important factor behind the Madrid and London bombings. The extent of support among European Muslims for radical views, and more specifically for terrorism, is difficult to gauge. A 2004 survey of British Muslims found that, while the overwhelming majority (73 per cent) strongly opposed terrorist attacks by Al-Qaeda and other organizations, a significant minority (13 per cent) believed further such attacks on the USA would be justified (Travis, 2004). Studies in Germany and the Netherlands have suggested that 5–10 per cent of the Muslim population sympathize with radical Islamic views (Sendagorta, 2005, p. 65). European counter-terrorism officials estimate that 1–2 per cent of the continent's Muslims – 250,000 to 500,000 people – are involved in some type of extremist activity (Savage, 2004, pp. 31–3). Even if only a very small proportion of Europe's Muslims might actually participate in or operationally support terrorism, the scale of the continent's Islamic population is nevertheless such that this provides a significant pool of potential terrorists.

The recognition that Europe faces a significant internal terrorist threat from within its own Islamic communities has led European governments to re-orientate counter-terrorism, intelligence and policing policies away from longer-standing ethno-national terrorist groups (such as the IRA and ETA) and towards the new threat from Islamic terrorism within Europe. In the longer term, however, addressing the terrorist threat from within European Islam will depend not on counter-terrorism, intelligence and police responses but rather on the degree to which Europe succeeds in integrating its growing Muslim population into its societies. Since 1945, European states have been divided between two broad approaches to integrating immigrant communities. The integrationist or assimilationist approach, of which France is viewed as the archetype, encourages and to some degree requires immigrants to adopt and adapt to their new society's existing values, culture and identity. The multicultural approach, symbolized by the UK, accepts and to some extent supports the development of multiple cultural identities. The increasing alienation of Europe's Islamic communities and the emergence of jihadi terrorism from within those communities, however, suggest that both approaches have failed in important ways. British-style multiculturalism has resulted in the emergence of separate, parallel societies and allowed extremism ('Londonistan') to flourish within parts of those societies. French-style integrationism has, however, also failed to truly integrate Islamic minorities, instead resulting in the marginalization and resentment that produced the violent riots of late 2005. In response to these failures, the European Union adopted a *Strategy for Combating Radicalization and Recruitment to Terrorism* in late 2005 (European Union, 2005b). The

EU's strategy called for limiting the activities of those promoting radicalization in places of education and worship, greater efforts to prevent people receiving terrorist training, empowering moderate voices within European Islam, and addressing structural factors that support radicalization by targeting inequalities and discrimination. The failure of both the integrationist and multicultural models suggests that a new approach to integration is needed, perhaps one that combines acceptance of certain core values (such as democracy and freedom of speech) with a recognition of distinctive cultures. More also arguably needs to be done to address the economic marginalization of Europe's Muslim populations.

Tensions between Europe and its Islamic population, and the threat of European Islamic terrorism, are likely to be growing problems, at least in the short-to-medium term. Alienation and discontent within Europe's Muslim communities and the sense of threat felt by Europe's majority populations create the risk of a vicious circle of escalating conflict that might be difficult to break. In the worst case, this could result in a deeply polarized division between the old ethnically 'white' Europe and Europe's newer Islamic population, endemic civil strife and increasingly widespread terrorism. Intensifying conflict between Europe and its Islamic communities should not, however, be viewed as inevitable. European Islam is a far from homogenous entity: it is divided between different branches of the Islamic faith (Sunnis, Shias and others), immigrants and their descendants from many different countries, and people in diverse socio-economic situations. While their may be growing discontent within Europe's Islamic communities, the majority of European Muslims have not rejected the core European values of individual freedom and democracy, nor do they support terrorism. The current debates over terrorism, security and identity, further, are leading at least some within European Islam to engage not in terrorism but in more traditional forms of political activity and social dialogue – exactly the kind of integration that may be necessary if a new modus vivendi is to be found between Europe and its Muslim communities (*The Economist*, 2006b, p. 34). Equally, although xenophobia may be on the rise in Europe, many people in old, 'white' Europe reject such views and are searching for new means of engaging with their Islamic fellow citizens. In short, there is a struggle within Europe between forces pushing Europe and its Islamic communities towards conflict, and forces that might integrate Muslims successfully into mainstream European society. This struggle involves very large questions of national and European identity, and its outcome will have a significant bearing on Europe's future. It will also be likely to have a significant impact on the relationship between Islam and the West at the global level. Intensifying conflict between Europe and its Islamic communities will reinforce the view elsewhere in the Islamic world that the West is irredeemably anti-Islamic, and that Muslims have little alternative but to use violent means to defend themselves. In contrast, the successful integration of Europe's Muslim minority will provide a powerful illustration of the possibility of a peaceful relationship between Islam and the West. The emergence of a new European Islam that combines the Muslim faith with the values of liberalism and democracy might also be an influential exemplar of how these two sets of values can coexist elsewhere in the Islam world.

Counter-terrorism II: foreign policy and the root causes of terrorism

The rise of global Islamic terrorism has prompted much debate on the underlying causes of terrorism and how they may be addressed. The reality that the 'new terrorism' is essentially a phenomenon of the Islamic world and has emerged predominantly from the Greater Middle East – the region stretching from North Africa to Afghanistan and Pakistan, and from the Caucasus and Central Asia to the Persian Gulf – has led to debate over how the strategic, political and socio-economic environment that has given rise to globalized Islamic terror-ism can be altered. After 9/11, the Bush Administration argued that the democratization of the Greater Middle East would be the most effec-tive long-term means of undercutting terrorism, and sought to put in place a strategy to achieve this goal. While the Bush Administration's strategy was open to many criticisms, it laid out (at least in theory) a radical new blueprint for the region. In contrast, neither individual European governments nor the EU have adopted such a clear or radi-cal overarching strategy to address the root causes of terrorism.

Nevertheless, European governments and the EU have engaged in variety of policy initiatives, both in the Greater Middle East and glob-ally, which may contribute to addressing the root causes of terrorism and are to varying degrees focused implicitly on that objective. As was seen in Chapter 4, this has included efforts to support a settlement of the Israeli–Palestinian conflict and the Euro-Mediterranean Partnership (EMP) relationship with the EU's southern neighbours. To the extent that a resolution of the Israeli–Palestinian conflict would address an important underlying cause of Islamic terrorism – and that argument is, of course, contentious – the EU's ability to support such an outcome has been rather limited. Similarly, although the EU now meets regularly with its EMP partners and has invested significant sums in functional co-operation projects, progress in democratization, improving the human rights situation, and economic development on the southern shore of the Mediterranean has been limited. The underlying relationship between the EU and its Mediterranean neighbours remains one of unequal partnership, and a significant degree of mutual mistrust exists. North Africa, in particular Morocco and Algeria, remains a major source of terrorist concern for Europe, in terms of both attacks on European targets in the region and terrorist infiltration into Europe.

In addition, to its involvement in the Israeli–Palestinian conflict and the EMP, the EU also has various bilateral trade and co-operation relationships with the other states in the Greater Middle East, as well as a formal dialogue with the Gulf Cooperation Council (GCC – which brings together Bahrain, Kuwait, Oman, Qatar, Saudi Arabia and the United Arab Emirates). In 2004, EU heads of state and government approved a report on an *EU Strategic Partnership with the Mediterranean and the Middle East*, which sought to provide more coherence to the EU's policies towards the region (European Union, 2004b). The EU is, however, likely to continue to face significant obstacles in addressing the root causes of terrorism in the Greater Middle East. The EU has had most success in using its influence in Central and Eastern Europe, where the combination of the post-1989 shift towards democracy, the attraction of the EU's model and the conditionality associated with EU membership gave it real power. In the Greater Middle East, the legacy of European imperialism means that most people are deeply wary of Europe's intentions, the majority of the region's regimes have not even begun the processes of democratization, and – with the important exception of Turkey – EU membership is not a realistic prospect. In contrast, the USA's role as the key provider of economic and/or military aid to Israel, Egypt and Saudi Arabia, and its capacity to intervene militarily, give it a much greater influence in the region. As Rosemary Hollis has concluded, the influence of the EU's 'soft power' on the Greater Middle East remains much less than that of American 'hard power' (Hollis, 2005). Like the USA, European governments also face the difficult dilemma that political change in the region may well result in increased instability – at least in the short-term – and bring to power Islamic political forces more anti-Western in outlook than many of the region's current regimes. France's support for Algeria's authoritarian regime, and the UK and France's close ties with Saudi Arabia and the other GCC states (in the form of arms sales, as well as other security and intelligence links) suggest that Europe is likely to remain at best a cautious champion of political change in the Greater Middle East.

At the global level also, many aspects of European foreign policy may be viewed as part of overall efforts to address the root causes of terrorism. For some decades, Europe (in terms of the EU member states plus the separate aid programmes of the EU) has been the leading provider of economic aid to the developing world. To the extent that poverty and economic underdevelopment are viewed as important underlying causes of terrorism, Europe thus plays a leading role in international efforts to tackle these problems. European development policies and their relationship with security are examined in more detail in the next chapter. It should be noted here, however, that while Europe is relatively generous as an aid provider, it has been much more reluctant to open its markets to goods from the developing world, and subsidies to European agriculture and industry mean that the developing world does not compete with European agriculture and industry on a level playing field. If Europe is serious about using development policy as a strategic means of addressing poverty as a root cause of terrorism, there is a powerful case that it should do much more to address the difficult economic issues of market access for goods from the developing world *vis-à-vis* European agricultural and industrial subsidies.

European states and the EU also play a prominent role in international efforts to address another challenge that some analysts view as a key part of the context for globalized Islamic terrorism: civil wars and failed states. Since the 1990s, the EU has developed a growing interest and role in the area of conflict prevention. In 2001, the Union adopted an *EU Programme for the Prevention of Violent Conflicts* (European Union, 2001). Within this context, the EU has sought both to pay greater attention to conflict prevention (for example, through the development of detailed conflict prevention Country Strategy Papers focusing on countries that have experienced, or may be particularly vulnerable to, violent conflict), and on mainstreaming conflict prevention in its wider relations with third countries (by trying to ensure that political, trade, aid, environmental and other aspects of these relations take into account their impact on potential conflicts). A number of European governments, such as those of Sweden and the UK, have also sought to promote conflict prevention. In 1999, the Swedish government adopted an action plan for preventing violent conflict. This sought to strengthen its activities and enhance co-operation with partners in the area of conflict prevention (Swedish Ministry for Foreign Affairs, 1999). In 2001, the British government established two conflict prevention 'pools' (one global and one focused specifically on Africa) which provide dedicated funding for conflict prevention activities, and seek to integrate the policies of the different branches of the British government (in particular the Foreign and Commonwealth Office, the Department for International Development and the Ministry of Defence) (Foreign and Commonwealth Office, 2003; Department for International Development, 2004).

Addressing the root causes of terrorism is inherently problematical. Our understanding of the causes of terrorism is limited and the question of what factors lie behind the emergence of globalized Islam terrorism is deeply contentious. Even if it is correct that conflicts in the Islamic world, failed states and economic underdevelopment are the key underlying causes of globalized Islamic terrorism, these are very large, long-term problems that will not be addressed easily. Europe's ability to influence, let along resolve, these problems is limited, and whether European leaders and publics are willing to provide the resources and take the difficult political decisions necessary to address these problems is open to serious doubt. While European governments may be correct to argue that the international community should do more to tackle the long-term causes of terrorism, translating that desire into effective action is likely to remain extremely challenging.

Conclusion

Europe is likely to face an ongoing major challenge from globalized Islamic terrorism: alongside the USA, European states are among the primary targets for external terrorism; parallel to this, alienation among significant sections of Europe's growing indigenous Muslim population means that the continent also faces a significant *internal* terrorist threat and threatens to make Europe one of the 'fields of jihad' of the twenty-first century.

European states and institutions, especially the EU, face major dilemmas in responding to the threat posed by globalized Islamic terrorism. The various internal and external security measures that European states have undertaken – nationally, collectively through the

EU, and together with the USA – have reopened the long-standing debate on the balance between security and libert, and calibrating that balance will be an ongoing challenge for governments and publics alike. Europe also faces major challenges in integrating its growing Muslim population: the limitations of both the assimilationist and the multicultural models suggests that a new approach is needed, but the debate on this question will involve fundamental issues of national and European identity.

The US 'war on terror' also poses major challenges for Europe. As this chapter has shown, Europeans are generally wary of, if not opposed to, central aspects of the US 'war on terror'. There is a powerful case that the US 'war on terror' has indeed produced an approach to counter-terrorism that is overly militarized and has exacerbated, rather than reduced, anti-Western sentiment and support for terrorism in the Islam world. While Europeans may be right to criticize central elements of the US approach to counter-terrorism post-9/11, articulating, let alone implementing, an alternative approach has proved to be more difficult. The development of a long-term approach to counter-terrorism, in particular one that addresses the root causes of terrorism, thus remains a central challenge for both individual European states and the EU as a whole.

Chapter 9

Soft Security

As discussed in Chapter 2, there has since the 1980s been a growing acceptance of the idea of a wider, non-military or soft security agenda. This redefinition of the concept of security has two elements. First, it is recognized increasingly that, while military means are central to war, the underlying causes of war and large-scale violent conflict are largely non-military, relating to political conflicts, economics and the environment. Second, non-military problems such as economic instability, environmental degradation and organized crime are increasingly viewed, in themselves, as major threats to the security of states and societies. The primary European security organizations have accepted the logic behind this new, wider security agenda and have to varying degrees been at the forefront of efforts to respond to the challenges it poses. Since it was established in the 1970s, the then Conference on (now Organization for) Security and Co-operation in Europe (C/OSCE) has pioneered the concept of a comprehensive security agenda, including issues such as human rights, democracy, economics and the environment. The EU's unique combination of political foreign policy co-operation, an emerging military role, justice and home affairs co-operation and economic, social and environmental competences means that it operates across the entire spectrum of issues that constitute the wider security agenda. Even NATO, which was (and arguably remains) an essentially military organization, is now 'committed to a broad approach to security, which recognizes the importance of political, economic, social and environmental factors' (NATO, 1999, para. 25). There is also increasing acceptance that the best long-term means of preventing violent conflict both between and within states are through political and economic co-operation and the promotion of democracy and good governance. In this context, the EU may be viewed as an unprecedented – and remarkably successful – exercise in long-term conflict prevention, having helped to transform much of Europe into the largely peaceful security community of the early twenty-first century. The EU is thus the leader and archetype of this new approach to security-building, and it is no coincidence that other

192

regional organizations – the Association of South East Asian Nations (ASEAN), the Southern Common Market (MERCOSUR) and the African Union (AU), for example – have to varying degrees sought to model themselves on the EU.

Although increasingly accepted by governments and international organizations, the concept of a wider, non-military security agenda is not unproblematical. The nature of the wider security agenda is amorphous: what does or does not constitute a security issue is unclear, as is the point at which a problem becomes (or should be viewed as) a security threat rather simply a part of normal politics. Defining a particular challenge – global warming, say, or organized crime – as a security threat or challenge, does not necessarily make any difference to the nature of that challenge, nor even perhaps to the way societies respond to it. The definition of an issue as a security threat or challenge – the process of securitization (Buzan *et al.*, 1998) – may also have negative consequences, importing undesirable security dynamics into previously non-security areas by encouraging a defensive fortress-type response.

Even if the widening of the security agenda to include a range of non-military challenges is sensible, the policy challenges of responding to the wider security agenda are very large indeed. Problems such as global poverty, economic instability, environmental degradation, weak states, mass migration and organized crime have deep roots and are not easily addressed. Addressing the wider security agenda is thus a massive, long-term challenge: a decades-long task requiring the mobilization of global political will and large-scale material resources. This chapter focuses on three key non-military security issues – economic development policy, global warming, and migration – exploring European engagement with these challenges.

Economic development policy

Economic underdevelopment and poverty are arguably at the heart of the new, wider security agenda. Economic underdevelopment and poverty contribute to the internal weakness of many states, civil wars and larger North–South tensions. As the EU's 2003 *European Security Strategy* put it:

> In much of the developing world, poverty and disease cause untold suffering and give rise to pressing security concerns. Almost 3 billion people, half the world's population, live on less than 2 Euros a day.

45 million die every year of hunger and malnutrition . . . In many cases, economic failure is linked to political problems and violent conflict . . . A number of countries and regions are caught in a cycle of conflict, insecurity and poverty. (European Union, 2003a)

Similarly, the Union's *European Consensus on Development*, adopted in 2005 as a new framework for EU development policy, argues that:

The context within which poverty eradication is pursued is an increasingly globalized world; this situation has created new opportunities but also new challenges. Combating global poverty is not only a moral obligation; it will also help to build a more stable, peaceful, prosperous and equitable world, reflecting the interdependency of its richer and poorer countries . . . without development and poverty eradication no sustainable peace will occur. (European Union, 2005c, pp. 3 and 12)

Europe, in particular the EU, is a key player in international economic development policy. The EU – considered as its member states plus the European Commission, which runs a separate EU development aid programme – is the largest donor of economic development to aid poor countries. Table 9.1 indicates levels of overseas development aid (ODA – the most widely used official definition of aid) provided by the EU, Japan and the USA – the main donor countries – since the 1980s. As can be seen from the table, EU member states have provided over half of the total ODA since the 1990s (the total EU figure is a little higher, as the table does not include the aid programme run by the European Commission). The EU's contribution of ODA relative to that the other leading aid donors has also increased significantly since the 1980s. In terms of ODA as a percentage of donors' gross national income (GNI) – one of the main ways of comparing aid – the average for EU member states was 0.3 per cent of GNI in 2003–4, compared to 0.16 per cent for the USA (the USA, of all the developed states, has since the 1980s consistently allocated the lowest percentage of GNI to aid) and 0.19 per cent for Japan. While the EU may be more generous as an aid provider than the USA and Japan, the EU's generosity should not be exaggerated. Since 1969, developed countries have, in theory, been committed to achieving a target of 0.7 per cent of GNP for aid within ten years – a target they have consistently failed to meet. While a small number of European states (Denmark, Luxembourg, the Netherlands, Norway and Sweden) have met this target, the majority

TABLE 9.1 *European, Japanese and US contributions to development aid*

	Volume of net ODA (mn US$ at 2003 prices and exchange rates)			Share of total DAC ODA (% at current prices and exchange rate)			ODA as percentage of GNI (two-year averages, net disbursements)		
	1983–94	1993–4	2003–4	1983–94	1993–4	2003–4	1983–94	1993–4	2003–4
EU members	27,179	34,333	37,661	43.0	51.8	53.8	0.34	0.30	0.25
Japan	8,832	10,194	8,689	14.7	21.3	12.0	0.33	0.28	0.19
USA	13,392	11,900	17,815	30.6	17.4	24.2	0.24	0.15	0.16
Total DAC	54,683	62,756	71,119	100	100	100	0.34	0.30	0.25

Notes: ODA = Overseas Development Aid; DAC = (members of) OECD Development Assistance Committee; DAC also includes other states.
Data from: Organisation for Economic Co-operation and Development (OECD) Development Assistance Committee (DAC), *Statistical Annex of the 2005 Development Co-operation Report*, OECD DAC website: www.oecd.org/dac/stats/dac/dcrannex (accessed 10 August 2006).

of EU member states have not come close to it, nor has the EU as a whole. Although the EU has increased its aid as a proportion of GNP/GNI since the early 2000s, EU aid levels are still less than they were in the 1980s and 1990s (Zupi, 2005, pp. 44–6).

Since the late 1990s there has been increasing debate on international development policy and economic aid. In 2000, the UN adopted the Millennium Development Goals (MDGs), a set of core development targets – including, for example, reducing by half the proportion of people living on less than one dollar a day, reducing by half the proportion of people who suffer hunger, and reducing by two-thirds the mortality rate for children under five – to be achieved by 2015. It is estimated that achieving the MDGs will require an additional US$50bn in aid per year – a near doubling of existing aid levels. In response to this, in May–June 2005 the EU committed to a major increase in ODA to 0.7 per cent of GNI for the fifteen 'old' EU member states by 2015, and 0.33 per cent of GNI for the ten states that joined the EU in 2004. Following this, at their July 2005 summit in Gleneagles, Scotland, the G8 (Group of 8) states committed to providing an additional US$50bn in aid per year by 2010. Critics have argued that a significant part of these initiatives, in particular from the G8, involves repackaging existing commitments and the double-counting of some activities (for example, by counting debt relief as aid) and that the real increase in aid will be substantially less than the $50bn headline figure. It remains to be seen how far the EU and other developed states will meet these commitments. If the EU achieves the 0.7 per cent of GNI target for aid, the Union's role as the leading provider of development assistance will be reinforced (unless, of course, there is a similar increase in US aid).

Parallel to the debate on aid since the 1990s has been a new debate about the relationship between trade and economic (under)development in poor countries. Most economists agree that trade liberalization – the reciprocal removal of barriers to free trade between states – promotes economic growth and development. In this context, the developed states of the world – the EU, but also the USA, Japan, Canada and Australia – have been subject to growing criticism regarding their protectionist trade practices towards developing countries, and in particular their use of subsidies to support agriculture (which means that developing countries do not compete on a level playing field) and trade barriers (which undermine the ability of poor countries to export goods to the developed world). It is estimated that the protectionist trade policies of developed countries cost poor countries over

US$100bn a year – twice what they receive in aid. Although all developing countries practise such protectionist policies, Oxfam estimates that of the 'quad' of major industrialized countries – the USA, the EU, Japan and Canada – the EU is marginally the most protectionist (Oxfam International, 2002, pp. 8–9, 96–101). In short, while the EU may be comparatively generous as a donor of development aid, there is a powerful argument that whatever good is done by European aid is undermined by European trade protectionism on an even larger scale.

The international response to growing criticism of developed countries' protectionism was the Doha development round of World Trade Organization (WTO) negotiations, launched in Doha, Qatar, in 2001. One of the central aims of the Doha round is to extend trade liberalization into the areas of greatest benefit to poor countries, in particular by removing tariffs and reducing subsidies in agriculture and textiles. The Doha round of WTO negotiations was thus a key test of multilateral trade liberalization as a means of benefiting the poorer countries of the world. Negotiations, however, broke down amid acrimony at meetings in Cancun, Mexico, in 2003 and again in Geneva in July 2006. Exact responsibility for the failure of these negotiations was controversial, but the underlying cause was the reluctance of the developing world, in particular the EU and the USA, to agree to reduce trade barriers and make far-reaching cuts in subsidies in relation to agriculture and textiles (Elliott, 2006). The 2006 breakdown in negotiations, further, raised the possibility of the Doha development round failing completely. The failure of the Doha development round would be a major, and perhaps permanent, setback to the goal of using multilateral trade liberalization as a key means of addressing poverty and underdevelopment in the Third World. As one of the world's two economic, trade and agricultural superpowers, alongside the USA, and a central actor within the WTO, the EU must bear a major share of the responsibility for the outcome of the Doha development round.

These debates on development and trade have in turn prompted growing discussion about the EU's Common Agricultural Policy (CAP). The CAP supports European agriculture, through a variety of subsidies, to the tune of more than €40bn annually. Critics argue that the CAP contributes to poverty in the Third World because it makes it impossible for developing-world farmers to compete with subsidized European agriculture, while the EU's reluctance to make a serious attempt at reforming the CAP has been a major obstacle to progress in the Doha WTO negotiations. Since the late 1990s there has been a series of reforms to the CAP, but these have been limited in nature, not altering the underlying reality that the EU continues to subsidize European agriculture on a massive scale. Some critics argue that agricultural subsidies should be phased out completely (*Guardian*, 2003). There remains strong support for the CAP, however, within some EU member states, in particular France and Germany. Any reform to the CAP faces the challenge of overcoming a powerful farming lobby, as well as an emotional attachment to the countryside. Jacques Delors, French politician and president of the European Commission in the 1980s and 1990s, for example, has argued that he would not sacrifice the French countryside on the altar of world trade (Charlemagne, 2003, p. 31). Given ongoing budgetary pressures, the CAP is likely to be the subject of further reforms. The extent and speed of CAP reform, however, will be a major test of the EU's willingness to give further substance to its commitment to supporting development in poorer parts of the world.

The EU has long played a central role in international development policy, as a donor of aid, through its bilateral and multilateral relationships with the developing world and in global trade negotiations. While the EU is a relatively generous donor of aid compared to the USA and some other developing countries, total EU aid levels have (until quite recently) fallen significantly, in real terms, since the 1980s. It remains to be seen how far the 2005 decision to meet the target of contributing 0.7 per cent of GNI to aid by 2015 will be achieved, but this commitment will – if achieved – amount to a doubling or more of EU aid. On trade, in contrast, the EU's record is much poorer, with its protectionist barriers and subsidies (in particular the CAP) acting as major obstacles to economic development in the Third World. The causes and cures of economic underdevelopment and poverty are, of course, the subject of a much larger debate, the scope of which cannot be addressed here. Nevertheless, aid and trade provide two major tests of Europe's willingness to translate its rhetoric on development into action that could help to lift millions of people in the Third World out of poverty.

Global warming

As was argued in Chapter 2, the most important global environmental security challenge is climate change or global warming (sometimes also referred to as the greenhouse effect). Global warming is the net increase in the earth's temperature resulting from the increased presence of so-called greenhouse gases (GHGs), such as carbon dioxide, methane and nitrous oxide, in the earth's atmosphere. Like a greenhouse, these gases trap heat in the atmosphere, resulting in an increase in the earth's temperature. There is a broad international scientific consensus that very significant global warming is occurring, and that human activity is largely responsible for this warming. Scientists estimate that concentrations of carbon dioxide (the main greenhouse gas) in the atmosphere are at their highest level for the last half a million years, and that the earth is warming more rapidly than at any time in at least the last thousand years. The Intergovernmental Panel on Climate Change (IPCC) – the global body co-ordinating scientific research on global warming – estimates that global temperatures rose by 0.6°C in the twentieth century and may rise by between 1.4°C and 5.8°C in the twenty-first century (Maslin, 2004, p. 1). The agricultural and industrial bases of modern human society have caused very large-scale GHG emissions, and there is a broad scientific consensus that anthropogenic GHG emissions – emissions resulting from human activity – are largely responsible for global warming. In particular, the use of fossil fuels (oil, gas and coal) for energy production, industrial processes and transport are the primary sources of anthropogenic GHG emissions.

Global warming is likely to have – indeed, is almost certainly already having – a number of major effects, most of which may either be viewed as security threats in their own right or will exacerbate other major security problems (such as new wars, mass migration and diseases) – see Box 9.1. Europe is less vulnerable to the consequences of global warming than much of the Third World, in particular Africa and parts of Asia and South America. Nevertheless, Europe will not be immune to the impact of global warming. The summer 2003 European heatwave, which may be attributed to global warming, caused more than 20,000 deaths. According to Stephen Tindale, the director of Greenpeace UK:

> There are two – equally bleak – scenarios for Europe. A gradual rise in temperatures could bring most of the continent within the range of tropical diseases such as malaria, and push southern Europe's regular shortages of fresh water to crisis levels. Global water shortages would affect perhaps three billion people, driving many millions of environmental refugees to mass at EU borders. Alternatively, the Gulf Stream could fail, tipping Europe into a new ice age. (Tindale, 2006, p. 1)

Box 9.1　The consequences of global warming

The emerging and likely future consequences of global warming include:

- *Rising sea levels*, which will threaten river delta-based regions and small island nations.
- *Altered weather patterns*, including more frequent and severe storms, hurricanes and tornadoes (resulting in a consequent increase in flooding), and more frequent and severe droughts and heatwaves.
- *The spread of diseases* into areas previously free from them; for example, as increased temperatures allow disease-carrying mosquitoes to move into these areas.
- *Eco-system disruption and loss of species diversity* as a result of climatic change.
- *Disruption of agriculture* as the climatic conditions and weather patterns on which it has rested alter.
- *Mass migration*, in particular as a result of rising sea levels but also as a consequence of other effects of global warming (such as the disruption of eco-systems and agriculture).
- *Increased likelihood of environmental and resource conflicts* as the effects of global warming increase competition for limited environmental and economic resources.

Data from: Mark Maslin, *Global Warming: A Very Short Introduction* (Oxford: Oxford University Press, 2004), pp. 83–101; and Natural Resources Defense Council (n.d.) *Consequences of Global Warming*, Natural Resources Defense Council website: http://www.nrdc.org/globalWarming/fcons.asp (accessed 16 August 2006).

There are two additional interrelated risks associated with global warming. The first is the possibility of a very major climatic shock. This risk relates to the possibility of massive and very rapid changes in global climate dynamics if the world's deep ocean (and related atmospheric) circulation patterns alter as a result of global warming. If the Gulf Stream, which warms Europe, is diverted – which is a possibility – much of the continent could be turned into an arctic or semi-arctic environment. The second danger is of so-called runaway global warming, where major additional increases in GHG emissions result in temperatures rising much more rapidly than currently predicted. In this scenario, global warming itself may cause further massive releases of GHGs – for example, from beneath the Siberian permafrost or the deep ocean seabeds – thereby dramatically accelerating the warming

process. The likelihood of these two developments are difficult to estimate and may be quite low, but both are real possibilities. Even if such
worst case scenarios do not come about, scientists argue that major
reductions in GHG emissions – up to 60 per cent of current levels – are
required in coming decades if global warming is to be contained and its
consequences mitigated (Maslin, 2004, pp. 118, 126).

Europe has played a central role in relation to global warming –
historically as a major producer of GHGs and since the 1990s as a leading force in international efforts to limit these emissions. The industrialized developed world, including Europe, has been responsible for the
majority of anthropogenic GHG emissions to date. Table 9.2 summarizes past, recent and projected future GHG emissions for the EU and a
number of other major developed and developing states. The EU
currently contributes about a fifth of total anthropogenic GHG emissions and Russia about a tenth, compared to about a third for the
United States (the world's largest producer). Given Europe's historic
and current role as a major GHG producer, there is an obvious case
that it should play a significant role in global efforts to reduce GHG
emissions. As China and India, the countries with the largest populations in the world, continue their economic and industrial development
in coming decades, their contribution – and that of other developing
counties – to GHG emissions will grow significantly. In the longer
term, therefore, reducing GHG emissions will also require the drawing
of developing states into reduction processes.

The EU has played a central role in efforts to establish an international regime to limit GHG emissions since negotiations began in the
late 1980s (Bretherton and Vogler, 2006, pp. 105–9). A UN
Framework Convention on Climate Change (UNFCCC) was agreed at
the Rio Earth Summit in 1992, establishing the goal of reducing GHG
emissions. Negotiations proceeded throughout the 1990s, with the EU
leading the case for legally binding emission reduction targets. The
Kyoto Protocol was signed in 1997, committing developed states to
reduce their GHG emissions by 5.2 per cent, compared to 1990 levels,
by 2012 (within this the EU was to reduce its GHG emissions by 8 per
cent and the USA by 7 per cent). Developing states were excluded from
legally binding emission reduction targets under the Kyoto agreement.
The Kyoto Protocol also includes other important elements, in particular a planned emissions trading scheme (under which GHG emission
rights can be bought and sold, thereby creating an incentive for countries and companies to reduce their GHG emissions and gain the right
to sell their spare capacity) and a Clean Development Mechanism

TABLE 9.2 Past, present and future greenhouse gas (GHG) emissions

Country/Group	Percentage of world GHG emissions 2000	Percentage of world population 2000	GHG emissions per capita 2000 (tons C equiv.)	Percentage of cumulative world GHG emissions 1850–2000	Emissions growth 1990–2000 (%)	Projected GHG emissions 2000–25 (% growth) – low and high growth estimates	
						Low	High
USA	20.6	4.7	6.6	29.8	18	20	52
China	14.8	20.9	1.1	7.3	39	50	181
EU-25	14.0	7.5	2.8	27.2	-3	-1*	39*
Russia	5.7	2.4	3.6	8.3	-22	37**	109**
India	5.5	16.8	0.5	2.0	64	73	225
Japan	4.0	2.1	2.9	4.1	12	4	46
Brazil	2.5	2.8	1.3	0.8	53	84	165
Mexico	1.5	1.6	1.4	1.0	25	68	215

Notes: * = EU-15; ** = Former Soviet Union.

Data from: Kevin Baumert and Jonathan Pershing, Climate Data: Insights and Observations (Arlington, Va.: Pew Center on Global Climate Change, 2004), http://www.pewclimate.org/docUploads/Climate%20Data%20new%20per%20cent2Epdf (accessed 18 August 2006).

(which allows developed countries or companies to implement GHG-reducing technologies in developing countries and gain the credit for such reductions). The USA, under the Clinton Administration, signed the Kyoto Protocol in 1997, but in the same year the Senate passed a resolution refusing to commit the USA to any reduction agreement that did not include binding targets for developing countries, making it clear that it would not ratify Kyoto. From this point in particular, the EU became the driving force behind the Kyoto Protocol. In 2001, the Bush Administration stated its unwillingness to ratify or implement the Kyoto Protocol, with US National Security Advisor Condoleezza Rice describing the agreement as 'dead' (Borger, 2001). The EU, however, continued to pursue the ratification and implementation of Kyoto. The EU was central to persuading other states, in particular Japan and Russia, to ratify the Kyoto Protocol – a key hurdle, since Kyoto could only come into force if fifty-five states accounting for at least 55 per cent of developed-world GHG emissions ratified the agreement. Russia agreed to ratify the agreement at a May 2004 EU–Russia summit and the Kyoto Protocol came into force in February 2005. Without the EU's leadership, there would have been no agreement with legally binding GHG emission reduction targets, and that agreement would not have been ratified or come into force.

The Kyoto Protocol, and by implication the EU's approach to global warming, is, however, an easy target for criticism. The Kyoto emission reduction target of 5.2 per cent for developed states is far below the 60 per cent that scientists suggest will be necessary to seriously curb global warming. It is unclear what will happen if states fail to meet their Kyoto emission reduction targets. The agreement is fundamentally weakened by the refusal of the USA, the world's largest GHG producer, to sign up to the process, and the absence of emission reduction targets for China, India and other developing states, which will be among the largest GHG producers in the future. Nevertheless, Kyoto can be viewed as a vital first step in a long-term process: it established the principles of global emission reduction targets and legally binding national targets within this, as well as other mechanisms that may be central to long-term global efforts to reduce GHG emissions (in particular, the emissions trading scheme and the Clean Development Mechanism). On the basis of the Kyoto Protocol, in 2005 the EU established its own emissions trading scheme (ETS), which will operate alongside national schemes in member states, but will also be open to participation by states and companies outside the Union (European Commission, 2005). As the first such regional scheme, the EU's ETS is likely to become the global standard and draw in states and companies from beyond the EU, including countries that are not signatories to the Kyoto Protocol. Emissions trading, and the EU's central role within this, may thus become one of the key mechanisms by which both Kyoto signatories and non-signatories are drawn into a longer-term GHG emission reduction process (Luterbacher, 2005, pp. 31–2).

While the EU played the leading role in the negotiation and ratification of the Kyoto Protocol, implementing the Kyoto GHG reduction targets has posed major challenges for the Union and its members. Table 9.3 summarizes GHG emissions in relationship to the Kyoto base year of 1990, the Kyoto target for the EU as a whole and for some of the Union's major members. The fifteen old EU member states accepted a collective GHG reduction target under Kyoto and then negotiated an internal EU burden-sharing agreement, under which some states agreed to make larger reductions while others were permitted GHG emission increases. The ten states that joined the Union in 2004, after the Kyoto agreement had been signed, have separate national targets. As can be seen, while some of the EU-15 (such as Germany and the UK) have reduced their GHG emissions significantly, others (such as Spain and Greece) have substantially increased theirs. The Central and Eastern European states that joined the Union in 2004 have reduced their GHG emissions by about a third, reflecting the industrial contraction they experienced immediately after the collapse of communism. The EU-15 reduced their collective GHG emissions by only 1.7 per cent between 1990 and 2003, but are projected to reduce emissions by 6.8 per cent of 1990 levels by 2010, leaving them 1.2 per cent short of the Kyoto target. GHG emissions by the EU-15, however, rose by 0.3 per cent between 2003 and 2004, with emissions increasing in ten of the fifteen member states (European Environment Agency, 2006). As of 2006, it was unclear whether the EU would reach its Kyoto target by the final deadline of 2012. Critics argue that EU member states have been far too slow and cautious in supporting alternative (non-fossil-fuel) energy production, energy conservation and new low-carbon technologies. The problems the EU has faced in implementing even the limited Kyoto GHG emission reductions suggest that achieving much larger, long-term reductions will pose a major challenge. Growing recognition of the scale of the problem posed by global warming, combined with increasing concern about rising oil prices and limited oil reserves, however, may generate the political momentum necessary to achieve more radical cuts in GHG emissions. In 2006, for example, the Swedish government announced plans to make Sweden an oil-free

TABLE 9.3 EU greenhouse gas emissions (GHG) and the Kyoto target

Country/Group	1990 – base year (Mt CO2)	2003 (Mt CO2)	Change 1990–2003 (% of base year)	EU burden-sharing and Kyoto targets (% of base year)	Projections for 2010, with additional policies and measures (% of base year)	Gap between projections and target (% of base year)
EU-15	4252.4	4179.6	-1.7	-8.0	-6.8	+1.2
EU-10	1099.8	745.5	-32.2	-6.7*	-19.6*	-12.8
EU-25	5352.2	4925.1	-8.0	-7.7*	-9.3*	-1.6
France	568.0	557.2	-1.9	0.0	-1.7	-1.7
Germany	1248.3	1017.5	-18.5	-21.0	-21.0	-0.0
Italy	510.3	569.8	+11.6	-6.5	+4.1	+10.6
Poland	565.3	384.0	-32.1	-6.0	-12.1	-6.1
Spain	286.1	402.3	+40.6	+15.0	+28.0	+13.0
UK	751.4	651.1	-13.3	-12.5	no data	no data

Note: * excludes Cyprus and Malta because they have no Kyoto targets.
Data from: European Commission, *Commission Staff Working Document: Annex to the Report from the Commission Progress Towards Achieving the Community's Kyoto Target*, Com(2005)655 Final (Brussels: Commission of the European Communities, 2005), 15 December, http://ec.europa.eu/environment/climat/pdf/comm_2005_655_anx.pdf (accessed 4 September 2006).

economy by 2020 (Vidal, 2006). Analysts argue that if the EU wants to achieve further reductions in GHG emissions it needs to ban subsidies to polluting energy sources (such as coal-fired power stations), direct funds towards renewable energy, and reform its ETS (where overall emission limits are too high and poorly policed) (Tindale, 2006).

As was noted above, limiting global warming will require much larger, long-term reductions in global GHG emissions than are required by the Kyoto Protocol. The Kyoto Protocol called for the initiation by the end of 2005 of international negotiations on a post-2012 climate change regime. In preparing for these negotiations, the EU called for 'the widest possible cooperation of all countries' – that is, including both the USA and developing countries – and argued that developed countries – that is, the EU, but also the US and other developed states – should pursue a GHG emission reduction pathway 'in the order of 15–30 per cent by 2020' compared to the 1990 Kyoto baseline (Council of the European Union, 2005, para. 46; see also Commission of the European Communities, 2005).

Negotiations in Montreal, Canada in November–December 2005 resulted in a commitment among the developed country signatories of the Kyoto Protocol to begin negotiations for a post-2012 agreement and a commitment among the larger group of members of the UNFCCC – including both the USA and developing countries – to 'engage in a dialogue . . . for long term cooperative action to address climate change' (UNFCCC, 2005a, 2005b). The latter agreement was an achievement for the EU, since it brought the USA and developing countries into the post-Kyoto negotiating process, although only on the basis of an 'open and non-binding exchange of views . . . [that] will not open any negotiations leading to new commitments' (Revkin, 2005; UNFCCC, 2005b). Meaningful long-term reductions in GHG emissions will, however, require the constructive involvement of both the USA and major developing countries such as China and India. The ability of the EU to bring these countries into future reduction processes will be one of the central challenges for Europe in responding to climate change – and a major test of the EU's pretensions to international leadership.

Population movements

The movement of people has become an increasingly prominent and controversial issue in European politics since the 1980s: questions relating to migration, refugees, asylum seekers, the free movement of labour, and border controls are now a central part of political debate in most European countries. These issues, furthermore, are increasingly discussed in security terms: as actual or potential threats to the security, welfare and identity of states and societies.

A number of trends in migration within and into Europe can be identified. Since the Second World War, Europe has 'experienced a historical shift from emigration to immigration' (International Organization for Migration, 2005, p. 141). Historically, European states were a major global source of emigrants, as they populated their colonies and empires as well as the new states of the USA, Canada, Australia and New Zealand. From the 1950s and 1960s, however, growing demand for labour made Western Europe a major destination for immigration (Weiner, 1995, pp. 21–5). Since then, immigration into Europe, primarily Western Europe, has increased significantly. The number of immigrants in Western Europe increased from 10 million in 1970 to 29 million in 2000, and for Europe as a whole – including Central and Eastern Europe and the former Soviet Union – from 19 million to 33 million (although a significant part of the latter increase is accounted for by the break-up of the Soviet Union, which overnight turned previously internal migrants into international migrants) (International Organization for Migration, 2005, p. 381). Other estimates suggested that by the early 2000s the immigrant population in Europe (excluding the former Soviet Union) was between 36 and 39 million (or 8 per cent of the total population), about a fifth of the world's total immigrant population (International Organization for Migration, 2005, pp. 144, 152).

Table 9.4 provides details of annual migration into the EU and a number of other major developed countries since the early 1990s (the years 1992, 1997 and 2001 are illustrative, and numbers of immigrants have been broadly similar since the early 1990s). As can be seen, well over 1 million migrants enter EU countries every year. As a consequence, since the early 1990s, many European countries have experienced major increases in migrant populations, with numbers of migrants more than doubling in Finland, Ireland, Italy, Portugal and Spain, and increasing by 50 per cent or more in Austria, Denmark, Luxembourg and the UK (International Organization for Migration, 2005, p. 385). In 2003, the European countries with the net largest immigration were Spain (+594,000), Italy (+511,000), Germany (+166,000), the UK (+103,000), Turkey (+98,000), Portugal (+64,000) and France (+55,000) (International Organization for Migration,

TABLE 9.4 *Migration: inflows of foreign population into EU and selected OECD countries (000s)*

Country/Group	1992	1997	2001
EU*	1,727.6	1,155.6	1,465.7
Australia**	107.4	85.8	88.9
Canada**	252.8	216.0	250.3
Japan	267.0	274.8	351.2
Switzerland	112.1	70.1	99.5
USA**	974.0	798.4	1,064.3

Notes: * EU figures exclude Austria, Greece, Ireland and Italy; ** permanent inflows (excludes temporary inflows).
Data from: Organisation for Economic Co-operation and Development (OECD), *Trends in International Migration* (Paris: OECD, 2003), table A.1.1, Inflows of foreign population into selected OECD countries; http://www.oecd.org/dataoecd/23/50/34641722.xls.

2005, p. 141). While a significant part of migration into EU countries is from other EU states, the majority of migrants are nevertheless third-country nationals: in 2000–1, for example, of 20 million migrants in EU-15 states, 14 million were third-country nationals (International Organization for Migration, 2005, p. 142). Southern Europe has the fastest-growing immigrant population in the early twenty-first century. In 2003, Spain had an estimated 2.66 million immigrants, and the large numbers of irregular immigrants in Spain, Italy, Portugal and Greece has led these countries to undertake periodic regularization programmes under which irregular immigrants are granted residence and work permits (International Organization for Migration, 2005, p. 147).

The interrelated issues of asylum seekers, refugees and illegal immigrants have also become increasingly controversial in Europe since the 1980s. It is estimated that the number of refugees in Europe (including the former Soviet Union) rose from 600,000 in 1970 to 2.4 million in 2000 (International Organization for Migration, 2005, p. 399). More significant, however, are the numbers of asylum seekers – that is, those claiming political asylum and seeking recognized refugee status. Table 9.5 provides details of the numbers of asylum seekers entering the EU and other major developed countries since the early 1990s. Between 250,000 and 500,000 asylum seekers have entered the EU annually

TABLE 9.5   *Inflows of asylum seekers into EU and selected OECD countries (000s)*

Country/Group	1993	1998	2002
EU	517.5	307.6	282.6
Australia	4.9	8.1	6.0
Canada	21.1	24.6	33.4
Japan	0.1	0.1	0.3
Switzerland	24.7	41.3	26.2
USA	144.2	55.4	63.4

Data from: Organisation for Economic Co-operation and Development (OECD), *Trends in International Migration* (Paris: OECD, 2003), table A.1.1. Inflows of asylum seekers into selected OECD countries, http://www.oecd.org/dataoecd/23/48/34641759.xls.

since the early 1990s. The EU receives approximately two-thirds of the total number of asylum seekers entering major developed countries. The majority of applications for refugee status are rejected and while some asylum seekers are returned to their countries of origin, many remain, with such 'disappeared asylum-seekers' becoming illegal immigrants.

Estimates of the numbers of illegal immigrants in Europe are inherently problematical. Illegal immigrants include those entering countries illegally, 'disappeared asylum-seekers' and those who overstay their legal visas. Jandl (2003) estimates that there are between 2.6 and 6.4 million illegal immigrants in Western Europe, with a medium estimate of 4 million, and that, as of the early 2000s, approximately 650,000 illegal immigrants were entering the EU-15 and 150,000 the ten states that joined the EU in 2004.

These trends in population movements into Europe reflect a long-term pattern discernible since the 1970s, the defining feature of which is the global migration of people from the poorer southern part of the world to the richer northern areas. The end of the Cold War, however, added an new dimension to population movements within Europe. The opening of the old Iron Curtain border allowed people to move between Eastern and Western Europe in significant numbers for the first time in four decades. The massive and uncontrolled movements of people from East to West which some observers feared might follow the end of the Cold War, however, did not happen. Western European states maintained relatively tight immigration policies and border controls, and the scale of both legal and illegal immigration from Eastern to Western Europe was thus limited. Germany was a partial exception to this trend, receiving between 280,000 and 500,000 migrants annually from post-communist Europe, not only ethnic Germans entitled to German citizenship but also other Eastern Europeans, from the mid-1980s onwards (International Organization for Migration, 1995, p. 384).

The Yugoslav wars of the 1990s did, however, create major conflict-driven population movements within Europe for the first time since the Second World War. Between 1991 and 1999, the Yugoslav wars generated over 3.7 million refugees and internally displaced persons (IDPs – people displaced from their homes but remaining in their country of origin) (Radovic, 2005, pp. 12–13). The first phases of the Yugoslav wars in Slovenia, Croatia and especially Bosnia between 1991 and 1995 created nearly 1.7 million refugees and 1.3 million IDPs. In the 1999 Kosovo war, nearly one million of Kosovo's two million population fled (primarily to neighbouring Macedonia, Albania and Montenegro) and another half a million were internally displaced within Kosovo. The majority of Kosovo's population, however, returned in the second half of 1999, following the deployment of a NATO peacekeeping force. The Kosovo war also illustrated the way in which population movements can exacerbate conflict situations in neighbouring states: the temporary influx of large numbers of Kosovar Albanians into Macedonia increased tensions between that country's majority Macedonian population and its own ethnic Albanian minority, while the porous Kosovo–Macedonia border allowed Albanian guerrillas in Kosovo and Macedonia to make common cause, resulting in low-level warfare between Albanian guerrillas and Macedonian government forces in 2001. The Yugoslav wars also left a significant long-term refugee/IDP problem: as of 2004, Bosnia still had over 309,000 IDPs and 229,000 Bosnian refugees outside the country, while Serbia-Montenegro had 276,000 refugees and 248,000 IDPs within its borders (UNHCR, 2004). It should be noted that the majority of refugees from the Yugoslav conflict moved into neighbouring states in the Balkans rather than Western Europe: with the exception of Germany which had accepted 345,000 Yugoslav refugees by 1995, other Western European states received much smaller numbers of refugees (Radovic, 2005, p. 12).

Similar patterns of conflict-driven migration have also occurred in the former Soviet Union – in particular, the Caucasus – since the early

1990s. The conflict between Armenia and Azerbaijan over Nagorno-Karabakh created refugee populations in both countries of over 200,000, and 600,000 IDPs within Azerbaijan; conflicts in Georgia generated more than 200,000 IDPs; and the conflict in Chechnya displaced about 500,000 people (UNHCR, 2004). This migration has essentially remained limited to the states/regions involved in the conflicts and their immediate neighbours, reflecting the reality that it is often difficult for refugees or IDPs to move further afield.

Conflict-driven migration has thus been a not insignificant force in post-Cold War Europe, but has essentially been limited to the Balkans and the Caucasus. If, as was argued at the beginning of this book, large-scale war is increasingly unlikely within Europe, then conflict-driven migration and its dangerous consequences – which remain large problems in some parts of the world, in particular Africa – may not be major challenges for Europe in the future.

The eastward enlargement of the EU in 2004 may, however, have opened a new era in migration *within* Europe. The free movement of workers – the right of citizens to work and reside in any member state of the EU – is a core principle of the Union, enshrined since the 1957 European Community Treaty. Concerns over the possible scale of East–West labour migration, however, led to the negotiation of transitional arrangements when the eight Central and Eastern European states (EU-8), plus Cyprus and Malta, joined the Union in 2004. EU-15 member states were allowed to apply national restrictions on the free movement of labour from EU-8 states up to 2009 (extendable to the latest date of 2011 if countries face serious labour market disturbances). The majority of EU-15 states chose to maintain such national restrictions, but Ireland, Sweden and the UK introduced free movement of labour for EU-8 citizens from 2004, and Finland, Greece, Portugal and Spain followed suit in 2006.

Prior to enlargement, the European Commission (and many economists) predicted that East–West labour migration would be limited in scale, with the Commission estimating that it would initially be between 70,000 and 80,000 a year, declining thereafter. In the event, the initial scale of East–West labour migration was much larger than expected: by 2006, the UK had received 450,000–600,000 workers from the eight Central and Eastern European states that joined the EU in 2004, and Ireland more than 100,000 (Kay, 2006).

The scale of migration following the 2004 EU enlargement generated concerns in the old EU-15 about possible job losses among indigenous workers, and the economic costs of social security provision for migrant workers from Central and Eastern Europe. These concerns were intensified by the prospect of Bulgaria and Romania joining the Union in 2007, these two countries being significantly poorer than the EU-8 states and therefore potentially likely to generate further large-scale labour migration. In response to such concerns, in August 2006 the British government announced that it would place restrictions on the rights of Bulgarians and Romanians to work in the UK when their countries joined the EU in 2007 (Woodward, 2006). Concern over labour migration has also called into question further enlargement of the EU to the Western Balkans, and in particular Turkey, whose large and growing population (over 70 million, predicted to grow to 80 million) and relative poverty might make it major source of such migration were it to join the Union. The European Commission and supporters of enlargement argue that the extension of free movement of labour to the enlarged EU will benefit both new and old member states (for example, the influx of workers from the EU-8 states into the UK and Ireland helped to fill labour market shortages in these countries and did not result in increased unemployment amongst indigenous workers) (Commission of the European Communities, 2006; Traser, 2006). The long-term scale of labour migration within the enlarging EU is difficult to predict, since it will depend on the speed with which new members' economies catch up with those of Western Europe, as well as on the extent of further enlargement of the Union.

How far these trends in population movements should be viewed as security problems or having significant security consequences is contentious. The most direct link between population movements and security is conflict-driven migration. The European experience in the former Yugoslavia and the former Soviet Union, however, suggests that the most serious effects of conflict-driven migration are usually limited to the states involved in conflicts and their immediate neighbours; while the declining likelihood of war in most of Europe is reducing this threat in any case. The linkage between other forms of migration – legal migration, refugees and illegal immigration – and security are more tenuous. Immigration can bring with it other threats (such as links to organized crime) and may be viewed as an economic security threat, with migrants threatening the job security of indigenous workers, contributing to the lowering of wages, and placing additional demands on welfare systems. The extent to which migration poses such an economic security threat is, however, controversial. Many economists argue that migration produces net benefits for the receiving countries. Many analysts also suggest that Europe faces a major economic demand for migration in the twenty-first century. Migration may also be perceived as a threat to existing national and/or European identities and values, or what Ole Waever and his colleagues call 'societal security' (Waever *et al.*, 1993).

European governments and the EU have adopted a number of policy responses to changing patterns of migration into and within Europe. Since the 1970s, most Western European states have had relatively restrictive immigration policies, allowing limited numbers of workers from outside Western Europe to enter either as permanent immigrants or on temporary work visas. Western European states have also sought to strengthen border controls through enhanced screening at entry points and intensified policing of land and sea borders. As discussed in Chapter 4, parallel to these national policies, under the Schengen regime, the majority of EU member states have agreed to abolish internal border controls and establish common external border controls and visa policies. The Schengen regime is now central to efforts to manage migration in much of Europe, with the Schengen border marking the boundary between an enlarging EU, in which there is free movement of persons, and third countries, whose citizens face strict limitations on their ability to enter the Schengen zone. The combination of relatively restrictive national immigration policies and the introduction of the Schengen regime are sometimes described as a 'fortress Europe': a defensive security response, closing Europe's borders in reaction to the perceived threat posed by migration.

The desire to contain immigration, in particular to limit the numbers of asylum seekers entering the EU, has led European political leaders and the EU to look for measures that might limit migration 'at source'. In the context of its Area of Freedom, Security and Justice (AFSJ), the EU has sought to develop co-operation with third countries in managing migration:

> EU policy should aim at assisting third countries . . . in their efforts to improve their capacity for migration management and refugee protection, prevent and combat illegal immigration, inform on legal channels for migration, resolve refugee situations by providing better access to durable solutions, build border-control capacity, enhance document security and tackle the problem of return. (European Union, 2004d, p. 11)

The EU provides various forms of financial and technical assistance to support states in addressing these issues, focusing in particular on neighbouring states in Africa, the Balkans and the former Soviet Union. Given the overwhelming economic imperatives behind migration, the problems of violent conflict and humans rights abuses, and the fact that many of these countries are weak states with severe governance problems, EU co-operation and assistance programmes are unlikely to have a significant impact on reducing migration. The EU has also pursued the conclusion of Readmission Agreements with third countries, under which countries agree to readmit nationals who have entered the EU illegally and (in some cases) third country nationals who have entered the Union illegally via the country concerned. As of 2006, the EU had concluded Readmission Agreements with Hong Kong, Macao, Sri Lanka, Albania and Russia, and was negotiating agreements with Morocco, Pakistan, Algeria, China and Ukraine (European Commission, 2006).

The difficulty of limiting the numbers of asylum seekers and illegal immigrants entering EU countries has led political leaders, such as British Prime Minister Tony Blair and Spanish Prime Minister José Maria Aznar in the early 2000s, to explore more radical measures, including cutting development aid to countries that fail to limit migration flows, establishing transit centres outside the EU where asylum seekers can be held while their applications for refugee status are assessed, and withdrawing from the 1951 Refugee Convention (under which signatories are bound to accept genuine refugees and consider the applications of asylum seekers for refugee status). Critics have argued that such measures would be both morally objectionable and ineffective, and they have not to date been adopted, but the fact that European political leaders have been willing to propose them indicates levels of public and elite concern over the issue.

European concern about migration from Africa, in particular North Africa, led to the holding of two special ministerial-level Africa–EU conferences on migration and development in 2006, the first in Rabat in July and the second in Tripoli in November. The latter resulted in the agreement of a wide range of measures to be taken by the EU and African states to manage migration, the establishment of an ongoing expert-level dialogue on the issue, and a commitment to hold a further EU–Africa Ministerial Conference on Migration and Development by 2009 (European Union, 2006). African analysts, however, argued that the EU was 'obsessed with fighting illegal immigration' and would need to come up with much more in terms of development aid if it wished to address the underlying economic causes of migration (Melander and Pfeiffer, 2006).

Given the overwhelming economic imperatives driving migration into Europe, European states and the EU are likely to face continuing large-scale immigration, both legal and illegal. European responses to migration, furthermore, are underpinned by a central contradiction: the public and politicians to some extent view migration as threat, yet European states are likely to need increasing numbers of migrants to meet labour market needs as Europe's indigenous population declines. Europe is therefore likely to face major challenges in balancing its need for immigration with continuing concern about the impact of that immigration.

Conclusion

As this chapter has shown, European governments and the EU are increasingly engaging with the soft or non-military security agenda. The extent and nature of soft security threats is, however, more problematical to assess. In many ways, Europe is much less vulnerable than most other regions of the world to soft security threats. The relatively internally strong character of most European states means that they are better able to respond to, or to resist, soft security threats than are weaker states in Africa, the Middle East, parts of Asia and Latin America. There are, however, significant variations in vulnerability to soft security threats within Europe: the weak states of the Balkans and the former Soviet Union have proved to be particularly vulnerable to some soft security threats (such economic instability and crime), a vulnerability reinforced by their relatively weak border controls.

In terms of responses to soft security threats, the examples of development policy and global warming examined here illustrate that Europe, and especially the EU, has played a significant global leadership role in recent years. Development policy, global warming and migration, however, also show that the EU faces major difficulties in responding to soft security challenges on two levels. First, EU members and the EU face significant domestic obstacles to the development of more effective policies in these areas. Support for protectionist trade policies remains strong within many EU states, and such policies are a major obstacle to the achievement of the Union's development goals. Similarly, although the EU has shown international leadership on the issue of global warming, most member states have failed to confront the major domestic challenges involved in seriously reducing greenhouse gas emissions. European leaders have also allowed an increasingly securitized debate on migration to development, if not having actively encouraged that debate, while failing to recognize or to explain to the public the reality that Europe will increasingly need migration to counterbalance the problem of an ageing and declining population. Second, at the international level, the problems of economic development and global warming illustrate that while the EU may be able to play a leadership role, it cannot address such problems alone. The EU thus faces a major foreign policy challenge in terms of persuading other states to join with it in order to take effective action in areas such as economic development and global warming. Soft security is thus likely to continue to pose major domestic and international challenges for European states and the EU.

Chapter 10

Conclusion

The new European security order

This book has examined security in contemporary – that is, post-Cold War and post-9/11 – Europe, and European responses to the new global security agenda. Its central thesis is that the nature of security within Europe has been transformed fundamentally by the development of a security community – a zone of peace where war is inconceivable and states no longer prepare for war against one another – that now covers all of Western, and much of Central and Eastern, Europe. The emergence of this security community has dramatically reduced the likelihood of great power war in Europe and moved much of the continent beyond its historic pattern of great power security competition, balance of power politics and rival alliances. At the time of writing, nearly two decades after the end of the Cold War, the European security community appears to be deeply entrenched: despite significant differences among its members over important issues (such as the Yugoslav conflict in the 1990s, the future direction of the EU, and the Iraq War), these differences have not given rise to old-fashioned, action–reaction competitive security dynamics. There are good reasons for believing Europe's peace will last: the various factors that underpin the European security community – democracy, relative economic prosperity, socio-economic interdependence and institutionalized international co-operation – are mutually reinforcing and deeply embedded. Short of the collapse of democracy in one or more of Western Euope's major powers, or an economic depression on the scale of that of the 1930s, a breakdown of the European security community and a return to the continent's historic pattern of great power security competition does not seem likely.

The European security community and its key institutions – the European Union and NATO – form the core of the new Europe: collectively they are the dominant political and economic force in the new Europe and they provide the framing context in which other states operate. Through the EU and NATO, the members of the European security community also increasingly adopt common policies towards the rest of Europe. Contemporary Europe is thus defined, to a significant degree, by a core–periphery relationship between the European security community and those states that remain outside that community. This relationship is, however, complicated by two further features. First, the core – the European security community – is not a hard entity like a traditional state, with clearly defined boundaries and a single centralized government, but is rather a soft, multi-level entity, with blurred and overlapping boundaries and decentralized governance. Jan Zielonka thus describes the EU as a neo-medieval empire (Zielonka, 2006). The multi-level, decentralized nature of the European security community significantly shapes its policies towards the rest of Europe, which tend to be complex, multi-layered and long-term in impact rather than the type of decisive application of hard power normally associated with great powers. Second, two states outside the European security community, Russia and Turkey, are major powers in their own right: the security community's relations with Russia and Turkey are thus a distinctive mix of core–periphery relationships between dominant and weaker powers on the one hand and more traditional relations between powerful international actors on the other.

Many of the greatest strategic uncertainties and central security policy challenges in contemporary Europe relate to the regions and countries on the periphery of the European security community. In the Western Balkans, the end of the Yugoslav wars has left a group of weak states under a form of Western suzerainty, and a situation where a return to violent conflict and warfare cannot be ruled out. The key question in the Western Balkans is the extent to which the West, and in particular the EU, which is assuming primary external responsibility for the region, can promote stability and integrate the region into the European security community. In this context, the issue of whether, and when, the Western Balkan states may join the EU is of central importance, because the prospect of EU membership is the primary means of external leverage over the region. In Turkey's case, while Turkey is a member of NATO, it is not a full part of the European security community and is torn between integration with that community and pursuing an independent policy as a power in its own right. Again, therefore, the prospect of EU membership is the primary means of external leverage over Turkey, and the issue of whether or not Turkey joins the EU may determine the long-term direction of its foreign policy and perhaps its politics more generally. As was seen in Chapter 5, Russia is not a member of the European security community and its relations with the West are characterized by an uneasy mix of co-operation and competition. In contrast to Turkey, however, Russia has little interest in or prospect of membership of NATO or the EU (except perhaps in the long term), and the ability of both institutions to influence Russia's direction is thus limited. The real question in Russo-Western relations is therefore not whether Russian may be integrated into the European security community, but rather the balance between co-operation and competition in the relations between the two, and the extent to which the West can restrain Russia's drift towards authoritarianism and encourage Russia to moderate its behaviour in the former Soviet Union. The other former Soviet states are, like the Western Balkan countries, weak states, where further instability and violent conflict cannot be ruled out. For the these states, the key question is whether the EU and/or NATO are really willing to consider them as potential members (which both organizations are currently reluctant to do, but have yet to make definitive decisions about) and what alternatives they have – in both the short and long-term – in the absence of EU and NATO membership. In short, issues relating to the European security community's ability to promote security and stability on its periphery, and the further enlargement of the EU and NATO, will pose major challenges and dilemmas in the coming years.

New threats?

The declining likelihood of war within much of Europe has focused attention on other types of security threat, in particular other forms of violent threat and non-military risk to security. In both cases, the nature, scale and implications of emerging threats, and the appropriate policy responses, are deeply contentious.

In terms of new forms of violent threat, 9/11 pushed the twin issues of terrorism and proliferation to the centre of the security agenda. In both cases, there is an argument that alarmist public debate has produced exaggerated threat perceptions and that the dangers posed by terrorism and proliferation are both limited and ones that European states will have to (and indeed can) learn to live with. The London and Madrid bombings made clear that Europe is a primary target of globalized Islamic terrorism, and that the threat is both external (coming from Islamic groups outside Europe) and internal (coming from sections of Europe's growing Islamic population). While the threat posed to Europe by terrorism is real and significant, it is, however, limited in important ways: it does not pose a risk of complete political subjugation, as past dangers of military invasion and occupation have; nor does it risk the wholesale destabilization of European societies. It is possible to envisage scenarios where the terrorist threat to Europe could grow significantly in scale – either in terms of much more wide-spread use of small-scale terrorist attacks (as Israel has experienced for some decades) or terrorist 'spectaculars' on a much larger scale (in the worst case using nuclear weapons) – but the likelihood of such a development may be reasonably low. The more likely scenario is that Europe will have to live with a long-term, persistent but limited level of terrorist threat: while protective security measures and longer-term preventive policies may contain that threat, the difficulty of preventing all attacks suggests that the threat – and periodic reality – of terrorist attacks will remain.

India and Pakistan's consolidation of their status as nuclear weapon states, North Korea's 2006 nuclear test and the likelihood that Iran may develop nuclear weapons suggest that Europe is also likely to face a continuing threat from WMD, especially nuclear weapons, proliferation. The nature of that threat may, however, be limited, at least in the short-to-medium term. The threat posed by chemical and biological weapons, though real, is limited in scale because of the difficulties of dispersing chemical agents or biological pathogens over large areas. A direct nuclear attack on Europe is probably unlikely, given the political and economic costs and the likely military retaliation any state undertaking such an attack would incur. The real impact of nuclear proliferation will probably be in constraining the freedom of the USA and European states to intervene militarily against states that have nuclear weapons. In the longer term, however, the greatest danger may be of more widespread nuclear proliferation and the possible erosion of the international taboo against the use of nuclear weapons. The difficulty of preventing determined states from developing nuclear weapons, and the reluctance of the established nuclear powers to explore seriously much more radical measures of nuclear disarmament, suggest that, as with terrorism, Europe is likely to have to live with at least limited nuclear proliferation.

Since the 1980s there has also been a growing debate on the issue of non-military threats to security. While it is clear that a range of non-military problems – economic instability and poverty, environmental degradation, migration, organized crime and diseases such as HIV/AIDS – pose significant challenges for Europe, either directly or in terms of a spillover from other parts of the world, whether these pose dangers to Europe's *security* is more contentious. Non-military problems may pose direct threats to peoples' lives, or major threats to the stability of states and societies, but the extent to which this is the case in much of Europe is debatable. The degree of vulnerability to non-military security threats also depends to a significant degree on the internal strength of states: the weak states of the Balkans and the former Soviet Union are particularly vulnerable to many non-military security challenges, whereas the capacity of Western European states and the EU as a whole to withstand or respond to such challenges is much greater. There is also a case that some issues have been unnecessarily or dangerously securitized: as was discussed in Chapter 9, European states have since the 1980s implemented increasingly defensive, securitized responses to migration, despite persuasive evidence that migration produces net economic gains and the fact that Europe increasingly needs migrants for its workforce. In other cases, however, there may be a strong argument that the scale of emerging non-military problems is such that they should be viewed as major threats to global security – as with global warming. The diverse range of issues usually bracketed together as part of the non-military security agenda make it difficult to draw conclusions that apply equally to different areas. Nevertheless, although the wider, non-military security agenda may be rather amorphous, European states and institutions have increasingly accepted its logic, and non-military issues are therefore likely to remain an important part of the European security agenda.

Europe and America, NATO and the EU

The end of the Cold War and the 9/11 attacks raised fundamental questions about the transatlantic relationship and NATO, which had been the bedrock of (Western) European security since the Second World War. Debate on the future of the transatlantic relationship has been split between those who argue that common interests, shared democratic values and institutionalized ties will hold the transatlantic relationship together, and those arguing that the loss of the 'Soviet threat' and divergent American and European approaches to security will increasingly undermine the transatlantic relationship. In Chapter 3 it was suggested that, in practice, a more mixed picture is emerging, with continued co-operation in some areas, but divergent approaches to security in others. The Bush Administration's post-9/11 foreign policy revolution and the Iraq War, however, caused a major deterioration in transatlantic relations, with many Europeans becoming increasingly concerned about central aspects of US approaches to the new security agenda. It remains to be seen how far a post-Iraq course correction in US foreign policy and a new US administration after 2008 may result in an improvement in transatlantic relations. Even if relations improve from their Bush era nadir, however, the transatlantic relationship is unlikely to return to the default partnership of the Cold War. While Europe and America share basic common values and interests, the relationship between the two is increasingly likely to be an elective partnership defined by shifting patterns of co-operation and divergence. Similarly, while NATO has been transformed since the end of the Cold War from a defence alliance into a broader security organization, it has also become simply one of a number of institutions, alongside the EU, the United Nations and others, that its members may choose to use to address the range of security challenges they face. While NATO will continue to take on important tasks (such as peacekeeping in Afghanistan), it is unlikely to become once again the central Western security institution that it was in the Cold War.

In contrast to the troubled transatlantic relationship and NATO's relative decline, the EU has assumed an increasingly prominent security role since the end of the Cold War. Since establishing its Common Foreign and Security Policy (CFSP) at the beginning of the 1990s, the EU has come to play a central foreign policy role on its own periphery, an emerging global role, a military role in various peacekeeping operations, and an expanding internal security role through its Area of Freedom, Security and Justice (AFSJ). Critics rightly point out that the Union is constrained by its largely intergovernmental, consensus decision-making in the area of foreign and security policy, highlighting key examples, such as the Yugoslav conflict and the Iraq war, where differences between member states have prevented the adoption of common EU policies. Nevertheless, the larger trend since the early 1990s has been towards the adoption and implementation of common EU policies across the spectrum of security issues. The EU, furthermore, is arguably a new type of power, quite different from traditional great powers: not a state, yet more than an international organization; a decentralized and multi-faceted power; and an actor which, while drawing on hard power, exercises influence as much through soft power and the attractiveness of its model and values. Despite its limitations, since the early 1990s the EU has begun to exercise continent-wide, and to some extent global, political leadership – a process that is likely to continue in future.

Europe and global security

The declining likelihood of war within Europe and the emergence of a new global security agenda have raised the question of what role Europe can and should play in addressing global security challenges beyond Europe. As was seen in Chapters 6 to 9, European states and in particular the EU are playing an increasing role in responding to new global security challenges. As these chapters also illustrated, European states and the EU are developing a distinctive European approach with an emphasis on multilateralism, the application of soft power and long-term conflict prevention and peace-building – or what can be characterized as an emerging European 'strategic culture' (Cornish and Edwards, 2005).

Europe's role in responding to global security challenges relates to larger questions of world order, debate over which has emerged with renewed vigour post-1989 and post-9/11. Kishore Mahbubani has described the current debate on world order as a choice between four competing visions: the Truman world order (an essentially liberal vision based on co-operation among sovereign states, underpinned after 1945 by American power); the Jiang Zemin world order (a multi-polar world in which China will eventually rise to become the world's leading power); the neo-conservative world order (based on the unilateral assertion of American power); and the Osama bin Laden world order (based on the overthrow of Western power in the Islamic world and the eventual establishment of an Islamic caliphate as the world's dominant force) (Mahbubani, 2005–6). During the Cold War, (Western) Europe largely supported the US-led vision of a liberal international order. After the end of the Cold War, however, while some in Europe viewed the EU as a counterweight to the USA (partly reflecting a balance-of-power realpolitik view), European support for a liberal international order largely continued. Since 9/11, the USA has to a significant degree abandoned the post-1945 Western liberal order, shifting towards a policy based on the unilateral assertion of American power. The extent to which US policy will shift back again towards support for a liberal international order remains to seen, but for the time being Europe has been left as the principal defender of that order. Europe has thus since the 1990s become the primary advocate of a liberal global order based international norms, multilateralism, constraints on power and the primacy of political and economic (rather than military) instruments – as illustrated by its support, in the face of US opposition, for the United Nations, multilateral arms control agreements, the Kyoto agreement and the International Criminal Court. Europe, however, lacks the power to achieve its vision of world order alone. The world of the twenty-first century will be one of multiple centres of power, of which Europe, primarily in the form of the EU, will be only one alongside the USA, China, India, Japan and Russia, as well as other emerging powers such as Brazil, Iran and South Africa. The viability of the European vision of a liberal international order will depend, in part, on Europe's ability to persuade other states to buy into and support that vision. One of the central challenges for Europe, and especially the EU, in the twenty-first century will therefore be to engage with other states and regions, including the USA, but also with other major powers (and in particular, perhaps, democracies such as India, Brazil and South Africa), in supporting the maintenance of a liberal international order.

Bibliography

Adler, Emmanuel and Barnett, Michael (eds) (1998) *Security Communities.* Cambridge, Cambridge University Press.

Allen, R. E. (ed.) (1990) *The Concise Oxford Dictionary of Current English*, 8th edn. Oxford, Clarendon Press.

Allin, Dana, H. (1995) 'Can Containment Work Again?', *Survival*, vol. 37, no. 1, pp. 53–65.

Allison, Graham (2006) 'The Nightmare This Time', *The Boston Globe*, 12 March. http://www.boston.com/news/globe/ideas/articles/2006/03/12/the_nightmare_this_time/? page=full (accessed 11 May 2006).

Andréani, Gilles (1999–2000) 'The Disarray of US Non-Proliferation Policy', *Survival*, vol. 41, no. 4, pp. 42–61.

Andréani, Gilles (2004) 'The "War on Terror": Good Cause, Wrong Concept', *Survival*, vol. 46, no. 4, pp. 31–50.

Anthony, Ian (2004) *The Role of the EU in International Non-Proliferation and Disarmament Assistance*, GCSP Occasional Paper Series No. 44. Geneva, Geneva Centre for Security Policy. http://www.gcsp.ch/e/publications/Other-pubs/Occ-papers/2004/44-Anthony.pdf.

Antonenko, Oksana (2001) 'Putin's Gamble', *Survival*, vol. 43, no. 4, pp. 49–59.

Arbatov, Alexei G. (1993) 'Russia's Foreign Policy Alternatives', *International Security*, vol. 18, no. 2, pp. 5–43.

Aron, Raymond (1954) *The Century of Total War*. New York, Doubleday.

Asmus, Ronald D. (2004) *Opening NATO's Door: How the Alliance Remade Itself for a New Era*. New York, Columbia University Press.

Asmus, Ronald D., Kugler, Richard L. and Larrabee, F. Stephen (1995) 'NATO Expansion: The Next Steps', *Survival*, vol. 37, no. 1, pp. 7–33.

Associated Press (2006) 'German, Polish Leaders Seek Friendlier Relations but Remain Apart on Key Issues', *International Herald Tribune*, 30 October. http://www.iht.com/articles/ap/2006/10/30/europe/EU_GEN_Germany_Poland.php (accessed 23 November 2006).

Aznar, Jose María, Durão Barroso, Jose-Manuel, Berlusconi, Silvio, Blair, Tony, Havel, Vaclav, Medgyessy, Peter, Miller, Leszek and Rasmussen, Anders Fogh (2003) 'United We Stand', *The Wall Street Journal*, 30 January, http://www.opinionjournal.com/extra/?id=110002994 (accessed 29 November 2006).

Baker, James A., III (2002) 'Russia in NATO?', *The Washington Quarterly*, vol. 25, no. 1, pp. 95–103.

Barber, Benjamin R. (1992) 'Jihad vs. McWorld', *The Atlantic Monthly*. http://www.theatlantic.com/doc/199203/barber (accessed 23 November 2006).

Barber, Benjamin R. (2003) *Jihad vs. McWorld: Terrorism's Challenge to Democracy*. London, Corgi.

Bergen, Peter (2005) 'Our Ally, Our Problem', *The New York Times*, 8 July. http://www.newamerica.net/publications/articles/2005/our_ally_our_probl em (accessed 26 February 2007)

Bildt, Carl (2004) 'If Europe Is to Keep Growing, It Must Think Big', *Financial Times*, 27 October.

Black, Ian (2003) 'Powell Calls on NATO to Send Troops to Iraq', *Guardian*, 5 December. http://www.guardian.co.uk/Iraq/Story/0,2763,1100481,00.html (accessed 6 December 2003).

Borger, Julian (2001) 'Bush Kills Global Warming Treaty', *Guardian*, 29 March. http://www.guardian.co.uk/international/story/0,3604,464902,00. html (accessed 4 September 2006).

Bretherton, Charlotte and Vogler, John (2006) *The European Union as a Global Actor*, 2nd edn, London/New York, Routledge.

Brown, Michael E. (1995) 'The Flawed Logic of NATO Expansion', *Survival*, vol. 37, no. 1, pp. 34–52.

Brown, Michael E. (1999) 'A Minimalist NATO', *Foreign Affairs*, vol. 78, no. 3, pp.205–18.

Brown, Michael E.(ed.) (2000) *The Rise of China*. Cambridge, Mass., MIT Press.

Brown, Michael E. (ed.) (2003) *Grave New World: Security Challenges in the 21st Century*. Washington, DC, Georgetown University Press.

Brown, Michael E., Lynn-Jones, Sean M. and Miller, Steven E. (eds) (1999) *Debating the Democratic Peace*. Cambridge, Mass., MIT Press.

Bunyan, Tony (2005) *While Europe Sleeps . . .*, ECLN Essays No. 11 (European Civil Liberties Network), reproduced on the Statewatch website. http://www.statewatch.org/news/2005/oct/ecln/essay-11.pdf (accessed 14 June 2006).

Burgess, Mark (2002) *In the Spotlight: Islamic Movement of Uzbekistan (IMU)*, CDI Terrorism Project, 25 March. Washington, DC, Centre for Defense Information). http://www.cdi.org/terrorism/imu.cfm (accessed 18 May 2006).

Burke, Jason (2004) *Al-Qaeda: The True Story of Radical Islam*. London, Penguin.

Bush, George W. (2002) *State of the Union Address*, 29 January. Washington, DC, The White House, Office of the Press Secretary. http://www. whitehouse.gov/news/releases/2002/01/20020129-11.html (accessed 24 November 2006).

Butler Committee (2004) *Review of Intelligence on Weapons of Mass Destruction: Report of a Committee of Privy Counsellors*, HC 898.

London, The Stationery Office. http://www.butlerreview.org.uk/report/report.pdf (accessed 18 November 2006).

Buzan, Barry (1991a) *People, States and Fear: An Agenda for International Security Studies in the Post-Cold War Era*, 2nd edn. Hemel Hempstead, Harvester Wheatsheaf.

Buzan, Barry (1991b) 'New Patterns of Global Security in the Twenty-First Century', *International Affairs*, vol. 67, no. 3, pp. 431–51.

Buzan, Barry, Kelstrup, Morten, Lemaitre, Pierre, Tromer, Elzbieta and Waever, Ole (1990) *The European Security Order Recast: Scenarios for the Post-Cold War Era*. London/New York, Pinter.

Buzan, Barry, Waever, Ole and de Wilde, Japp (1998) *Security: A New Framework for Analysis*. Boulder, Col./London, Lynne Rienner.

Carnegie Commission on Preventing Deadly Conflict (1997) *Preventing Deadly Conflict: Final Report with Executive Summary*. Washington, DC, CCPDC.

Carter, Ashton B. and Perry, William J. (1999) *Preventive Defense: A New Security Strategy for America*. Washington, DC, Brookings Institution.

Carter, Ashton B., Perry, William J. and Steinbruner, John D. (1992) *A New Concept of Cooperative Security*, Brookings Occasional Papers. Washington, DC, Brookings Institution.

Charlemagne (2003) 'Let Them Eat Foie Gras', *The Economist*, 21 June, p. 31.

Charlemagne (2004) 'A European Superpower', *The Economist*, 13 November, p. 38.

Charlemagne (2005) 'The End of Enlargement?', 16 July, *The Economist*.

Charlemagne (2006) 'Playing Soft or Hard Cop', *The Economist*, 21 January, p. 33.

Chyba, Christopher F. and Greninger, Alex L. (2004) 'Biotechnology and Bioterrorism: An Unprecedented World', *Survival*, vol. 46, no. 2, pp. 143–62.

Colombani, Jean-Marie (2001) 'We Are All Americans', *Le Monde*, 12 September, reproduced in *World Press Review*, vol. 48, no. 11, November. http://www.worldpress.org/1101we_are_all_americans.htm (accessed 22 May 2006).

Commission of the European Communities (2005) *Communication from the Commission to the Council, the European Parliament, the European Economic and Social Council and the Committee of the Regions: Winning the Battle Against Global Climate Change*, COM(2005) 35 final, 9 February. Brussels, Commission of the European Communities. http://eur-lex.europa.eu/LexUriServ/site/en/com/2005/com2005_0035en01.pdf (accessed 6 September 2006).

Commission of the European Communities (2006) *Communication from the Commission to the Council, the European Parliament, the European Economic and Social Council and the Committee of the Regions: Report on the Functioning of the Transitional Arrangements set out in the 2003 Accession Treaty (Period 1 May 2004–30 April 3006)*, COM(2006) 38 final, 8 February. Brussels, Commission of the European Communities. http://eur-lex.europa.eu/LexUriServ/site/en/com/2006/com2006_0048en01.pdf (accessed 19 September 2006).

Commission on Human Security (2003) *Human Security Now*. New York, Commission on Human Security.

Commission on the Intelligence Capabilities of the United States Regarding Weapons of Mass Destruction (2005) *Commission on the Intelligence Capabilities of the United States Regarding Weapons of Mass Destruction: Report to the President of the United States*. Washington, DC, Commission on the Intelligence Capabilities of the United States Regarding Weapons of Mass Destruction. http://www.wmd.gov/report/wmd_report.pdf (accessed 18 November 2006).

Commission to Assess the Ballistic Missile Threat to the United States (1998) *Report of the Commission to Assess the Ballistic Missile Threat to the United States: Executive Summary*. http://www.fas.org/irp/threat/missile/rumsfeld (accessed 26 Februaru 2007).

Cooper, Julian (1998) 'The Military Expenditure of the USSR and the Russian Federation, 1987–97', in Stockholm International Peace Research Institute (SIPRI), *SIPRI Yearbook 1998: Armaments, Disarmament and International Security*. Oxford, Oxford University Press, pp. 243–61.

Cornish, Paul and Edwards, Geoffrey (2005) 'The Strategic Culture of the European Union: A Progress Report', *International Affairs*, vol. 81, no. 4, pp. 801–20.

Cottey, Andrew (1995) *East–Central Europe after the Cold War: Poland, the Czech Republic, Slovakia and Hungary in Search of Security*. London, Macmillan.

Cottey, Andrew (ed.) (1999a) *Subregional Cooperation in the New Europe: Building Security, Prosperity and Solidarity from the Barents to the Black Sea*. London, Macmillan.

Cottey, Andrew (1999b) 'Central Europe Transformed: Security and Cooperation on NATO's New Frontier', *Contemporary Security Policy*, vol. 20, no 2, pp. 1–30.

Cottey, Andrew (2004) 'NATO: Globalisation or Redundancy?', *Contemporary Security Policy*, vol. 25, no. 3, pp. 1–18.

Cottey, Andrew and Bikin-kita, Ted (2006) 'The Military and Humanitarianism: Emerging Patterns of Intervention and Engagement', in Victoria Wheeler and Adele Harmer (eds), *Resetting the Rules of Engagement: Trends and Issues in MilitaryHumanitarian Relations*, HPG Report 21. London, Humanitarian Policy Group, Overseas Development Institute, 21–38.

Council of the European Union (2005) *European Council, Brussels, 22 and 23 March 2005: Presidency Conclusions*. Brussels, European Union. http://ec.europa.eu/environment/climt/pdf/spring_2005.pdf (accessed 6 September 2006).

Cox, Michael (1995) *US Foreign Policy After the Cold War: Superpower Without a Mission?* London, Pinter.

Cox, Michael, Booth, Ken and Dunne, Tim (1999) 'Introduction: The Interregnum: Controversies in World Politics, 1989–99', *Review of International Studies*, vol. 25, Special Issue, pp. 3–19.

Croft, Stuart, Redmond, John, Rees, G. Wyn and Webber, Mark (1999) *The Enlargement of Europe*. Manchester, Manchester University Press.

Cumings, Bruce (1999) 'Still the American Century', *Review of International Studies*, vol. 25, Special Issue, pp. 271–99.

Daalder, Ivo H. and Lindsay, James M. (2003) *America Unbound: The Bush Revolution in Foreign Policy*. Washington, DC, Brookings Institution.

Dando, Malcolm (2005) 'The Bioterrorist Cookbook', *Bulletin of the Atomic Scientists*, vol. 61, no. 1, pp. 34–9, http://www.thebulletin.org/article. php?art_ofn=nd05dando (accessed 21 November 2006).

Dannreuther, Roland (ed.) (2004) *European Union Foreign and Security Policy: Towards a Neighbourhood Strategy*. London/New York, Routledge.

Dassu, Marta and Whyte, Nicholas (2001) 'America's Balkan Disengagement?', *Survival*, vol. 43, no. 4, pp. 123–36.

Davis, Ian (2004) *A Long Way from Consensus: Threat Perceptions in European NATO and the Future of Missile Defence*, Presentation to the Conference on Transatlantic Missile Defence, sponsored by the George C. Marshall European Center for Security Studies, in co-operation with Office of Secretary of Defense for International Security Policy, Garmisch-Partenkirchen, Germany, 5–7 April. London/Washington, DC, The British American Security Information Council. http://www.basicint.org/nuclear/ NMD/marshall.htm (accessed 15 July 2004).

Defense Threat Reduction Agency (2006) *Threat Reduction Scorecard (as of 6 April 2006)*. Washington, DC: Defense Threat Reduction Agency.

Department for International Development (2004) *The Africa Conflict Prevention Pool: A Joint UK Government Approach to Preventing and Reducing Conflict in Sub-Saharan Africa*. London, Department for International Development. Foreign and Commonwealth Office website: http://www.fco.gov.uk/Files/kfile/ACPP%20Information%20Doc%20- %20final.pd (accessed 9 July 2006).

Department of Defense (2002) *Secretary Rumsfeld Speaks on '21st Century Transformation' of U.S. Armed Forces (transcript of remarks and question and answer period) Remarks as Delivered by Secretary of Defense Donald Rumsfeld, National Defense University, Fort McNair, Washington, D.C., Thursday, January 31, 2002*. http://www.defenselink.mil/speeches/2002/ s20020131-secdef.html (accessed 24 November 2006).

Department of Defense (2003) *Secretary Rumsfeld Briefs at the Foreign Press Center, 22 January, Department of Defense News Transcript*. http://www.defenselink.mil/transcripts/2003/t01232003_t0122sdfpc.html (accessed 24 November 2006).

de Nevers, Renée (1994) *Russia's Strategic Renovation*, Adelphi Paper 289. London, Brassey's for International Institute for Strategic Studies.

DeSutter, Paula A. (2006) *International Cooperation on Missile Defense Capabilities Growing, Prepared Remarks, Delivered at the National Defense University Foundation Congressional Breakfast Seminar Series, Washington DC, 4 April*. Washington, DC, US Department of State. http://usinfo.state.gov/xarchives/display.html?p=washfile-english&y=2006&m=April&x=20060404160654idybeekcm0.2211725 (accessed 26 February 2007).

Deutsch, Karl W; Burrell, Sidney A.; Kann, Robert A.; Lee, Maurice, Jr.; Lichterman, Martin; Lindgren, Raymond E.; Loewenheim, Francis L.; and Van Wagenen, Richard W. (1969) *Political Community in the North Atlantic Area: International Organization in the Light of Historical Experience*. New York, Greenwood Press.

Dombrowski, Peter and Payne, Rodger A. (2006) 'The Emerging Consensus for Preventive War', *Survival*, vol. 48, no. 2, pp. 115–36.

Duchene, François (1972) 'Europe's Role in World Peace', in Mayne, Richard (ed.), *Europe Tomorrow: Sixteen Europeans Look Ahead*. London, Fontana, pp. 32–47.

Duffield, Mark (2001) *Global Governance and the New Wars*. London, Zed Books.

Duke, Simon (2000) *The Elusive Quest for European Security: From EDC to CFSP*. Basingstoke, Palgrave Macmillan.

Eberstadt, Nicholas (1999) 'Russia: Too Sick to Matter?', *Policy Review*, vol. 95. http://www.policyreview.com/jun99/eberstadt.html (accessed 5 December 2006).

Economist, The (2006a) 'Tales from Eurabia', *The Economist*, 24 June, p. 11.

Economist, The (2006b) 'Special Report: Islam, America and Europe – Look Out, Europe, They Say', *The Economist*, 24 June, pp. 29–34.

Elbe, Stefan (2003) *Strategic Implications of HIV/AIDS*, Adelphi Paper 357. Oxford, Oxford University Press for International Institute of Strategic Studies.

Elliott, Larry (2006) 'It Will Take Years to Revive Trade Talks', *Guardian*, 31 July. http://business.guardian.co.uk/story/0,,1833708,00.html (accessed 14 August 2006).

Elworthy, Scilla and Rogers, Paul (2001) *The United States, Europe and the Majority World After 11 September*. Oxford, Oxford Research Group. http://www.oxfordresearchgroup.org.uk/publications/briefings/sept11brief ing.pdf (accessed 23 November 2006).

European Commission (2001) *Country Strategy Paper 2002–2006, National Indicative Programme 2002–2003: Russian Federation*. Brussels, European Commission. EU website: http://ec.europa.eu/comm/external_relations/russia/csp/02-06_en.pdf (accessed 5 December 2006).

European Commission (2004) *Communication from the Commission: European Neighbourhood Policy Strategy Paper*, COM(2004) 373 Final.

Brussels, European Commission. EU website: http://ec.europa.eu/world/
enp/pdf/strategy/strategy_paper_en.pdf (accessed 30 November 2006).

European Commission (2005) *EU Action Against Climate Change: EU
Emissions Trading – An Open Scheme Promoting Global Innovation.*
Brussels, European Commission. EU website: http://ec.europa.eu/environ-
ment/climat/pdf/emission_trading3_en.pdf (accessed 17 August 2006).

European Commission (2006) *A Framework for Cooperation with Third
Countries on Migration Issues*, updated July 2006. Brussels, European
Commission. EU website: http://ec.europa.eu/justice_home/fsj/immigration/
relations/fsj_immigration_relations_en.htm (accessed 29 October 2006).

European Environment Agency (2006) *EU Greenhouse Gas Emissions
Increase for Second Year in a Row*, Press Release, 22 June, European
Environment Agency. http://org.eea.europa.eu/documents/newsreleases/
GHG2006-en (accessed 4 September 2006).

European Union (1992) *The Maastricht Treaty: Treaty on European Union*,
Maastricht, 7 February 1992. http://www.eurotreaties.com/maastrichtext.
html (accessed 1 March 2007).

European Union (1993) European Council in Copenhagen, 21–22 June 1993,
Conclusions of the Presidency, SN 180/1/93 REV 1. http://www.consilium.
europa.eu/ueDocs/cms_Data/docs/pressData/en/ec/72921.pdf (accessed 29
September 2006).

European Union (1997) *The Amsterdam Treaty – Amending the Treaty on
European Union, The Treaties Establishing the European Communities
and Certain Related Acts*, Amsterdam, 2 October 1997. http://
eurotreaties.com/amsterdamtreay.pdf (accessed 1 December 2006).

European Union (1999) 'European Council, Cologne, 3–4 June 1999,
Declaration of the European Council on Strengthening the Common
European Policy on Security and Defence', in Maartje Rutten, *From St-Malo
to Nice – European Defence: Core Documents*, Chaillot Paper 47. Paris,
Institute for Security Studies, Western European Union, May 2001, pp. 41–5.

European Union (2001) *EU Programme for the Prevention of Violent
Conflicts, adopted by the General Affairs Council on 11–12 June 2001 and
endorsed by the European Council at Gotborg 15–16 June 2001.* EU
website: http://www.eu2001.se/static/eng/pdf/violent.PDF (accessed 30
November 2006).

European Union (2003a) *European Security Strategy: A More Secure Europe
in a Better World.* http://ue.eu.int/uedocs/cmsUpload/78367.pdf.

European Union (2003b) *European Strategy Against Proliferation of Weapons
of Mass Destruction*, Brussels, 12 December. EU website: http://register.
consilium.europa.eu/pdf/en/03/st15/st15708.en03.pdf (accessed 1 March
2007).

European Union (2004a) *Headline Goal 2010: Approved by General Affairs
and External Relations Council on 17 May 2004 and Endorsed by the
European Council of 17 and 18 June 2004.* http://ue/eu.int/eudocs/
cmsUpload/2010%20Headline%20Goal.pdf.

European Union (2004b) *Final Report (approved by the European Council in June 2004) on an EU Strategic Partnership with the Mediterranean and the Middle East*. Brussels, European Union, June. EU website: http://www.consilium.europa.eu/uedocs/cmsUpload/Partnership%20Medi terranean%20and%20Middle%20East.pdf (accessed 7 July 2006).

European Union (2004c) *Text of the Treaty Establishing a Constitution for Europe, 29 October 2004*. http://www.eurotreaties.com/constitutiontext. html (accessed 29 November 2006).

European Union (2004d) *The Hague Programme: Strengthening Freedom, Security and Justice in the European Union*, 16054/50. Brussels, European Union, 13 December. EU website: http://ec.europa.eu/justice_home/doc_ centre/doc/hague_programme_en.pdf (accessed 14 January 2007).

European Union (2005a) *European Union Factsheet: The Euro-Mediterranean Partnership (EMP) – The Barcelona Process*. Brussels, European Union, February. EU website: http://www.consilium.europa.eu/uedocs/cmsUpload/ MEDIT.pdf (accessed 7 July 2006).

European Union (2005b) *European Union Factsheet: The Fight Against Terrorism*. Brussels, European Union, June. EU website: http://www. consilium.europa.eu/uedocs/cmsUpload/3Counterterrorfinal170605.pdf (accessed 28 May 2006).

European Union (2005c) *The European Union Strategy for Combating Radicalisation and Terrorism*. Brussels, European Union, 24 November. http://register.consilium.eu.int/pdf/en/05/st14/st14781-re01.en05.pdf (accessed 29 June 2006).

European Union (2005d) *The European Consensus on Development: Joint statement by the Council and the Representatives of the Governments of the Member States meeting within the Council, the European Parliament and the Commission on the European Union Development Policy. 20 December*. EU website: http://ec.europa.eu/comm/development/body/ development_policy_statement/docs/edp_declaration_signed_20_12_2005 _en.pdf#zoom=125 (accessed 14 August 2006).

European Union (2006) *Joint Africa–EU Declaration on Migration and Development, Tripoli, 22–23 November 2006*. EU website: http://ec.europa.eu/development/body/tmp_docs/2006/Joint_declaration_ 22110_AUEU.pdf (accessed 14 January 2007).

Evans, Michael (2005) 'MI5 Analysts Admit Link between Iraq War and Bombings', *The Times*, 28 July. http://www.timesonline.co.uk/article/ 0,,22989-1711093,00.html (accessed 23 May 2006).

Fenwick, Helen (2002) 'Responding to 11 September: Detention without Trial under the Anti-Terrorism, Crime and Security Act 2001', in Lawrence Freedman (ed.), *Superterrorism: Policy Responses*. Oxford, Blackwell, pp. 80–104.

Fishman, Boris (2003) *Wild East: Stories from the Last Frontier*. Boston, Mass., Justin, Charles & Co.

Foreign and Commonwealth Office (2003) *The Global Conflict Prevention Pool: A Joint UK Government Approach to Reducing Conflict.* London, Foreign and Commonwealth Office. http://www.fco.gov.uk/Files/kfile/43896_Conflict%20Broc,0.pdf (accessed 9 July 2006).

Foreign and Commonwealth Office (2005) *Counter-Terrorism Legislation and Practice: A Survey of Selected Countries*, FCO Research Paper. London, Foreign and Commonwealth Office. http://www.fco.gov.uk/Files/kfile/QS%20Draft%2010%20FINAL1.pdf (accessed 14 June 2006).

Forster, Anthony (2006) *Armed Forces and Society in Europe.* Basingstoke, Palgrave Macmillan.

Freedman, Lawrence (2001) 'The Third World War?', *Survival*, vol. 43, no. 4, pp. 61–87.

French Ministry of Foreign Affairs (2003) *Iraq: Declaration Russia–Germany–France, 5 March 2003*, Permanent Mission of France to the United Nations. http://www.un.int/france/documents_anglais/030305_mae_france_irak.htm (accessed 24 November 2006).

Frost, Robin M. (2005) *Nuclear Terrorism After 9/11*, Adelphi Paper 378. London, Routledge for International Institute for Strategic Studies.

G8 (2002) *Statement by G8 Leaders, The G8 Global Partnership Against the Spread of Weapons and Materials of Mass Destruction, Kananaskis, June 27*, http://www.g7.utoronto.ca/summit/2002kananaskis/arms.html, (accessed 1 March 2007).

Gaddis, John Lewis (1986) 'The Long Peace: Elements of Stability in the Postwar International System', *International Security*, vol. 10, no. 4, pp. 99–142.

Gaddis, John Lewis (1998) 'History, Grand Strategy and NATO Enlargement', *Survival*, vol. 40, no. 1, pp. 145–51.

Galeotti, Mark (2002) 'The Challenge of "Soft Security": Crime, Corruption and Chaos', in Andrew Cottey and Derek Averre (eds), *New Security Challenges in Postcommunist Europe: Securing Europe's East.* Manchester/New York, Manchester University Press, pp. 151–71.

Gambles, Ian (ed.) (1995) *A Lasting Peace in Central Europe?*, Chaillot Paper 20. Paris, Institute for Security Studies, Western European Union.

Gardner Feldman, Lily (1999) 'The Principle and Practice of "Reconciliation" in German Foreign Policy: Relations with France, Israel, Poland and the Czech Republic', *International Affairs, vol.* 75, no. 2, pp. 333–56.

Garton Ash, Timothy (2005) *Free World: Why a Crisis of the West Reveals the Opportunity of Our Time.* London, Penguin.

Gleick, Peter H. (1993) 'Water and Conflict: Fresh Water Resources and International Security', *International Security*, vol. 18, no. 1, pp. 79–112.

Gnesotto, Nicole (2002–3) 'Reacting to America', *Survival*, vol. 44, no. 4, pp. 99–106.

Gnesotto, Nicole (ed.) (2004) *EU Security and Defence Policy: The First Five Years (1999–2004).* Paris, European Union Institute for Security Studies.

Gnesotto, Nicole and Grevi, Giovanni (eds) (2006) *The New Global Puzzle: What World for the EU in 2025*. Paris, European Union Institute for Security Studies.

Goldgeier, James M. and McFaul, Michael (1992) 'A Tale of Two Worlds: Core and Periphery in the Post-Cold War Era', *International Organization*, vol. 46, no. 2, pp. 467–91.

Gompert, David and Kugler, Richard (1995) 'Free-Rider Redux: NATO Needs to Project Power (And Europe Can Help)', *Foreign Affairs*, vol. 74, no. 1, 7–12.

Goodson, Roy (2003) 'Transnational Crime, Corruption, and Security', in Michael E. Brown (ed.), *Grave New World: Security Challenges in the 21st Century*. Washington, DC, Georgetown University Press, pp. 259–78.

Gordon, Philip H. (1997–8) 'Europe's Uncommon Foreign Policy', *International Security*, vol. 22, no. 3, pp. 74–100.

Gordon, Philip H. (2002) *Iraq: The Transatlantic Debate*, Occasional Paper 39. Paris, European Union Institute for Security Studies.

Gordon, Michael R. (2000) 'Bush Would Stop US Peacekeeping in Balkan Fights', *New York Times*, 21 October.

Gormley, Denis M. (2004) 'The Limits of Intelligence: Iraq's Lessons', *Survival*, vol. 46, no. 3, pp. 7–28.

Grabbe, Heather (2006) *The EU's Transformative Power: Europeanization through Conditionality in Central and Eastern Europe*. Basingstoke, Palgrave Macmillan.

Graham, Thomas E. (1999) 'The Prospect of Russian Disintegration is Low', *European Security*, vol. 8, no. 2, pp. 1–14.

Graham, Thomas, Jr (1999) *World without Russia?*, Jamestown Foundation Conference. Washington, DC, Carnegie Endowment for International Peace. http://www.carngieendowment.org/publications/index.cfm?fa=view&id=285 (accessed 17 January 2006).

Grand, Camille (2000) *The European Union and the Non-Proliferation of Nuclear Weapons*, Chaillot Papers 37. Paris, Western European Union Institute for Security Studies.

Gray, Colin S. (1999) *The Second Nuclear Age*. Boulder, Col., Lynne Rienner.

Grgic, Borut (2004) 'There Are Worse Things than a Nuclear Iran', *International Herald Tribune*, 2 December. Global Policy Forum website: http://www.globalpolicy.org/security/sanction/iran.1202worsethings.htm (accessed 6 December 2004).

Guardian (2003) 'Kicking the Subsidies: Third World Farmers Need a Fair Deal', *Guardian*, 18 August. http://www.guardian.co.uk/wto/article/0,2763,1020721,00.html (accessed 14 August 2006).

Guelke, Adrian (1998) *The Age of Terrorism and the International System*. London, I. B. Tauris.

Harbom, Lotta and Wallensteen, Peter (2006) 'Patterns of Major Armed Conflicts, 1990–2005', Appendix 2A in Stockholm International Peace

Research Institute, *SIPRI Yearbook 2006: Armaments, Disarmament and International Security*. Oxford, SIPRI/Oxford University Press, pp. 108–19.

Harris, Martha (2003) 'Energy and Security', in Brown, Michael E. (ed.), *Grave New World: Security Challenges in the 21st Century*. Washington, DC, Georgetown University Press, pp. 157–77.

Hart, Douglas and Simon, Steven (2006) 'Thinking Straight and Talking Straight: Problems of Intelligence Analysis', *Survival*, vol. 48, no. 1, pp. 35–60.

Heisbourg, François (1992) 'The Future of the Atlantic Alliance: Whither NATO, Whether NATO?', *The Washington Quarterly*, vol. 15, no. 2, pp. 127–39.

Herspring, Dale R. (2002) 'Deprofessionalising the Russian Armed Forces', in Anthony Forster, Timothy Edmunds and Andrew Cottey (eds), *The Challenge of Military Reform in Postcommunist Europe: Building Professional Armed Forces*. Basingstoke, Palgrave Macmillan, pp. 197–210.

Herz, John H. (1950) 'Idealist Internationalism and the Security Dilemma', *World Politics*, vol. 2, pp. 157–80.

Hill, Fiona (2002) 'Russia: The 21st Century's Energy Superpower', *The Brookings Review*, vol. 20, no. 2, pp. 28–31. http://www. brookings.edu/press/review/spring2002/hill.htm (accessed 3 December 2006).

Hill, Fiona (2004) *Energy Empire: Oil, Gas and Russia's Revival*. London, Foreign Policy Centre. http://fpc.org.uk/fsblob/307.pdf (accessed 3 December 2006).

Hoge, James F., Jr. (2004) 'A Global Power Shift in the Making', *Foreign Affairs,* vol. 83, no. 4, pp. 2–7.

Holbrooke, Richard (1995) 'America: A European Power', *Foreign Affairs,* vol.74, no. 2, pp. 38–51.

Hollis, Rosemary (2005) 'The Greater Middle East', ch. 5 in Stockholm International Peace Research Institute, *SIPRI Yearbook 2005: Armaments, Disarmament and International Security*. Oxford, Oxford University Press.

Home Office (n.d.) 'Terrorism and the Law'. Home Office website: http://www.homeoffice.gov.uk/security/terrorism-and-the-law/?version=1 (accessed 14 June 2006).

Homer-Dixon, Thomas F. (1991) 'On the Threshold: Environmental Changes as Causes of Acute Conflict', *International Security*, vol. 16, no.2, pp. 76–116.

Homer-Dixon, Thomas F. (1994) 'Environmental Scarcities and Violent Conflict', *International Security*, vol. 19, no. 1, pp.5–40.

Houghton, John (2003) 'Global Warming Is Now a Weapon of Mass Destruction', *Guardian*, 28 July. http://www.guardian.co.uk/comment/story/0,3604,1007042,00.html.

Howard, Michael (2002) 'What's In a Name? How to Fight Terrorism', *Foreign Affairs*, vol. 81, no. 1, pp.8–13.

Howorth, Jolyon (2003–4) 'France, Britain and the Euro-Atlantic Crisis', *Survival*, vol. 45, no. 4, pp. 173–92.

Human Rights Watch (2005) *Proposed Anti-Terrorism Measures Threaten Fundamental Rights*, 10 August, reproduced on Global Policy Forum website: http://www.globalpolicy.org/empire/terrorwar/liberties/2005/0810ukterrormeasures.htm (accessed 17 January 2005).

Human Security Centre (2005) *Human Security Report 2005: War and Peace in the 21st Century*. Oxford, Oxford University Press. http://www.humansecurityreport.info/ (accessed 21 November 2006).

Hunter, Robert E. (1999) 'Maximizing NATO', *Foreign Affairs*, vol. 78, no. 3. pp. 190–203.

Huntington, Samuel P. (1993) 'The Clash of Civilizations?', *Foreign Affairs*, vol. 72, no. 3, pp. 22–49.

ICISS (International Commission on Intervention and State Sovereignty) (2001) *The Responsibility to Protect: Report of the International Commission on Intervention and State Sovereignty*. Ottawa, ICISS/International Development Research Centre.

IISS (International Institute for Strategic Studies) (1991) *The Military Balance 1991–92*. London, Brassey's for the IISS.

IISS (International Institute for Strategic Studies) (1995) 'Transnational Crime: A New Security Threat?', in *Strategic Survey 1994–95*. Oxford: Oxford University Press for the IISS, pp. 25–33.

IISS (International Institute for Strategic Studies) (2000) *The Military Balance 2000–2001*. Oxford, Oxford University Press for the IISS.

IISS (International Institute for Strategic Studies) (2001) 'Global Trends: The Spread of Infectious Diseases', in *Strategic Survey 2000–01*. Oxford, Oxford University Press for the IISS, Strategic Geography section, pp. xxviii–ix.

IISS (International Institute for Strategic Studies) (2004a) *Strategic Survey 2003–4*. Oxford, Oxford University Press for the IISS.

IISS (International Institute for Strategic Studies) (2004b) *The Military Balance 2004–2005*. Oxford, Oxford University Press for the IISS.

IISS (International Institute for Strategic Studies) (2004c) 'The US Global Posture Review', *Strategic Comments*, vol. 10, no. 7.

IISS (International Institute for Strategic Studies) (2006) *The Military Balance 2006*. London, Routledge for the IISS.

International Crisis Group (2001) *HIV/AIDS as a Security Issue*, ICG Report. Washington, DC/Brussels, International Crisis Group. http://crisisgroup.org/library/documents/report_archive/A400321_19062001.pdf (accessed 1 March 2007).

Ikenberry, G. John (2001) *After Victory: Institutions, Strategic Restraint and the Rebuilding of Order After Major Wars*. Princeton, NJ/Oxford, Princeton University Press.

International Organization for Migration (2005) *World Migration 2005: Costs and Benefits of International Migration*, vol. 3 – IOM World

Migration Report Series. Geneva, International Organization for Migration. http://www.iom.int/jahia/Jahia/cache/bypass/pid/8?entryId=932 (accessed 21 September 2006)

Jandl, Michael (2003) *Estimates on the Numbers of Illegal and Smuggled Immigrants in Europe: Presentation at Workshop 1.6, 8th International Metropolis Conference, 17 September 2003*, PowerPoint presentation. Vienna, International Centre for Migration Policy Development. http://www.icmpd.org/uploading/Metropolis%20Presentation%2D2003%2DMJ%2D1.pdf (accessed 21 September 2006).

Jehl, Douglas (2005) 'Iraq May Be Prime Place for Training of Militants, C.I.A. Report Concludes', *The New York Times*, 22 June. http://www.nytimes.com/2005/06/22/international/middleeast/22intel.html?ex=1277092800&en=cca56f7374b2b81a&ei=5090&partner=rssuserland&emc=rss (accessed 23 May 2006).

Jentleson, Bruce W. (ed.) (2000) *Opportunities Missed, Opportunities Seized: Preventive Diplomacy in the Post-Cold War World*. Lanham, Rowman & Littlefield.

Jervis, Robert (1976) *Perception and Misperception in International Politics*. Princeton, NJ, Princeton University Press.

Jervis, Robert (1978) 'Cooperation Under the Security Dilemma', *World Politics*, vol. 30, no. 2, pp. 167–214.

Jervis, Robert (1982) 'Security Regimes', *International Organization*, vol. 36, no. 2, pp. 357–78.

Jervis, Robert (1985) 'From Balance to Concert: A Study of International Security Cooperation', *World Politics*, vol. XXXVIII, no. 1, pp. 58–79.

Jervis, Robert (1991–2) 'The Future of World Politics: Will It Resemble the Past', *International Security*, vol. 16, no. 3, pp. 39–73.

Jervis, Robert (1997) *System Effects: Complexity in Political and Social Life*. Princeton, NJ, Princeton University Press.

Jervis, Robert (2002) 'Theories of War in an Era of Leading-Power Peace: Presidential Address, American Political Science Association, 2001', *American Political Science Review*, vol. 96, no. 1, pp. 1–14.

Johnson, Chalmers (2000) *Blowback: The Costs and Consequences of American Empire*. New York, Metropolitan Books.

Judah, Tim (2000) *Kosovo: War and Revenge*. New Haven, Conn./London, Yale University Press.

Kagan, Robert (2002) 'Power and Weakness', *Policy Review*, vol. 113. http://www.policyreview.org/JUN02/kagan.html.

Kagan, Robert (2003) *Paradise and Power: America and Europe in the New World Order*. London, Atlantic Books.

Kaldor, Mary (2001) *New and Old Wars: Organized Violence in a Global Era*. Cambridge, Polity Press.

Kalicki, Jan H. and Goldwyn, David L. (eds) (2005) *Energy and Security: Toward a New Foreign Policy Strategy*. Baltimore, Md., Johns Hopkins University Press.

Kaplan, Robert D. (1994) 'The Coming Anarchy', *The Atlantic Monthly*, vol. 273, no. 2, pp. 44–76.

Kay, John (2006) 'How the Migration Estimates Turned Out Wrong', *Financial Times*, 6 September. Reproduced at http://www.johnkay.com/print/459.html (accessed 19 September 2006).

Kaysen, Carl (1990) 'Is War Obsolete? A Review Essay', *International Security*, vol. 14, no. 4, pp.42–64.

Kegley, Charles W., Jr. (1991) *The Long Postwar Peace: Contending Explanations and Projections*. New York, HarperCollins.

Kennedy, Paul (1988) *The Rise and Fall of the Great Powers: Economic Change and Military Conflict from 1500 to 2000*. London, Fontana.

Keohane, Daniel (2005) 'One Step Forward, Two Steps Back', *E!Sharp*, November–December, pp. 37–8. Centre for European Reform website: http://www.cer.org.uk/pdf/article_keohane_esharp_nov05.pdf.

Keohane, Robert O. and Martin, Lisa L. (1995) 'The Promise of Institutionalist Theory', *International Security*, vol. 20, no. 1, pp. 39–51.

Keohane, Robert O. and Nye, Joseph S. (2001) *Power and Interdependence*, 3rd edn. New York, Longman.

Keohane, Robert O., Nye, Joseph S. and Hoffman, Stanley (1993) *After the Cold War: International Institutions and State Strategies in Europe, 1989–1991*. Cambridge, Mass., Harvard University Press.

Krause, Joachim (1996) 'The Proliferation of Weapons of Mass Destruction: The Risks for Europe', in Paul Cornish, Peter van Ham and Joachim Krause (eds), *Europe and the Challenge of Proliferation*, Chaillot Papers 24. Paris, Western European Union Institute for Security Studies, pp. 5–21.

Krause, Keith and Williams, Michael C. (eds) (1997) *Critical Security Studies: Concepts and Cases*. London, UCL Press.

Krauthammer, Charles (1990–1) 'The Unipolar Moment', *Foreign Affairs*, vol. 70, no. 1, pp. 23–33.

Kremenyuk, Viktor (2002) 'Russia's Defence Diplomacy in Europe: Containing Threat Without Confronation', in Andrew Cottey and Derek Averre (eds), *New Security Challenges in Postcommunist Europe: Securing Europe's East*. Manchester /New York, Manchester University Press), pp. 98–111.

Layne, Christopher (1993) 'The Unipolar Illussion', *International Security*, vol. 17, no. 4, pp. 5–51.

Lehne, Stefan (2004) 'Has the "Hour of Europe" Come at Last? The EU's Strategy for the Balkans', in Judy Batt(ed.), *The Western Balkans: Moving On*, Chaillot Papers 70. Paris, European Union Institute for Security Studies, pp. 111–24.

Levy, Jack (1989) 'Domestic Politics and War', in Robert I. Rotberg, and Theodore K. Rabb, *The Origin and Prevention of Major Wars*. Cambridge, Cambridge University Press, pp. 79–99.

Levy, Marc A. (1995) 'Is the Environment a National Security Issue?', *International Security*, vol. 20, no. 2, pp. 35–62.

Lindley-French, Julian (2002) *Terms of Engagement: The Paradox of American Power and the Transatlantic Dilemma Post-11 September*, Chaillot Paper No. 52. Paris, European Union Institute for Security Studies.

Lipset, Seymour Martin (1990) *Continental Divide: The Values and Institutions of the United States and Canada*. London, Routledge & Kegan Paul.

Loescher, Gil and Milner, James (2005) *Protracted Refugee Situations: Domestic and International Security Implications*, Adelphi Paper 375. Abingdon, Routledge for International Institute for Strategic Studies.

Lugar, Richard G. (1993) *NATO: Out of Area or Out of Business – A Call for US Leadership to Revive and Redefine the Alliance*, Presentation to the Open Forum of the US Department of State, 2 August.

Lugar, Richard G. (2005) *The Lugar Survey on Proliferation Threats and Responses*. Washington, DC, US Senate. http://lugar.senate.gov/reports/NPSurvey.pdf (accessed 1 March 2007).

Lungescu, Oana (2003) 'Chirac Blasts EU Candidates', BBC News website, 18 February. http://news.bbc.co.uk/1/hi/world/europe/2774139.stm (accessed 2 December 2006).

Luterbacher, Urs (2005) 'Degradation – Environment, Climate Change, and the Kyoto Protocol', in Antonio Missiroli (ed.), *Disasters, Diseases, Disruptions: A New D-Drive for the EU*, Chaillot Paper No. 83. Paris, European Union Institute for Security Studies, pp. 21–36.

Lukasik, Stephen J., Goodman, Seymour E. and Longhurst, David W. (2003) *Protecting Critical Infrastructure Against Cyber-Attack*, Adelphi Paper 359. Oxford, Oxford University Press for International Institute for Strategic Studies.

Lynch, Dov (2003) *Russia Faces Europe*, Chaillot Papers No. 60. Paris, European Union Institute for Security Studies.

Mahbubani, Kishore (2005–6) 'The Impending Demise of the Postwar System', *Survival*, vol. 47, no. 4, pp. 7–18.

Mandelbaum, Michael (1998–9) 'Is Major War Obsolete?', *Survival*, vol. 40, no. 4, pp. 20–38.

Manners, Ian (2002) 'Normative Power Europe: A Contradiction in Terms?', *Journal of Common Market Studies*, vol. 40, no. 2, pp. 235–58.

Manners, Ian and Whitman, Richard (eds) (2000) *The Foreign Policies of European Union Member States*. Manchester, Manchester University Press.

Mansfield, Edward D. and Snyder, Jack (1995) 'Democratization and the Danger of War', *International Security*, vol. 20, no. 1, pp. 5–38.

Maslin, Mark (2004) *Global Warming: A Very Short Introduction*. Oxford, Oxford University Press.

Mayhew, Alan (1998) *Recreating Europe: The European Union's Policy Towards Central and Eastern Europe*. Cambridge, Cambridge University Press.

Mearsheimer, John J. (1990) 'Back to the Future: Instability in Europe After the Cold War', *International Security*, vol. 15, no. 1, pp. 5–56.

Melander, Ingrid and Pfeiffer, Tom (2006) 'EU–Africa Summit Reveals Differences', *Dawn*, 14 July. http://www.dawn.com/2006/07/14/int15.htm (accessed 14 January 2007).

Melvin, Neil (1995) *Russians Beyond Russia: The Politics of National Identity*, Chatham House Papers. London, Cassell/Royal Institute of International Affairs.

Micklethwait, John and Wooldridge, Adrian (2004) *The Right Nation: Why America Is Different*. London, Allen Lane.

Miller, Steven E. (1992) 'Western Diplomacy and the Soviet Nuclear Legacy', *Survival*, vol. 34, no.3, pp. 3–27.

Minogue, Kenneth (2000) *Politics: A Very Short Introduction*. Oxford, Oxford University Press.

Mohan, C. Raja (2006) 'India and the Balance of Power', *Foreign Affairs*, vol. 85, no. 4, pp.17–32.

Morgenthau, Hans J. (1985) *Politics Among Nations: The Struggle for Power and Peace*, 6th edn. New York, McGraw-Hill.

Mueller, John (1990) *Retreat from Doomsday: The Obsolescence of Major War*. New York, Basic Books.

Muller, Harald (2003) *Terrorism, Proliferation: A European Threat Assessment*, Chaillot Papers No. 58. Paris, European Union Institute for Security Studies.

National Commission on Terrorist Attacks Upon the United States (2004) *The 9/11 Commission Report: Final Report of the National Commission on Terrorist Attacks Upon the United States*. New York/London, W. W. Norton.

NATO (1991) *The Alliance's New Strategic Concept, Agreed by the Heads of State and Government participating in the meeting of the North Atlantic Council in Rome, on 7th–8th November 1991*. http://www.nato.int/docu/comm/49-95/c911107a.htm (accessed 24 November 2006).

NATO (1999) *The Alliance's Strategic Concept, Approved by the Heads of State and Government participating in the meeting of the North Atlantic Council in Washington D.C., on 23rd and 24th April 1999*, Press Release NAC-S(99)65, 24 April. http://www.nato.int/docu/pr/1999/p99-065e.htm (accessed 9 August 2006).

NATO (2001) Statement by the North Atlantic Council, Press Release (2001)124, 12 September. http://www.nato.int/docu/pr/2001/p01-124e.htm (accessed 22 May 2006).

NATO (2002) *Prague Summit Declaration: Issued by the Heads of State and Government participating in the meeting of the North Atlantic Council in Prague on 21 November 2002*, Press Release (2002)127. http://www.nato.int/docu/pr/2002/p02-127e.htm (accessed 15 May 2006).

NATO (2005) *The NATO Response Force – NRF*, Supreme Headquarters Allied Powers Europe (SHAPE) Issues, updated 7 January 2005. http://www.nato.int/shape/issues/shape_nrf/nrf_intro.htm.

NATO (2006a) *NATO Missile Defence Feasibility Study Results Delivered*, Press Release (2006)048, 10 May. http://www.nato.int/docu/pr/2006/p06-048e.htm (accessed 12 May 2006).

NATO (2006b) NATO, *Missile Defence*, updated 10 May. http://www.nato.int/issues/missile_defence/index.html (accessed 12 May 2006).

NATO (2006c) *NATO–EU: A Strategic Partnership*, updated 12 October 2006. http://www.nato.int/issues/nato-eu/index.html (accessed 24 November 2006).

NATO (2006d) ISAF Key Figures, 10 November. http://www2.hq.nato.int/ISAF/media/pdf/placemat_isaf.pdf (accessed 8 December 2006).

NATO (n.d.) *NATO Response Force: Land Component Command*, (Varese, Italy: NATO Rapid Deployable Corps – Public Information Office). http://www.nato.int/nrdc-it/docu/brochure/041001.pdf (accessed 1 March 2007).

Natural Resources Defense Council (n.d.) *Consequences of Global Warming*. Natural Resources Defense Council website: http://www.nrdc.org/globalWarming/fcons.asp (accessed 16 August 2006).

Nelson, Daniel N. (1991) 'Europe's Unstable East, *Foreign Policy*, vol. 82, pp. 137–58.

Norton-Taylor, Richard (2006) 'Iraq War "Motivated London Bombers"', *Guardian*, 3 April.

Nye, Joseph S., Jr. (1996) 'Conflicts After the Cold War', *The Washington Quarterly*, vol. 19, no. 1, pp. 5–24.

Nye, Joseph S., Jr. (2000) 'The US and Europe: Continental Drift?', *International Affairs*, vol. 76, no. 1, pp. 51–9.

Nye, Joseph S., Jr. (2002) *The Paradox of American Power: Why the World's Only Superpower Can't Go It Alone*. Oxford, Oxford University Press.

O'Hanlon, Michael and Singer, P. W. (2004) 'The Humanitarian Transformation: Expanding Global Intervention Capacity', *Survival*, vol. 46, no. 1, pp. 77–100.

Ortega, Martin (2002) *Iraq: A European Point of View*, Occasional Paper 40. Paris, European Union Institute for Security Studies.

OSCE (Organization for Security and Co-operation in Europe) (2005) *Survey of OSCE Long-Term Missions and other OSCE Field Activities*. Vienna, OSCE Secretariat, Conflict Prevention Centre. 25 August 2005.

Oxfam International (2002) *Rigged Rules and Double Standards: Trade, Globalisation and The Fight Against Poverty*. Oxford, Oxfam.

Palme Commission (1982) *Common Security: A Programme for Disarmament*. London, Pan.

Perkovich, George (2003) 'Bush's Nuclear Revolution: A Regime Change in Non-proliferation', *Foreign Affairs*, vol. 82, no. 2, pp. 2–8.

Perkovich, George (2004) *Deconflating 'WMD'*, Published study No. 17. Stockholm, Weapons of Mass Destruction Commission. http://www.wmdcommission.org/ (accessed 24 November 2006).

Persbo, Anders and Davis, Ian. (2004) *Sailing into Uncharted Waters: The Proliferation Security Initiative and the Law of the Sea*, BASIC Research

Report 2004.2. London/Washington, DC, British American Security Information Council.

Peterson, John (2004) 'Europe, America, Iraq: Worst Ever, Ever Worsening?', Journal of Common Market Studies, vol. 42, Issue s1 (The JCMS Annual Review of the European Union in 2005), pp. 9–26.

Pew Global Attitudes Project (2005) *American Character Gets Mixed Reviews: US Image up Slightly but Still Negative – 16-Nation Pew Global Attitudes Survey*. Washington, DC, Pew Research Center, 23 June. http://pewglobal.org/reports/pdf/247.pdf (accessed 23 May 2006).

Pirozzi, Nicoletta (2006) *UN Peacekeeping in Lebanon: Europe's Contribution*, European Security Review, No. 30. Brussels, International Security Information Service (ISIS) Europe. http://www.isis-europe.org/ftp/Download/ESR30.Lebanon.pdf (accessed 8 December 2006).

Pollack, Kenneth M. (2002) 'Next Stop Baghdad?', Foreign Affairs, vol. 81, no. 2, pp. 32–47.

Radovic, Borislav (2005) 'A Brief Retrospective on the Problem of Refugees in the Yugoslav Wars 1991–99', in Goran Opačić, Ivana Vidaković and Branko Vujadinović, *Living in Post-War Communities*. Belgrade, IAN – International Aid Network, pp. 11–26. http://www.ian.org.yu/publikacije/posleratnezajednice/book/book.pdf (accessed 19 October 2006).

Record, Jeffrey (2003) *Bounding the Global War on Terrorism*. Carlisle, Pa., Strategic Studies Institute of the US Army War College. http://www.strategicstudiesinstitute.army.mil/pdffiles/PUB207.pdf (accessed 21 November 2006).

Rees, Wyn (2006) *Transatlantic Counter-Terrorism Cooperation: The New Imperative*. London, Routledge.

Revkin, Andrew C. (2005) 'News Analysis: Emissions Talks End in Modest Gains', *New York Times*, 11 December. *International Herald Tribune* website: http://www.iht.com/bin/print_ipub.php?file=/articles/2005/12/11/news/climate.php (accessed 4 September 2006).

Rice, Condolezza (2000) 'Campaign 2000: Promoting the National Interest', *Foreign Affairs*, vol. 79, no. 1, pp.45–62.

Risse-Kappen, Thomas (1996) 'Identity in a Democratic Security Community: The Case of NATO', in Peter Katzenstein (ed.), *The Culture of National Security*. New York, Columbia University Press, pp. 359–99.

Roberts, Adam (2005) 'The "War on Terror" in Historical Perspective', *Survival*, vol. 47, no. 2, pp. 101–30.

Robertson, Lord George (2003) *NATO's Transformation: Remarks by NATO Secretary-General Lord Roberston at the Geneva Centre for Security Policy*, 13 October. http://www.nato.int/docu/speech/2003/s031013a.htm (accessed 9 December 2006).

Ruppe, David (2005) 'Biological Terrorism Dangers Overstated, Expert Says', *Global Security Newswire*. Nuclear Threat Initiative website, http://www.nti.org/d_newswire/issues/2005_12_7.html#C03902CA (accessed 1 March 2007).

Russett, Bruce (1982) 'Defense Expenditures and National Well Being', *American Political Science Review*, vol. 76, pp. 767–77.

Russett, Bruce (1993) *Grasping the Democratic Peace: Principles for a Post-Cold War Era*. Princeton, NJ, Princeton University Press.

Russett, Bruce and Oneal, John R. (2001) *Triangulating Peace: Democracy, Interdependence, and International Organizations*. New York, W. W. Norton.

Salmon, Trevor C. (1992) 'Testing Times for European Political Cooperation: The Gulf and Yugoslavia, 1990–1992', *International Affairs*, vol. 68, no. 2, pp 233–53.

Sample, Ian (2003) 'You Ain't Seen Nothing Yet', *Guardian*, 19 June. http://www.guardian.co.uk/life/feature/story/0,13026,980048,00.html.

Sasse, Gwendolyn (2006) 'Where Did It All Go Wrong in Ukraine?', *Guardian Unlimited*, 4 August. http://www.guardian.co.uk/ukraine/story/0,,1837596,00.html (accessed 23 November 2006).

Savage, Timothy M. (2004) 'Europe and Islam: Crescent Waxing, Cultures Clashing', *The Washington Quarterly*, vol. 27, no. 3, pp. 25–50.

Schmitt, Burkhard (2003) 'Conclusions', in Gustav Lindstrom and Burkhard Schmitt (eds)., *Fighting Proliferation: European Perspectives*, Chaillot Papers No. 66. Paris, European Union Institute for Security Studies, pp. 89–92.

Schmitt, Burkhard (2004) 'European Capabilities: How Many Divisions?', in Nicole Gnesotto (ed.), *EU Security and Defence Policy: The First Five Years (1999–2004)*. Paris, European Union Institute for Security Studies, pp. 89–110.

Schmitt, Burkhard (2005) *Information Security: A New Challenge for the EU*, Chaillot Paper No. 76. Paris, European Union Institute for Security Studies.

Sendagorta, Fidel (2005) 'Jihad in Europe: The Wider Context', *Survival*, vol. 47, no. 3, pp. 63–71.

Shapiro, Jeremy and Suzan, Benedicte (2003) 'The French Experience of Counter-terrorism', *Survival*, vol. 45, no. 1, pp. 67–98.

Silber, Laura and Little, Allen (1995) *The Death of Yugoslavia*. London, Penguin /BBC Books.

Simms, Brendan (2002) *Unfinest Hour: Britain and the Destruction of Bosnia*. London, Penguin.

Simon, Steven and Benjamin, Daniel (2000) 'America and the New Terrorism', *Survival*, vol. 42, no. 1, pp. 59–75.

Simon, Steven and Benjamin, Daniel (2001–2) 'The Terror', *Survival*, vol. 43, no. 4, pp. 5–18.

Singer, Max and Wildavsky, Aaron (1993) *The Real World Order: Zones of Peace/Zones of Turmoil*. Chatham, NJ, Chatham House.

Simpson, Victor L. (2005) 'Allies Resist America Taking Away Their Terrorism Suspects', *Associated Press*, 20 June. Global Policy Forum website: http://www.globalpolicy.org/empire/terrorwar/analysis/2005/0620rendition.htm (accessed 27 June 2005).

Sjursen, Helene (2004) 'On the Identity of NATO', *International Affairs*, vol. 80, no. 4, pp. 687–703.

Stalenheim, Petter, Fruchart, Damien, Omitoogun, Wuyi and Perdomo, Catalina (2006) 'Military Expenditure', ch. 8 in Stockholm International Peace Research Institute, *SIPRI Yearbook 2006: Armaments, Disarmament and International Security*. Oxford, SIPRI/Oxford University Press, pp. 295–324.

Smith, Laura (2006) 'Attorney General Calls for Guantánamo to Close', *Guardian*, 10 May. http://www.guardian.co.uk/guantanamo/story/0,,1771926,00.html (accessed 23 May 2006).

Smith, Mark (1991) *The Soviet Fault Line: Ethnic Insecurity and Territorial Dispute in the Former USSR*, Whitehall Paper Series. London, Royal United Services Institute for Defence Studies.

Smyth, Jamie (2006) 'EU Faces Challenge to Secure Energy Supplies', *The Irish Times*, 6 January.

Solana, Javier (1997) *NATO–Russia Relations at the Turn of the Century, Speech by the Secretary General at the Konrad Adenauer Foundation, Berlin, 7 November*. http://www.nato.int/docu/speech/1997/s971107a.htm (accessed 24 November 2006).

Steinberg, James B. (2003) 'An Elective Partnership: Salvaging Transatlantic Relations', *Survival*, vol. 45, no. 2, pp. 113–46.

Stevenson, Jonathan (2004) *Counter-terrorism: Containment and Beyond*, Adelphi Paper 367. Oxford, Oxford University Press for International Institute for Strategic Studies.

Stiglitz, Joseph (2002) *Globalization and its Discontents*. London, Penguin.

Strange, Susan (1987) 'The Persistent Myth of Lost Hegemony', *International Organization*, vol. 41, no. 4, pp. 551–74.

Sturcke, James (2006) 'EU: US Access to Flight Data Unlawful', *Guardian*, 30 May. http://www.guardian.co.uk/eu/story/0,,1786002,00.html (accessed 12 July 2006).

Swedish Ministry for Foreign Affairs (1999) *Preventing Violent Conflict: A Swedish Action Plan*. Stockholm, Ministry for Foreign Affairs. http://www.sweden.gov.se/content/1/c6/02/01/61/aad1f9e6.pdf (accessed 9 July 2006).

Swift, Richard (2004) 'The Wild East', *New Internationalist*, April, Issue 366. http://newint.org/features/2004/04/01/keynote/ (accessed 23 November 2006).

Tindale, Stephen (2006) 'The EU Must Do More on Climate Change', *CER Bulletin*, Issue 46. London, Centre for European Reform. http://www.cer.org.uk/articles/46_tindale.html (accessed 21 August 2006).

Tonra, Ben (2001) *The Europeanisation of National Foreign Policy: Dutch, Danish and Irish Foreign Policy in the European Union*. Aldershot, Ashgate.

Townsend, Mark and Harris, Paul (2004) 'Now the Pentagon Tells Bush: Climate Change Will Destroy Us', *The Observer*, 22 February. http://observer.guardian.co.uk/international/story/0,,1153513,00.html.

Tran, Mark (1999) ' "I'm Not Going to Start Third World War for You," Jackson told Clark', *Guardian Unlimited*, 2 August. http://www.guardian. co.uk/Kosovo/Story/0,2763,208120,00.html (accessed 4 December 2006).

Traser, Julianna (2006) *Who's Still Afraid of EU Enlargement?*, 5 September. Brussels, European Citizen Action Service. http://ecas.org/file_uploads/ 1182.pdf (accessed 19 September 2006).

Travis, Alan (2004) 'Muslims Abandon Labour over Iraq War', *Guardian*, 15 March. http://politics.guardian.co.uk/iraq/story/0,12956,1169486,00.html (accessed 28 June 2006).

Travis, Alan and Norton-Taylor, Richard (2006) 'Evidence Points to al-Qaida Link to 7/7 Bombs', *Guardian*, 12 May. http://www.guardian.co.uk/attack-onlondon/story/0,,1773194,00.html.

Traynor, Ian (2005) 'Warsaw Seeks Shelter of "Son of Star Wars" ', *Guardian*, 16 November.

Traynor, Ian, Astill, James and Aglionby, John (2004) 'Secret network passed on nuclear design', *The Guardian*, 6 February.

Tuchman Mathews, Jessica (1989) 'Redefining Security', *Foreign Affairs*, vol. 68, no. 2, pp. 162–77.

UK Ministry of Defence (1998) *Strategic Defence Review: Modern Forces for a Modern World*. London, Ministry of Defence.

UNAIDS (2004) *2004 Report on the Global AIDS Epidemic: Executive Summary*. Geneva, UNAIDS – Joint United Nations Programme on HIV/AIDS. http://www.unaids.org/bangkok2004/GAR2004_pdf/GAR2004_ Execsumm_en.pdf.

UNFCCC (UN Framework Convention on Climate Change) (2005a) *United Nations Climate Change Conference (COP 11 and COP/MOP 1) 28 November to 9 December 2005, Palais des Congrès de Montréal, Decision -/CMP.1 Consideration of commitments for subsequent periods for Parties included in Annex I to the Convention under Article 3, paragraph 9, of the Kyoto Protocol. UNFCCC website:* http://unfccc.int/files/meetings/cop_11/ application/pdf/cmp1_00_consideration_of_commitments_under_3.9.pdf (accessed 6 September 2006)

UNFCCC () (2005b) *United Nations Climate Change Conference (COP 11 and COP/MOP 1) 28 November to 9 December 2005, Palais des Congrès de Montréal, Decision -/CP.11 Dialogue on long-term cooperative action to address climate change by enhancing implementation of the Convention. UNFCCC website:* http://unfccc.int/files/meetings/cop_11/application/pdf/ cop11_00_dialogue_on_long-term_coop_action.pdf (accessed 6 September 2006).

UNHCR (United Nations High Commissioner for Refugees) (2004) *2004 UNHCR Statistical Yearbook: Country Data Sheets*. Geneva, UNHCR. http://www.unhcr.org/statistics (accessed 19 October 2006).

United Nations (1945) *Charter of the United Nations.* http://www.un.org/aboutun/charter/index.html (accessed 28 March 2006).

United Nations (2003) *Report of the Secretary-General: Implementation of the United Nations Millennium Declaration,* 2 September, UN General Assembly, Fifty-eighth Session, A/58/323. New York, United Nations. UN website, http://www.un.org/millenniumgoals/sgreport2003.pdf?OpenElement (accessed 1 March 2007).

United Nations (2004a) *Implementation of the United Nations Millennium Declaration: Report of the Secretary-General,* United Nations A/59/282, General Assembly, Fifty-ninth session, 27 August. New York, United Nations. UN website: http://www.un.org/millenniumgoals/sgreport2004.pdf?OpenElement (accessed 10 August 2006).

United Nations (2004b) *A More Secure World: Our Shared Responsibility: Report of the Secretary-General's High-Level Panel on Threats, Challenges and Change,* 2 December, UN General Assembly, A/59/565. New York, United Nations. http://www.un.org/secureworld/report.pdf (accessed 21 November 2006).

United Nations (2005) *2005 World Summit Outcome,* United Nations General Assembly A/60/L.1, 15 September. New York, United Nations. http://daccessdds.un.org/doc/UNDOC/GEN/N05/487/60/PDF/N0548760.pdf?OpenElement (accessed 1 March 2007).

United States (2002) *The National Security Strategy of the United States of America.* http://www.whitehouse.gov/nsc/nss.pdf (accessed 1 March 2007).

United States (2006) *The National Security Strategy of the United States of America.* http://www.whitehouse.gov/nsc/nss/2006/nss2006.pdf (accessed 16 March 2006).

US Commission on National Security in the 21st Century (1999) *New World Coming: American Security in the 21st Century – The Phase I Report on the Emerging Global Security Environment for the First Quarter of the 21st Century.* http://www.fas.org/man/docs/nwc/nwc.htm.

van de Linde, Erik; O'Brien, Kevin; Lindstrom, Gustav; De Spiegeleire, Stephan; Vayrynen, Mikko (2002) *Quick Scan of Post-9/11 National Counter-terrorism Policymaking and Implementation in Selected European Countries,* Research Project for the Netherlands Ministry of Justice, MR-1590. Leiden, RAND Europe. http://www.rand.org/pubs/monograph_reports/2005/MR1590.pdf (accessed 29 May 2006).

Valencia, Mark J. (2005) *The Proliferation Security Initiative: Making Waves in Asia,* Adelphi Paper 376. London, Routledge for International Institute for Strategic Studies.

Van Evera, Stephen (1990–1) 'Primed for Peace: Europe After the Cold War', *International Security,* vol. 15, no.3, pp. 7–57

Vidal, John (2006) 'Sweden Plans to Be World's First Oil-Free Economy', *Guardian,* 8 February. http,//www.guardian.co.uk/oil/story/0,,1704954,00.html (accessed 4 September 2006).

Vilnius Group (2003) 'Statement of the Vilnius Group Countries in Response to the Presentation by the United States Secretary of State to the United Nations Security Council Concerning Iraq, 5 February 2003', in Antonio Missiroli, (ed.), *From Copenhagen to Brussels: European Defence: Core Documents*, Chaillot Papers 67. Paris, European Union Institute for Security Studies), p. 345.

Waever, Ole, Buzan, Barry, Kelstrup, Morten, and Lemaitre, Pierre (1993) *Identity, Migration and the New Security Agenda*. London, Pinter.

Wallensteen, Peter and Axell, Karin (1993) 'Armed Conflict at the End of the Cold War, 1989–92', *Journal of Peace Research*, vol. 30, no. 3, pp. 331–46.

Walt, Stephen M. (1991)'The Renaissance of Security Studies', *International Studies Quarterly*, vol. 35, no. 2, pp. 211–39.

Walt, Stephen M. (1997) 'Why Alliances Endure or Collapse', *Survival*, vol. 39, no. 1, pp. 156–79.

Waltz, Kenneth N. (1979) *Theory of International Politics*. New York, McGraw-Hill.

Waltz, Kenneth N. (1993) 'The Emerging Structure of International Politics', *International Security*, vol. 18, no. 2.

Weiner, Myron (1995) *The Global Migration Crisis: Challenge to States and to Human Rights*. New York, HarperCollins.

Weiss, Thomas G. (2005) *Military–Civilian Interactions: Humanitarian Crises and the Responsibility to Protect*, 2nd edn. Lanham, Rowman & Littlefield.

Weitz, Richard (2005) *Revitalising US–Russian Security Cooperation*, Adelphi Paper 377. Abingdon, Routledge for International Institute for Strategic Studies.

Wheeler, N. J. (2000) *Saving Strangers: Humanitarian Intervention in International Society*. Oxford, Oxford University Press.

White House (2002) *The President's Trip to Europe and Russia, Fact Sheet: Threat Reduction Assistance – United States Government Non-proliferation/Threat Reduction Assistance to Russia*. White House, Office of the Press Secretary, 24 May. http://www.whitehouse.gov/news/releases/2002/05/20020524-16.html.

Whitlock, Craig and Smiley, Shannon (2005) 'Germans Arrest 22 in Anti-Terror Raids', *The Washington Post*, 13 January. Reproduced on Global Policy Forum website: http://www.globalpolicy.org/empire/terrorwar/analysis/2005/1013german.htm (accessed 17 January 2005).

Willerton, John P. and Cokerham, Geoffrey (2003) 'Russia, the CIS and Eurasian Interconnections', in James Sperling, Sean Kay and S. Victor Papacosma, *Limiting Institutions? The Challenge of Eurasian Security Governance*. Manchester/New York, Manchester University Press), pp. 185–207.

Wilkinson, Paul (2000) Terrorism Versus Democracy: The Liberal State Response. London, Frank Cass.

Wilkinson, Paul (2005) *International Terrorism: The Changing Threat and the EU's Response*, Chaillot Paper No. 84. Paris, European Union Institute for Security Studies.

Wimmer, Andreas (2003–4) 'Democracy and Ethno-religious Conflict in Iraq', *Survival*, vol. 45, no. 4, pp. 111–34.

Wohlfeld, Monika (1997) *The Effects of Enlargement on Bilateral Relations in Central and Eastern Europe*, Chaillot Papers 26. Paris, European Union Institute for Security Studies of Western.

Wolfers, Arnold (1962) *Discord and Collaboration: Essays on International Politics*. Baltimore, Md., Johns Hopkins University Press.

Woodall, Pam (2006) 'The New Titans: A Survey of the World Economy', *The Economist*, 16 September.

Woodward, Will (2006) 'Romanians and Bulgarians Face Immigration Curbs', *The Guardian*. http://politics.guardian.co.uk/eu/story/0,,1854777,00.html (accessed 19 September 2006).

Woollacott, Martin (2005) 'A Bigger Threat Than the Bomb', *Guardian*, 13 May.

World Bank (2005) *Dying Too Young: Addressing Premature Mortality and Ill Health Due to Non-Communicable Diseases in the Russian Federation*. World Bank, Human Development Department, Europe and Central Asia. http://www_wds.worldbank.org/servlet/WDSContentServer?WDSP/IB/2006/02/10/000160016_20060210125603/Rendered/PDF/323770v10RU0Wh1ung1Summary01PUBLIC1.pdf (accessed 15 February 2006).

World Health Organization (WHO) (2005) *Climate and Health Fact Sheet*. Geneva, World Health Organization. http://www.who.int/globalchange/news/fsclimandhealth/en/print.html (accessed 22 May 2006).

Yost, David S. (1999) *The US and Nuclear Deterrence in Europe*, Adelphi Paper 326. Oxford, Oxford University Press for International Institute for Strategic Studies.

Yost, David S. (2005) 'France's Evolving Nuclear Strategy', *Survival*, vol. 47, no. 3, pp. 117–46.

Younge, Gary (2005) 'US Reaction: Newspapers Warn of Threat to America from "Londonistan" ', *Guardian*, 12 July.

Zakaria, Fareed (1997) 'The Rise of Illiberal Democracy', *Foreign Affairs*, vol. 76, no. 6, pp. 22–43

Zakaria, Fareed (2003) *The Future of Freedom: Illiberal Democracy at Home and Abroad*. New York, W. W. Norton.

Zartman, I. William and Kremenyuk, Victor A. (eds) (1995) *Cooperative Security: Reducing Third World Wars*. Syracuse, NY, Syracuse University Press.

Zielonka, Jan (2006) *Europe as Empire: The Nature of the Enlarged European Union*. Oxford, Oxford University Press.

Zelikow, Philip (1996) 'The Masque of Institutions', *Survival*, vol. 38, no. 1, pp. 6–18.

Zelikow, Philip D. and Rice, Condoleezza (1995) *Germany Unified and Europe Transformed: A Study in Statecraft.* Cambridge, Mass., Harvard University Press.
Zelikow, Philip (1996) 'The Masque of Institutions', *Survival*, vol. 38, no. 1, pp. 6–18.
Zupi, Marco (2005) 'Deprivation – Poverty and Foreign Policy, in Antonio Missiroli (ed.), *Disasters, Diseases, Disruptions: A New D-Drive for the EU*, Chaillot Paper No. 83. Paris, European Union Institute for Security Studies, pp. 37–50.

Index

11 September 2001 terrorist attacks
(also 9/11)   1, 2, 10, 31, 40, 41,
50, 52, 58, 62, 106, 127, 130,
149, 169, 171, 172, 174, 180,
187, 219, 221, 223

Abu Ghraib   175
Aceh   142
Afghanistan   37, 43, 44, 62–3, 66,
68, 106, 123, 127, 129, 130, 137,
138, 169, 171, 172, 173, 175,
187, 222
   role in emergence of Islamic
   terrorism   9
Africa   79, 93, 96, 190, 199, 214,
215
African Union (AU)   93, 130, 193
aid (also Overseas Development
Assistance – ODA)   194–6
Albania   18, 23, 68, 80, 183, 210,
214
Algeria   90, 136, 171, 173, 184, 188,
189, 214
Al-Qaeda   32, 34, 40, 42, 43, 44, 45,
138, 152, 171, 173, 174, 175,
177
American century   50
Andreani, Gilles   154, 174
Annan, Kofi, UN Secretary-General
46, 55
Anti-Ballistic Missile (ABM) Treaty
164
Arbatov, Alexei   104
Argentina   152
Armenia   91, 113, 114, 210
arms control   155–8, 167, 224
Asia   34, 35, 36, 96, 165, 199, 215
Association of South East Asian
Nations (ASEAN)   193
August 1991 Soviet coup   103
Australia   33, 66, 196, 207
Austria   83, 84, 87, 136, 207
Aum Shinrikyo   42, 154

'axis of evil' (Iran, Iraq and North
Korea)   44–5, 63
Azerbaijan   91, 114, 173, 183, 210
Aznar, José Maria, Spanish Prime
Minister   87, 214

Baker, James, US Secretary of State
60
balance of power
   politics   12, 14, 29, 33
   global   35–6, 51, 108
Balkans   4, 18, 61, 62, 66–7, 68, 77,
79, 85, 87, 88, 89, 96, 130,
130–3, 138, 146, 173, 183, 214,
215, 221
Baltic states   103, 114, 115
   and Russia   15
Barber, Benjamin   34
Basque country and terrorism   42
Belarus   25, 90, 91, 113, 114, 115
Belgium   69, 81, 84, 86, 97, 136,
137, 177
Berlusconi, Silvio, Italian Prime
Minister   129
Beslan hostage crisis (2004)   173
Bildt, Carl, former Swedish Prime
Minister   24
Biological and Toxin Weapons
Convention (BTWC)   149, 155,
156
biological weapons   40, 41, 153, 220
Black Sea Economic Co-operation
group   16
Blair, Tony, British Prime Minister,
129, 214
blowback, phenomenon   9
Bosnia   60, 61, 66, 68, 96, 110, 124,
127, 131, 133, 142, 173, 177,
183, 210
Brazil   36, 152, 224
Britain   see United Kingdom
Bulgaria   15, 19, 27, 68, 89, 183,
212

Bush Administration (2001–) 44, 44–5, 50, 52, 53, 63, 64, 65, 75, 76, 77, 87, 128, 138, 160, 161, 187, 221–2
  foreign policy 'revolution' 63
  National Security Strategy (2002) 45, 63, 128
  National Security Strategy (2006) 128
  non-proliferation policy 149–50
Bush Administration, first (1989–92) 59–60
Bush, George, US President (1989–92) 60
Bush, George W., US President (2001–8) 62, 75, 164
  State of the Union speech, January 2002 63

Canada 33, 138, 159, 196, 197, 207
Caucasus 18, 27–8, 37, 38, 91, 107, 173, 187, 210–11
Central America 38
Central Asia 18, 27–8, 66, 106, 107, 114, 121, 173, 183, 187
Central and Eastern Europe 12, 14, 15, 16, 17, 18, 19, 21, 22, 23, 28, 29, 61, 64, 65, 68, 79, 83, 84, 87, 88–9, 91, 97, 106, 107, 111, 112, 124, 165, 207, 211, 217
Chechnya 43, 103, 106, 108, 111, 125, 133, 173–4, 184, 210
chemical weapons 40, 41, 153, 220
Chemical Weapons Convention (CWC) 149, 155, 156
China 27, 33, 34, 35, 36, 37, 39, 48, 50, 53, 62, 72, 73, 93, 104, 106, 115, 120, 123, 125, 150, 156, 157, 166, 201, 203, 214, 224
Chirac, Jacques, French President 84, 164
'clash of civilizations' 34
climate change *see* global warming
Clinton Administration 60–1, 87, 160, 203
Clinton, Bill, US President (1992–2000) 60
Cold War 2, 5, 6, 10, 11, 13, 22, 29, 77, 86, 102, 104, 123, 136, 164, 223

end of 2, 5, 13, 14, 21, 22, 29, 33, 39, 50, 58, 59, 67, 86, 102, 120, 123, 124, 136, 209, 217, 221, 222
Collective Security Treaty Organization (CSTO) 113
Colombia 37, 48
'colour revolutions' 114, 115, 122, 173
'coming anarchy' 37
Commission on Human Security 46
Commonwealth of Independent States (CIS) 113, 114
Comprehensive Test Ban Treaty (CTBT) 61, 62, 149, 156
Concert of Europe 16
Conference on Security and Cooperation in Europe (CSCE) (*see also* Organization for Security and Cooperation in Europe, OSCE) 16–17, 192
Cooperative Threat Reduction (CTR) 158–60
core–periphery, feature of international order 33–4
Council of Baltic Sea States 16
Council of Europe 17, 28, 176
crime, as a security problem 32, 48, 118
critical infrastructure security/protection 32, 49
Croatia 68, 84, 131, 210
Cuba 34
Cyprus 26, 27, 83, 89, 211
Czech Republic 19, 38, 84, 89
Czechoslovakia 136

Darfur 126, 130
Dayton agreement 61, 132
de Gaulle, Charles, French President 86
Delors, Jacques 198
democracy, global spread of 33
democratic peace 14
Democratic Republic of Congo (DRC) 142
Denmark 64, 84, 86, 136, 194, 207
deterrence 164
diseases and security 32, 48
Doha round 197
Duchene, François 80

East Asia   35, 123
East Timor   37, 124, 137
economic development policy   193–8
economics and security   46–7
Egypt   40, 43, 90, 171, 188
energy security   32, 47–8
enlargement of 'Europe'   18–28, 30, 219
  and insider/outside, inclusion/exclusion dynamics   22
environment and security   47
Estonia   19, 68, 89, 114
Euro-atlanticism   86–8
Euro-Gaullism   86–8
Euro-Mediterranean Partnership (EMP, also 'Barcelona Process')   90, 187–8
European Coal and Steel Community (ECSC)   81
European Convention on Human Rights   180
European Court of Justice   181
European Defence Community (EDC)   81
European Union (EU)   4, 12, 16, 17, 19, 22, 120, 132, 166, 169, 191, 192, 192–3, 196, 197, 201, 203, 204, 206, 207, 208–9, 214, 217–18, 218, 221, 222, 223, 224
  Amsterdam Treaty   82, 97, 99
  Area of Freedom Security and Justice (AFSJ)   79, 97–9, 180, 213–14, 222
  battlegroups   146
  Central and Eastern Europe, policy towards   88–9
  'civilian power'   80
  Committee of Permanent Representatives (COREPER)   82
  Common Agricultural Policy (CAP)   197–98
  Common Foreign and Security Policy (CFSP), 16, 60, 79, 80, 80–6, 222
  Constitutional Treaty   82–3, 85–6, 91–2, 101
  Copenhagen criteria   89
  defence policy/role   60, 61, 66, 69, 79, 95–6
  enlargement   84, 88–9, 90, 91–2, 111, 211–12

European Union (*cont.*)
European Commission   82, 99, 159, 194, 211, 212
European Consensus on Development   194
European Council   82
European Defence Agency (EDA)   146
European Political Co-operation (EPC) process   81
European Neighbourhood Policy (ENP)   90–1
European Parliament   176
European Security Strategy document   45, 65, 85, 92, 129, 150, 162, 193–4
European Strategy Against Proliferation of Weapons of Mass Destruction   150, 155, 159, 162
EU Programme for the Prevention of Violent Conflicts   189
EU Strategic Partnership with the Mediterranean and the Middle East   188
External Action Service   83
External Affairs Commissioner   83
'external relations'   82
former Soviet Union, policy towards   89–90
General Affairs and External Relations Council   82
'Helsinki Headline Goal'   95
High Representative for the CFSP   82, 83
global security role   79, 80, 92–5
Justice and Home Affairs (JHA) co-operation   79, 81, 97
Maastricht Treaty   60, 79, 81, 82, 97
Military Committee (EUMC)   95–6
Military Staff (EUMS)   96
neighbourhood politics/policy   88–92
Nice Treaty   82
Partnership and Co-operation Agreements (PCAs)   28, 90, 110
and peacekeeping/intervention   93, 124, 127, 130, 131, 131–2, 133, 142–6, 147
Policy Planning and Early Warning Unit   82

European Union (*cont.*)
  Political and Security Committee
    (PSC/COPS) 82, 95
  and Russia 90, 91, 110–12, 119
  security role 3, 4
  Stabilization and Association
    Agreements 89
  Strategy for Combating
    Radicalization and Recruitment to
    Terrorism 185–6
  and terrorism 98, 178–79, 180, 181
  Western Balkans, policy towards 89
  'extraordinary rendition' 175

Finland 83, 87, 136, 207, 211
Fissile Material Cut-Off Treaty
    (FMCT) 156
former Soviet Union 4, 14, 18, 27,
    37, 67, 68, 79, 88, 89–90, 91,
    102, 103, 106, 108, 111, 112–16,
    119, 120, 121, 133–5, 146–7,
    158, 167, 183, 207, 210–11, 212,
    204, 215, 219, 221
former Yugoslavia/former Yugoslav
    states 18, 23, 35, 38, 89, 212
France 58, 64, 65, 69, 76, 77, 80, 81,
    83, 84, 86, 88, 94, 97, 101, 106,
    124, 136, 137, 147, 150, 152,
    155, 157, 159, 161, 164, 166,
    168, 170, 171, 173, 177, 183,
    185, 189, 198, 207

G8 (Group of 8) 159, 196
Gaidar, Yegor, Russian Prime Minister
    104
Georgia 28, 44, 68, 91, 103, 113, 114,
    115, 121, 128, 133, 142, 210
German re-unification 59, 81
Germany 13, 58, 59, 64, 65, 66, 67,
    69, 76, 80, 81, 83, 84, 86, 94, 97,
    101, 106, 137, 138, 150, 152,
    159, 161, 170, 177, 182, 183,
    185, 198, 204, 207, 210
  and Poland, 15
Global Partnership Against the Spread
    of Weapons and Materials of
    Mass Destruction 159
global security, European role 3, 4,
    31, 56–7, 223–4
Global Threat Reduction Initiative
    (GTRI) 160

global warming 32, 55, 56, 58,
    198–206, 221
  emissions trading scheme (ETS)
    203–4
globalization 35
Goldsmith, Lord, UK Attorney-
    General 176
Gorbachev, Mikhail, Soviet President
    103
Graham, Thomas, Jr 116
Grand, Camille 157
Greece 26, 27, 87, 136, 170, 204,
    208, 211
Gros, Daniel 112
GUAM/GUUAM (Georgia, Ukraine,
    (Uzbekistan), Azerbaijan,
    Moldova group) 114
Guantanamo Bay 175
Gulf Cooperation Council (GCC)
    188, 189
Gulf War, 1990–1 39, 79, 83–4, 136,
    152
Gray, Colin 40

Haiti 124, 127, 130
Hart–Rudman Commission 62
hegemonic threats (to European
    security) 11–12
HIV/AIDS 32, 48, 55, 103, 117–18
Holbrooke, Richard 61
Hollis, Rosemary 188
homeland security 44, 177–82
Houghton, Sir John 47
humanitarian intervention 124–7,
    133, 137
Hungary 19, 68, 84, 89, 136
  and its neighbours 15
Huntington, Samuel 34
Hussein, Saddam 64, 128

Iceland 97
Illegal immigration 209
'illiberal democracies' 35, 105
Implementation Force (IFOR) 132
India 27, 35, 36, 39, 40, 48, 50, 53,
    93, 104, 106, 123, 149, 157, 163,
    168, 201, 203, 220, 224
Intergovernmental Panel on Climate
    Change (IPCC) 199
International Atomic Energy Agency
    (IAEA) 40, 41

International Commission on
    Intervention and State Sovereignty
    (ICISS)   126
International Criminal Court (ICC)
    58, 61, 62, 79, 94, 95, 224
International Monetary Fund (IMF)
    93, 107, 127
international order, Western-
    dominated   32, 33, 36
international politics, post-Cold War
    2
International Security Assistance Force
    (ISAF)   138
Iran   27, 34, 40, 41, 45, 63, 104, 108,
    121, 128, 149–50, 150, 152, 154,
    155, 156, 157, 160, 162, 163,
    167, 168, 224
Iraq   39, 40, 41, 43, 45, 52, 53, 63,
    64, 124, 137, 142, 156, 157, 160,
    161
Iraq War (2003–)   3, 35, 41, 52, 58,
    64–5, 69, 76, 80, 84, 86, 87, 94,
    100, 106, 110, 127, 128, 129,
    129–30, 137, 142, 148, 149, 149,
    150, 152, 160, 161, 161–2, 167,
    174–5, 221–2, 222
    intelligence failures relating to   9,
    65
Ireland   83, 87, 136, 137, 207, 211,
    212
Islam   72, 73
    Europe and   183–87
Islamic terrorism, globalized   43–4,
    54, 55, 72, 107, 169, 171, 172,
    174, 190, 219–20
Israel   39, 90, 94, 157, 161, 167, 188
Israeli–Palestinian conflict   56, 94,
    187–8
Italy   64, 81, 84, 86, 94, 136, 137,
    138, 159, 162, 170, 175, 177,
    207, 208

Jackson, Sir Michael, British General
    110
Japan   33, 40, 50, 53, 66, 93, 123,
    152, 159, 194, 196, 197, 203, 224
'Jihad versus McWorld'   34
Jordan   90

Kagan, Robert   71–2, 74
Kaliningrad   111

Kaplan, Robert   37
Kashmir   43, 184
Kazakhstan   113, 115, 173, 183
Kerry, John, US Senator/Presidential
    candidate 2004   75
Korean War   136
Kosovo   23, 24, 62, 67, 110, 131,
    133, 173
    Kosovo Force (KFOR)   132
    Kosovo war, 1999   25, 61, 95, 110,
    124, 125, 127, 132, 210
Kozyrev, Andrei, Russian Foreign
    Minister   104
Kyoto Protocol   61, 62, 79, 94, 95,
    201–6, 224
Kyrgyzstan   66, 113, 115, 121, 173,
    183

Latvia   19, 68, 89, 113, 114
League of Nations   16
Lebanon   90, 130, 137
'Letter of the Eight'   84
Liberal Democratic Party (Russia)
    104
liberal international order   223–4
liberal theories (of international
    relations)   13–14, 72, 73–4, 77,
    85
Libya   40, 90, 156, 161
Lithuania   19, 68, 89, 111, 114
London terrorist attacks, July 2005
    56, 169, 172, 178, 182, 184,
    219
'Londonistan'   172, 185
'loose nukes'   158–60
Lugar, Richard, US Senator   68, 153,
    158
Lukashenko, Alexander, Belarusian
    President   25
Luxembourg   81, 86, 97, 194, 207
Luxor Massacre (1997)   171

Macedonia   66, 68, 96, 131, 132,
    142, 183, 210
Madrid terrorist attacks, March 2004
    1, 56, 87, 169, 171, 171–2, 180,
    182, 184, 219
Mahbubani, Kishore   223
Malta   83, 89, 211
major war, obsolescence of   36–7
market economics   33

Mediterranean   70, 83, 88, 90, 91, 188
MERCOSUR (Southern Common
    Market)   93, 193
Middle East   34, 39, 58, 64, 70, 94,
    106, 123, 152, 154, 162, 165,
    168, 171, 173, 174, 187, 188,
    189, 215
Millennium Development Goals
    (MDGs)   196
Milosevic, Slobodan, Yugoslav/Serbian
    leader   132
missile defences   41, 62, 164–6
Missile Technology Control Regime
    (MTCR)   155
Moldova   24, 25, 91, 103, 113, 114,
    115, 133
Monde, Le   62
Montenegro   131, 210
Morocco   90, 188, 214
Muller, Harald   154
multilateralism   4, 223
Myanmar (Burma)   34

Netherlands   64, 81, 86, 97, 136,
    137, 138, 177, 183, 185, 194
neutral/non-aligned states   83, 87
'new Europe'   58, 66
new (global) security agenda   1, 33,
    56, 61
'new terrorism'   32, 42–4, 61, 169,
    171–2, 174, 187
new wars   32, 36–9, 56, 123, 146
New Zealand   207
non-military security   1, 6–7, 14,
    45–9, 55, 192–3, 215, 220–21
North Africa   173
North Atlantic Treaty Organization
    (NATO)   12, 16, 17, 18–19, 22,
    59, 61, 67, 67–71, 72, 80, 81, 96,
    111, 133, 146, 164, 165, 166,
    192, 217–18, 221, 222
  and 9/11   62–3, 69
  and Afghanistan   62–3, 69, 70
  and Balkans   61, 66–7
  'Berlin-plus' arrangements   69
  Cold War   70
  Combined Joint Task Force (CJTF)
    concept   61
  enlargement/expansion   23, 68,
    107, 109
  Istanbul Co-operation Initiative   70

NATO (*cont.*)
  NATO Response Force (NRF)   70,
    139
  new strategic concept (1991)   60
  'out of area' role   68
  and peacekeeping/intervention
    124, 127, 130, 131, 132, 138–42,
    142, 147
  Rome summit, November 1991   59
  –Russia relationship   68–9, 109–10
North East Asia   154, 162, 168
North Korea   34, 40, 41, 45, 63, 128,
    149, 150, 152, 155, 156, 157,
    160, 162, 163, 167, 168, 220
Northern Ireland   42
Norway   97, 136, 137, 194
Nuclear Non-Proliferation Treaty
    (NPT)   40, 41, 93, 149, 155,
    156, 157, 160–1
Nuclear Suppliers Group (NSG)   155
nuclear weapons   36–7, 168, 220
  'nuclear leakage'   39
Nunn, Sam, US Senator   158
Nye, Joseph   75

'old Europe'   58, 66
Organization for Security and
    Cooperation in Europe (OSCE –
    see also Conference on Security
    and Co-operation in Europe,
    CSCE)   16–17, 28, 133, 192
Oxfam   197

Pakistan   34, 39, 40, 123, 149, 156,
    157, 163, 168, 172, 173, 187,
    214, 220
Palestine/Palestinian Authority   43,
    90, 94, 184
Palestinian terrorism   42, 170, 171
Partnership for Peace (PfP)   19, 28,
    61, 68
Passenger Name Records (PNR) data
    180–1
PATRIOT Act   177
Peacebuilding Commission   127
peacekeeping   123–4, 126–7, 130,
    136, 137, 147
  European role in   10, 136–7
Philippines   44, 128
Poland   15, 19, 64, 66, 68, 84, 89,
    90, 111, 136
  and eastern neighbours   15

population movements   32, 48, 206–15
Portugal   84, 86, 136, 137, 207, 208, 211
preventive (also pre-emptive) war doctrine (US)   63, 128–30
proliferation (of weapons of mass destruction)   4, 32, 39–42, 54, 61, 63, 94, 107, 149, 154–5, 167, 219, 220
   European policies towards   150, 155–6, 157–8, 158–9, 161–2
Proliferation Security Initiative (PSI)   66, 162
Putin, Vladimir, Russian President   103, 105, 106, 107

realist theories (of international relations)   13, 29, 52, 71–2, 73, 77
Refugee Convention (1951)   214
refugees   208
'responsibility to protect', concept   126
revolutionary threats (to European security)   11–12
Rice, Condoleezza, US National Security Advisor   62, 203
Rio Earth Summit   201
Roberston, Lord George, NATO Secretary-General   147
Roberts, Adam   174
'rogue states'   44–5, 63, 127
Romania   15, 19, 68, 89, 212
Rumsfeld, Donald, US Secretary of Defense   58, 63
Rumsfeld Commission   62
Russia   3, 18, 25, 25–6, 27, 29, 33, 35, 37, 39, 48, 50, 53, 58, 61, 62, 64, 66, 67, 68, 72, 73, 77, 90, 94, 125, 133, 147, 150, 155, 156, 157, 158, 159, 161, 162, 164, 166, 168, 183, 203, 214, 218, 224
   'a world without Russia'   116
   crime   118
   democracy   105
   demographic decline   117
   Duma   104, 105
   economic/financial collapse (1998)   103, 104–5, 116, 118
   economy   116

Russia (*cont.*)
   'energy superpower'   103, 105, 106, 112, 119, 120, 121
   environment   118
   and EU   90, 91, 110–12, 119
   foreign policy   102, 103–7
   governance problems   116–17
   health problems   117–18
   military   104, 118
   military forces in Transdnistria   25
   and NATO   24, 109–10
   and NATO enlargement   23, 68–9, 109
   North Caucasus   117, 119, 183
   presidential election, March 2004   105
   weakness as security problem   116–20
   'Weimar Russia'   102, 104
   and the West   102, 107–9, 120
   and Western security community   25–6, 27, 108, 218–19
   and Yugoslav wars   25
Rwanda   37, 123, 125, 137, 147

SARS (severe acute respiratory syndrome)   48
Saudi Arabia   40, 43, 152, 171, 188, 189
Schengen Agreement   97, 98, 99, 111, 178, 213
'second nuclear age'   40
securitization, process   7, 49, 193, 221
security   6–11
   –freedom trade-off   10
   human   46
   open to abuse   10–11
   policy choices   9
   policy trade-offs   9–10
   'referent objects' of   7
   soft, 6–7, 32, 45–9
   traditional/narrow definition of   6
   –welfare trade-off   10
security community   36, 39, 123, 217–19
   definition of   2, 12
   enlargement of   14–16, 19, 22, 30
   European   4, 5, 11–16, 17, 18, 19, 25, 28–9, 30, 108, 120
   global   12–13

security co-operation 7–8, 16–17, 29–30
security institutions 14, 17
Serbia 27, 60, 131, 183
Shanghai Co-operation Organization (SCO) 115
Sierra Leone 124, 137, 147
Singapore 66
Slovakia 19, 68, 89
Slovenia 19, 68, 84, 89, 130–1, 210
soft power 4, 76, 80, 87, 159, 162, 167, 188, 223
Solana, Javier, EU High Representative for the CFSP 82
Somalia 37, 124, 125, 137
South Africa 36, 48, 152, 224
South America 34, 199
South Korea 40, 152
Southern Africa 37
Southern Europe 208
Soviet Union (*see also* former Soviet Union) 103, 106, 112, 158
Spain 42, 64, 84, 86, 136, 155, 162, 175, 177, 183, 204, 207, 208, 211
Srebrenica massacre (1995) 131
Stabilization Force (SFOR) 132
Steinberg, James 75
Stevenson, Jonathan 172
strategic culture, European 223
Sudan 37, 126, 142
Suez War 136
subregional co-operation/institutions 15–16, 17
Sweden 83, 84, 87, 136, 152, 175, 189–90, 194, 204–6, 211
Syria 34, 40, 90, 128

Taiwan 37, 39, 152
Tajikistan 113, 115, 133, 173, 183
terrorism 4, 63, 167, 219–20
'age of terrorism' 170
'catastrophic' 44
cyber-terrorism 49
European responses 1
French 'sanctuary doctrine' 170–1
WMD terrorism 41, 153–4, 154–5
UN Counter-Terrorism Committee 44
Third World 38
'Third World War' 45
Tibet 125

Tindale, Stephen 199
threat assessment, problems of 8–9
Tokyo underground terrorist attack 42, 154
trade and development 196–8
transatlantic relations 3, 57, 176, 221–2
'elective partnership' 75, 78, 222
Transdnistria region (of Moldova) 25
'Trevi Group' 97
Turkmenistan 173, 183
Tunisia 90
Turkey 18, 25, 26, 29, 40, 64, 66, 69, 77, 84, 90, 92, 120, 136, 170, 183, 207, 212, 218
relations with Greece 26
and Western security community 25, 26, 218

Ukraine 23, 24–5, 90, 91, 103, 106, 111, 113, 114, 115, 121, 214
United Kingdom 52, 64, 65, 66, 76, 80, 83, 84, 86, 88, 97, 101, 115, 124, 136, 137, 138, 147, 150, 152, 157, 159, 160, 162, 164, 165, 166, 168, 172, 173, 175, 177–9, 180, 182, 185, 189, 189–90, 204, 211, 212
United Nations (UN) 36, 93, 94, 123–4, 125, 126, 126–7, 127, 131, 133, 146, 223
UN Framework Convention on Climate Change (UNFCCC) 201
UN World Summit, September 2005 126, 127
United Nations Protection Force (UNPROFOR) 131
United States of America (USA) 33, 37, 39, 41, 43, 63, 66, 68, 73, 80, 81, 86, 94, 106, 114, 120, 123, 131, 132, 136, 139, 150, 152, 159, 160, 164, 166, 167, 171, 190, 191, 194, 196, 197, 203, 206, 207, 222, 223, 224
Congressional elections, 1994 61
Department of Homeland Security 44, 177
defence spending 49, 50–1, 53, 63
disengagement from Europe 58–9, 66–7, 77, 81

258   Index

United States of America (USA)
(*cont.*)
 global power (also hegemony)   3,
  30–1, 32, 44, 49–54, 57
 post-9/11 foreign policy debate   54,
  77, 127
 Presidential election, 2004   75
 unilateralism   55, 63, 64, 75, 76
Uzbekistan   66, 113, 114, 115, 173,
 183

Van Gogh, Theo   184
Venezuela   106
Vietnam War   136
Vilnius group letter   84
Visegrad group   15
Vojvodina   131

'war on terror'   1, 42, 44–5, 59,
 76, 87, 136, 169, 174–6, 180,
 191
weapons of mass destruction (WMD)
 1, 4, 40–1, 63, 66, 149, 152, 153,
 220
West Africa   37
Western Balkans   18, 23, 24, 84, 90,
 91, 92, 212, 218

Western former Soviet Union   18, 24–5
'wild east'   14
World Bank   93, 127
world order   223–4
World Trade Organization (WTO)
 36, 92, 197

Yeltsin, Boris, Russian President   103,
 104, 105, 118
Yemen   44
Yanukovich, Viktor, Ukrainian Prime
 Minister   24–5
Yugoslav wars/conflict (*see also* former
 Yugoslavia)   1, 14–15, 23, 25,
 38, 60, 61, 68, 79, 81, 84, 85,
 100, 107, 109–10, 123, 124,
 130–1, 146, 210, 218, 222
Yushchenko, Viktor, Ukrainian
 President   24

Zakaria, Fareed   35
Zangger Committee   155
Zapatero, José Luis Rodriguez,
 Spanish Prime Minister   87
Zhirinovsky, Vladimir   104
Zielonka, Jan   218
'zones of turmoil'   34